SO-BSZ-197

The Children of
Renaissance Florence

Unless Recalled Earlier

DATE DUE

DEMCO, INC. 38-2931

Pou

in F

The Children of Renaissance Florence

Power and Dependence
in Renaissance Florence
Volume 1

Richard C. Trexler

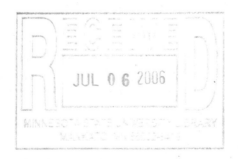

Medieval & Renaissance Texts & Studies

Binghamton, New York

1993

HN
488
.F56
T74
1993
v.1

© Copyright 1993
Center for Medieval and Early Renaissance Studies
State University of New York at Binghamton

Library of Congress Cataloging-in-Publication Data

Trexler, Richard C., 1932–
   Power and dependence in Renaissance Florence / Richard C. Trexler.
      p. cm.
   Includes bibliographical references.
   Contents: v. 1. The Children of Renaissance Florence—v. 2. The women of
Renaissance Florence—v. 3. The workers of Renaissance Florence.
   ISBN 0–86698–156–X (v. 1). —ISBN 0–86698–157–8 (v. 2).
—ISBN 0–86698–158–6 (v. 3)
   1. Florence (Italy)—Social conditions. 2. Children—Italy—Florence—History.
3. Youth—Italy—Florence—History.   4. Women—Italy—Florence—History.
5. Working class—Italy—Florence—History. I. Title.
HN488.F56T74 1992
306'.0945'51—dc20   92– 44785
                                                                     CIP

Printed in the United States of America

For my friend and sister

Marie

Flourishing

Contents

Introduction

HOW MANY SPECTATORS OF THE RENAISSANCE PAGEANT HAVE SAID OR sensed it: the Renaissance discovered children and youth! In this view, the angelic *putto*, the blonde adolescent, and the liveried fineyoungman of Tuscan quattrocento art show how irrevocably Florentines had unmasked the physical and psychological stages of the pre-adult world. Yet one may ask: how much do we actually know about the life of children and the young in this age? And what do we mean by "children"? Do we mean males or females, or both? Do we mean infants and the very young (*pueri*), adolescents, or "youth," as contemporaries called twenty-year-olds? And what of social status? Are we talking about the pampered darlings of the well-off, about street-smart urchins who nonetheless had the benefits of roof, table, and perhaps even school; or do we mean those thousands of poor and disadvantaged kids whose only nourishing parent was the commune itself?

The present collection bridges the chasm of social difference between some of these different groups in quest of an overview of Florentine attitudes toward that part of the city's residents who, despite their differences, had this in common: they were dependent upon the adult world because of their young age. Some were bastards and others legitimate; infants among them might be incapable of feeding themselves, youth certainly could. Females obviously were at a greater disadvantage than were males; and there was a massive difference between orphans and those dependents, even in their late twenties, who came from powerful Florentine families but still could not sign certain contracts. Still, these dependents were young. Among the three volumes of essays I have edited on power and dependence in Florence, it is this volume that turns its attention to those youngsters who, because of their youth, were not emancipated.

This survey begins by exploring the frame of the image of Renaissance Florence that many of its citizens, and indeed many of its students, have wanted to project to the world. To frame that flattering image, the proper people of Florence had to define who was going to be included within the image, and who not. Since the honor of the city consisted of the honor of its "decent" families, the latter had to determine either before or right after birth which children to include or exclude from their own familial images. True, many families could put off a decision on family identity by sending their newborn infants off to wet nurses for about two years, thus excluding them from the family image for the time being. Foundling homes and suffocation were, however, two other answers to the problem of what to do with those children that parents decided they did not want around or could not support, at least for the time being. It is these two instruments of "honor control" that are the difficult subjects of the first two studies in this collection.

Only the rare visitor to Florence fails to walk past the so-called hospital or *spedale degli Innocenti*, the great foundling home built by the architect Brunelleschi for the commune of Florence in the 1420s and 1430s. It would be a place, the city chancellor Leonardo Bruni promised the government of Florence on the eve of its construction, "where [citizens would] be able to hide, and wipe from their brows, that shame which cannot be hidden ... from God."[1] To cut right to the quick, this means that city fathers needed a home for their bastard children because without one, as Bruni implies, their honor and that of their families stood to be attacked by the infants' mothers. Thus, in a complex but important way, the honor of fathers, which alone made it possible to procure honorable partners for their daughters, depended upon an honorable home in which to hide their illegitimate, or otherwise infirm, paternity.

Doubtless, the citizenry hoped that the Innocenti would end the inveterate habit of killing or wasting infants; such was the motivation repeatedly given for foundling homes. Basically, the new home would provide an alternate familial setting for these "innocents," one large enough to house ever-increasing numbers. Boys and girls left there in secret by a parent or other agent would, with no questions asked, be wet-nursed, educated, and taught skills until they reached an age when the boys would leave and support themselves, while the girls, with the financial assistance of the government, would marry.

The necessary sources have survived to allow me to study how these children were cared for. Details must await the reader of the essays themselves, of course; at this point I will simply summarize the findings. First, once the massive home filled up, death rates skyrocketed: by late in the fifteenth century, some nine of ten infants placed in the home died soon after admission. Clearly, for all the good will and money of the Florentines, the sheer numbers of matriculants, combined with at times flagging material support and inferior medical care, defeated any hope of saving lives. Second, our calculations make it certain that no matter the measurement, the care, and thus the chances of survival, of girls were inferior to those of boys. Third, over the

---

[1] From Bruni's address to the government on 25 October 1421; see note 63 of "Foundlings."

course of the fifteenth and early sixteenth centuries a large number of females defied all odds and grew to womanhood in the house. Unable to find husbands as had been hoped, these young women soon realized that the Florentine welfare system would be unable to support them. To keep the house open for infant foundlings, these mature girls were sometimes turned out into the streets—with predictable results. The *Innocentine*, as they were called, became part of the patriarchy's general problem of women.

The Innocenti, with its terrible history in the fifteenth and sixteenth centuries—the so-called Renaissance—was but one particularly imposing attempt to solve the massive problem of caring for or disposing of unwanted or insupportable children, more than half of whom were, as we shall see, female. As mentioned, another temporary solution was to put one's infants to one after another wet nurse until they reached about two years of age. Rich parents might hire a nurse to live in, but for those who could afford it, sending them abroad, often to the Casentino hills east of Florence, was the absolutely normal route. Most of these parents certainly looked forward to the day the toddlers entered the parental hearth, but in the meantime, wet-nursing outside the home solved many domestic problems. One was a problem of reputation, for it was considered dishonorable for a woman to nurse. Still, these solutions came at a price: the risk that the child would not live through those early years was higher. Indeed, it was well known that wet nurses at times starved infants.

The second essay in this collection confronts the problem of infanticide, as it emerges in early sixteenth-century episcopal documents from Fiesole, a suburb of Florence. Needless to say, the frequent incidence of female mortality in the wet-nursing industry already makes one suspect infanticide; for how, otherwise, can one account for these girls' fate? Indeed, this suspicion is replaced by certainty in the light of the bishops' records, which show that in the wake of tough new episcopal legislation against the suffocation of children, couples began to come forward to church authorities and plead that an infant had accidentally suffocated as it lay sleeping in bed with them. To be absolved, these couples, who usually were *not* the parents of the infant, received the exemplary punishment of public humiliation, being forced to stand outside a church and rue their "carelessness."

Given the number of cases involved, there can be no doubt that intent and not mere accident was involved, especially when we recall that perhaps nine in ten of these couples were *not* the parents of the dead children, but merely had charge of them. Almost certainly, these couples were, as some indeed stated, wet-nursing the infants by agreement either with the infant's actual parents or with the Innocenti foundling home. The fact that in these very years episcopal legislators extended their warnings against sleeping with children beyond parents to include third parties, appears to provide an explanation for what was happening. In a world where putting out children had become practically a mass industry, church authorities aimed at effectively forbidding the wet nurse (*balia*) and her husband (*balio*) from (profitably) abandoning one charge so as to take on a new one.

As difficult as it may be for students in modern middle America to imagine themselves a part of the world these essays describe, students from elsewhere on the planet will have no difficulty whatever. Let us not forget, after all, that the gap between the actual care given to children and our sentiments toward them can be immense. The rate of child mortality in the United States, for example, is much higher than in several other countries despite the charitable sentiments and institutions Americans pride themselves on. Elsewhere, increases in child prostitution, indeed instances of selling the children of whole islands to wealthy visitors, can be verified in the daily newspapers. Sentiments about children may have been revolutionized over recent centuries, but it is not clear that the fate of children has improved.

After the quantitative essays, it is to these sentiments that the second set of essays in this volume turns, sentiments to begin with toward males twenty years of age and younger. One of the phenomena that the reader will already have encountered in the essays on unwanted infants is that early sixteenth-century European legislators, for the first time in history, began to manifest a certain type of pathos toward childhood: would poor child X survive adult cruelty? Was a witch responsible for the untimely death of child Y? And even, how dare an unwed mother abort fetus Z!

Not for a moment should the reader doubt that the poor and powerless, such as young women who aborted fetuses or abandoned newborns, and not the rich and powerful, were the victims of these new sentiments. Nevertheless, these sentiments, which inform a series of sixteenth-century laws said to protect infants and the young, are an important phenomenon. What becomes evident is that, as so often, fifteenth-century Florentines were out in front shaping this new pathos and the institutions that mirrored it.

Salvation is now the operative word. In the essay on quattrocento adolescents, the high point arrives when one politician realizes in 1492 that something quite new had occurred in the previous decades: from seeing itself as a self-reliant republic run by adult political males, Florence had come to believe that only through its children's intercession with the Christian god could the city fathers survive. How had things come to that pass?

An answer to this question begins with the fact that early in the fifteenth century, a group of clubs or confraternities started to function whose membership, if not its "captains" or leaders, was strictly limited to the young. The highlights of their activity were oratorical, dramatic, and processional in character. In other words, youngsters were trained to be able to speak, act, and march publicly, to the enormous gratification of their parents. The young could be socialized and acculturated so that they would become "good citizens." By then, in the early years of the Medici, that meant obedient and not obstreperous.

The last decade of the fifteenth century violently compromised this vision of the child and adolescent. Opponents expelled the Medici from the city, and the great preacher Savonarola to some extent assumed the mantle of Lorenzo the Magnificent. The Dominican clearly saw the potential of the young, but bemoaned their historic association with the hated Medici. Finding that the older boys, those twenty-year-olds contemporaries called "youth" (*giovani*), were opposed to his rigorous morality and his politics, Savonarola amazingly began to attract very young children, of an age not previously courted by the movement, to his side. By the time the Florentines executed him in 1498, a full-fledged ideological battle had been joined between Savonarola's young saviors and the older, militarily more potent "youth" who talked of saving the commune by taking arms against the foreigners who were flooding into Italy. Needless to say, granting arms to its youngsters was a luxury that the gerontocracies of Italian republican cities had not been able to afford for centuries.

The last essay in this collection leads up to this decisive turn in the city's history, but, originally written for a conference on the European *charivari*, it begins by stating that until 1530, the Florentine republic gave its children and youth little room for boyish assertiveness or inversion. Precisely because they feared the young, city fathers historically rejected occasions on which boys and youth, usually in the subversive interest of their own relatives, might act against the established order.

Perhaps the most significant indicator of this culture's attitude toward young men is the common linguistic formulation *giovani e garzoni*, that is, youth—those between twenty and forty years of age—and working men or laborers, who in this culture as in many others were called "boys" whatever their age (cf. *garçon, Knecht*, etc.). Elder citizens associated certain psychological and behavioral patterns of the one set of boys (for example, liberality) with those of the working "boys" (wastrels), and feared conspiracies that could unite the two groups against them.

The citizens' fears were to some extent well founded, because no matter how vast the social cleft there might be between one "boy" and another, both groups were dependents and often felt a common resentment toward the possessing city fathers. There were also political experiences to drive the lesson home. In 1342 and 1343, the so-called tyrant Walter of Brienne, in order to crush his opposition, allied himself with a group of upper-class *giovani* against their fathers *and* with a mass of workers or *garzoni*; the latter won their first political rights when Brienne organized them into fraternities that threatened the establishment. Then in 1378 the insurrectionary Ciompi terrified the possessing classes, in part through an unholy alliance with aristocratic youth. "Respectable" fifteenth-century males regarded both these historical precedents as events that had almost ended all law and order.

Fears such as these moved the political class in Florence to work against any union between *giovani e garzoni*, and also to suppress neighborhood, as distinct from city-wide, solidarities. For is it not evident that neighborhood would appear the alpha and omega of self-protection to dependent classes or groups to whom civic or city-wide representation was foreclosed? Obviously the families of the civic regimes, who dared not participate directly in neighborhood imbroglios, used these dependents to make their neighborhoods fortresses of their power, whatever the communal limits on such parochialism. For the dependents themselves, neighborhoods were of elemental importance; and they were, for that reason, opposed in principal by the political classes.

What happened after the mid-fifteenth century was, first, that *giovani e gar-*

zoni re-emerged onto the citywide stage to a great extent as representatives of neighborhoods, and second, that they did so legally. These new parochialisms were supported by the Medici and allied families. Especially during the years of Lorenzo de' Medici (1469–1492)—who himself died before he was old enough to hold the highest civil office—youth was fashionable, and it flaunted its influence with *il Magnifico*. At the same time, a type of bucolic vaunting of the working man was in, and so the *garzoni* of Florence, parading or processing through the streets, also emerged as a public force.

Thus the reputation of young men, including their avocation as fighters, was slowly recouped, to reach its peak in the early sixteenth century, when they boasted of having brought down Savonarola and ended his moral terror. This is the context in which Niccolò Machiavelli, who in his *Prince* would demand that Italians reject mercenaries and learn to defend themselves against foreigners, recommended that Florence's fathers arm their youth to similar ends. The right moment arrived when Florence, under siege, was forced to rely on its young men as saviors. During the Last Republic (1527–1530), the air was filled with the praise not of the children and adolescents, but of the twenty-year-olds, saviors, it was said, of the Republic.

With the fall of the Republic and the rise of the Medici Principate, a new phase of Florentine history began. But in the previous two centuries much had changed. At the ideological level, neighborhood solidarities were now in the ascendancy—under the control of the grand dukes of Tuscany! And in Florence, as in most of Europe, a new positive legal attitude toward youth and children had been put in place. At the institutional level, in the development of the modern foundling home, a complex welfare institution for the housing and training of abandoned children had taken root. Perhaps not completely separate, in the schools and confraternities new instruments for the indoctrination of young boys had been developed. Finally, the important notion of the young saving the old had emerged.

Still, at the start of the sixteenth century, the intellectual, medical, and financial wherewithal to care for a mass of institutionalized children was nowhere to be found. Florentines had indeed learned how to frame familial images that could be maintained through welfare institutions, abandoning children to foundling homes and nunneries so that the nuclear profiles of these family images were limited and manageable. Yet now these institutions, guarantors of familial honor, were at the edge of collapse and horror. Pathos toward the young, in this capital of the Renaissance, was born in suffering.

The Foundlings of Florence, 1395-1455[*]

C HARITY IS AN AMBIGUOUS HUMAN ACTIVITY. INDIVIDUAL KINDNESS documents the power of the giver and the weakness of the recipient. Giving to a charitable institution seems to denote altruism, but in fact permits a tax write-off. Interning the helpless appears to aid them; it also atrophies the human sentiment of solidarity.

This rich man's problem is particularly great when the recipient is an infant who, for whatever reasons, cannot be supported by her parents. Without institutionalization, the infant dies. Having been interned, she has no individual defender, no real civil status—we call her an "it"—nor is she capable of opposing the order which mistreats her. Contributing nothing to the commonweal, she has no claim upon it. She is the child of the state, and the state is a fickle parent.

Foundling homes have always aimed at stabilizing the public order by syphoning off mouths which threaten family and state survival. A Florentine dictum of 1513 gets to the heart of the matter:

> If we were to confess the truth, one can absolutely say that [the foundling home of the Innocenti and the hospital of Santa Maria Nuova] have been and are two firm and solid columns maintaining this sublime Republic and its liberty.[1]

The salvation of unwanted newborn infants did, however, serve other purposes, ones just as important to medieval and early modern society as social preservation. Failure to take in the unwanted newborns increased infanticide and simple abandonment; and as a moral censor, the Florentine commune

---

[*] This essay appeared previously in *History of Childhood Quarterly* 1 (1973): 259–84. I wish to thank Frederic Jaher for his criticism of this paper. The American Philosophical Society helped finance the necessary research.
[1] Cited in F. Del Migliore, *Firenze Città Nobilissima Illustrata* (Florence, 1684), 313.

could not tolerate such practices, for they set a bad example for citizens. Just as important, the absence of foundling homes denied heaven to the unbaptized children who died as a result of this lack.

The moral and material benefits that were derived from foundling homes were as inextricably bound together as were the disadvantages attendant upon their absence. They could help increase population, and at the same time increase God's blessing upon the city:

> One may firmly believe that through these [foundlings] and because of the prayers of these infants, who shine in purity, our most high and omnipotent God in his piety and mercy will not only deign to conserve this his city and state, but allow it to grow daily.[2]

The mixture of motivations was patent. If the commune failed to save unwanted children, the family unit was threatened and the citizenry scandalized by infanticide and desertion. By creating and supporting foundling homes, citizens created merit—making opportunities for themselves, which in turn led to divine support for the city. What could be more altruistic than to allow children to live; what more useful than the prayers of innocents?

The most haunting implication of the care of unwanted children by foundling homes was not directly motivational but institutional. Infants put out to nurse were given to mothers whose own infants had either died, been abandoned, or themselves been given to wet nurses (balie). The lives of the innocents, like those of any child put to nurse, depended on the death or dislocation of their peers. By feeding its charges back into the rural family, the urban foundling home, whose purpose was to stabilize the family unit, inexorably contributed to its dissolution, and to the deaths of other children.[3]

Much has been written in the last century on the social problem of abandonment since the population explosion of the eighteenth and nineteenth century. There is no lack of statistics, tables, and autopsy reports for this period.[4] Yet the sheer enormity of the modern problem has stunted attention to the living human beings caught in the web of an unequal social order. Little is known about the individual mother or father who deserted the nineteenth-century child.

The study of foundling homes in earlier centuries has scarcely begun.[5] The present article examines the constituency of the foundling homes of Flor-

---

[2] *Archivio di Stato, Firenze, Provvisioni* (hereafter *ASF, Prov.*) 147, fols. 169v–171r (29 December 1456). On the concept of salvation by innocents, see "Ritual in Florence: Adolescence and Salvation in the Renaissance," in the present volume.

[3] See "Infanticide in Florence: New Sources and First Results," in the present volume.

[4] Bibliography is to be found ibid., n. 2.

[5] Semichon's and Hügel's works are cited ibid., n. 7; L. Lallemand, *Histoire des enfants abandonnés et délaissés* (Paris, 1885); W. Platz, *Geschichte des Verbrechens der Aussetzung* (Stuttgart, 1876). For Florence, see now P. Gavitt, *Charity and Children in Renaissance Florence: The Ospedale degli Innocenti, 1410–1536* (Ann Arbor, 1990). Unfortunately, this work is often unreliable. See now also the general work of J. Boswell, *The Kindness of Strangers: The Abandonment of Children in Western Europe from Late Antiquity to the Renaissance* (New York, 1988).

ence in the first half of the fifteenth century. It tries where possible to get behind the raw data of sex and age to the textures of abandonment and care, even to the sensibilities of parents forced to desert their infants. From a description of the qualitative as well as the quantitative configurations of foundling care, the uncertainty of life and the ambiguity of motives in dealing with children in this age can be appreciated.

The basic public institutions of Florentine child welfare developed between the thirteenth and early sixteenth centuries. First to surface were receptacles for unwanted children. Of these, Santa Maria da San Gallo was the earliest, appearing in documents dating from the end of the thirteenth century. It had probably accepted infants long before that date.[6] Santa Maria della Scala followed, founded by private donation in 1316.[7] Both institutions received the sick poor as well as infants. By the early fifteenth century, the older facilities had proven inadequate, and in 1419 the commune of Florence in conjunction with the silk guild decided to build a home specifically for foundlings. Santa Maria degl'Innocenti, as this great asylum was called, opened in 1445 and quickly became the central caritative institution for infants in Florence, and indeed for the Florentine dominion.[8]

A clearing house for lost or deserted children was also instituted at an early point. From at least mid-trecento the confraternity of the Misericordia took in lost or abandoned children, caring for them until they were claimed by their frantic parents or until it was certain they had been abandoned. A famous fresco of 1386 pictures the children placed on display by the captains. Overjoyed parents rush to claim their little ones. Other children sit disconsolately by, waiting in vain for parents who will not appear.[9] Such unfortunates, "having remained some days in the house of the said Misericordia, and not being sought after," were sent to one of the foundling homes.[10] In 1389 the hospital of the Scala implied that its foundlings consisted mainly of those who were brought there after "having been lost for a certain period of time."[11]

The Camaldolan monk Ambrogio Traversari described the Scala and its operative plan in a letter of 1435:

There is within the walls of the city of Florence a place, called a brephotrophium in Greek, where exposed infants of uncertain parentage are

---

[6] *ASF, Prov.* 4, fol. 8r (19 May 1294); printed in L. Passerini, *Storia degli stabilimenti di beneficenza e d'istruzione elementare della città di Firenze* (Florence, 1853), 935ff.

[7] *ASF, Prov.* 14, fols. 176v–177r (17 May 1316). In 1319 the hospital was caring for infants; ibid. 16, fols. 47v–48r (26 March 1319).

[8] Passerini, *Storia*, 685–94; his 1444 date of opening resulted from failure to convert the Florentine year, which ended on 25 Mar. (hereafter *sf*) to the modern chronology (hereafter *sc*).

[9] The date of and confraternity pictured in this painting were determined by Passerini (*Storia*, 455ff.).

[10] *Archivio degl'Innocenti, Firenze* (hereafter *AIF*), II,6, fol. 130v (1396).

[11] "In educando et alendo pueros qui ad dictum hospitale deferuntur, tamquam certo tempore carentes" (*ASF, Prov.* 77, fols. 312r–314r [19 February 1388*sf*]).

cared for, more than 200 of both sexes. Customarily they are first given over to wet nurses for breast feeding. When they are weaned, they are diligently cared for within this institution. Boys are sent to learn their letters; girls learn womanly things. When they later become adults, the boys learn a trade which will support them; the girls are married, with the institution providing a dowry.[12]

Boys might wander the streets if they could not find work. Girls should not. The failure to successfully integrate female innocents and even legitimate girls into general society on their reaching adolescence led to the creation of conservatories or warehouses for unwanted adolescents. These institutions did not fully develop until the cinquecento, but the need for them was already pressing a century earlier. In 1454, only nine years after the opening of the Innocenti, a pious confraternity described the situation in no uncertain terms. Due to poverty or a lack of parents, many young girls could not be reared "as honor required." If grown, they could not find husbands equal to their own social position.[13] The conservatory which the brotherhood intended to build would take in indigent young girls, provide them with a dowry, and keep them until a husband could be found. As a result, both poor and dignified families of the city would be relieved, prostitution would be discouraged, and through the "infinite marriages" to be arranged, population would increase.[14]

---

[12] The letter does not name the Scala. Mehus identified it with the Innocenti, but this is impossible for chronological reasons. The occasion of the letter was an indulgence for an adolescent confraternity which met in the hospital. The Scala was the only hospital hosting such a group; see Ambrogio Traversari, *Latinae epistolae* . . . , ed. L. Mehus, 2 (Florence, 1759), col. 39.

[13] The confraternity was the Tempio, in charge of the consolation of condemned criminals (*ASF, Prov.* 145, fols. 97v–100r [20 July 1454]).

[14] "Unum monasterium sive locus aptus pro retinendo puellas et conservando eas in vita honesta et bonorum morum. . . . Cum quotidie per experientiam dignoscatur, quod plurime tum ob defectum parentum, tum ob paupertatem et defectum substantie, non possint nutriri neque conduci eo modo et forma prout secundum honestatem exigeretur, nec postea nutrite ad honorem conduci, cum plurime remaneant innupte et sepe in malum exitum tendunt, quia male conducuntur. Unde ut provideatur et detur remedium quod talia inconvenientia non sequantur et ad hoc ut altissimus deus, mediantibus talibus operibus misericordie et caritatis, subveniat casibus et indigentiis nostre civitatis. . . . Et adtento etiam quanto sit utile rei publice, quia ex predictis sequi habent infinita matrimonia et fieri nuptie, et per consequens repleri et multiplicari hec civitas populo, et resultabit etiam ex hoc novo pietatis opere, fama et reputatio magna huic civitati" ibid. ("A nunnery or place suitable for housing girls and preserving their decency and good morals. . . . For daily experience tells us that due either to the absence of relatives or because of poverty and an absence of wealth, they cannot be reared or guided as decency requires, nor having been reared be honorably married off, many remain unmarried and often end badly, because they are badly guided. So that a remedy is provided so that such things do not happen, and so that the high God, as a result of such works of mercy and charity, will help the households and indigents of our city. . . . And seeing as well how useful it is to the republic, since from the aforesaid will follow and be made infinite marriages, with the result that this city will be replenished and multiplied in populace, and from this new pious work will result great fame and reputation for this city").

As far as can be determined, this particular institution never materialized. Partly as a result of its failure, legitimate unwanted girls from upstanding families started to flow into nunneries, which became another prime Florentine welfare institution. By the early sixteenth century, thirteen percent of all the females in the city were ensconced behind monastic walls.[15] Similar arrangements for legitimate poor girls and grown foundlings were long in coming. In 1518, a Florentine testator endowed the building of a nunnery at the Innocenti for those female innocents who "do not want to marry and who want to preserve their virginity." Those girls closest to puberty were to be favored.[16] At that late date, the asylum still had no effective method to prevent girls from slipping into prostitution after puberty.

A final institution for child care was developed toward mid-cinquecento. Homes for children past weaning but not yet adolescent, those three to ten years old, became an absolute necessity in the 1530s when hordes of these children were deserted by their parents and begged in the streets of Florence. Pleading that those unfortunates were also human beings, the first grand duke of Tuscany instituted homes and asylums for them during the 1540s.[17]

The present state of Florentine historical research does not permit definitive correlations between the evolution of child-welfare institutions and changing social fact. In certain areas, the import of environmental factors cannot be ignored. During the quattrocento the late marriage age of men certainly encouraged the generation of illegitimate children.[18] But was this late age of marriage new? High marriage dowries and the commune's inability to cope with the problem clearly increased the number of unwanted girls in the quattrocento. But had not Dante referred to this problem a century before?[19] The list of contributing factors could be extended: immigration and emigration patterns, military affairs, distributions of wealth. All of these influenced the birth and disposition of children. None has been studied from their point of view.

The relevance of the slave and servant population of Florence to the problem is more difficult to establish. Some writers have made the presence of

[15] R. Trexler, "Le célibat à la fin du Moyen Age: Les religieuses de Florence," *Annales E.S.C.* 27 (1972): 1329–50.

[16] *ASF, Diplomatico, Santa Maria degl'Innocenti*, 22 February 1517sf.

[17] A. D'Addario, *Aspetti della controriforma a Firenze* (Rome, 1972), 464–71, esp. 468.

[18] D. Herlihy, "Vieillir à Florence au Quattrocento," *Annales E.S.C.* 24 (1969): 1341f., 1346.

[19] "Non faceva, nascendo, ancor paura
   la figlia al padre, ché il tempo e la dote
   non fuggían quinci e quindi la misura
Non avea case di famiglia vòte;
   non v'era giunto ancor Sardanapalo
   a mostrar ciò che in camera si puote" (*Paradiso*, 15:103) ("Nor yet did the daughter at her birth cause fear to the father, for the time and the dowry did not outrun due measure on this side and that. Houses empty of family there were none, nor had Sardanapalus arrived yet to show what could be done in the chamber").

slaves in the city responsible for the thoughtless production of bastards.[20] But were the free servant girls of Florence less promiscuous or more respected than their unfree sisters? Not only does the demography of these two groups remain uncertain; their social impact upon the city has scarcely been scientifically examined.[21]

Any future explanation of child-welfare chronology must be based on such material factors, but it will not ignore the relation of the problem to its perception. It is at least conceivable, for example, that earlier centuries had no "child problem" in part because infanticide was tolerated. Or it may become clear that the law conspired against infants by its ignorance of a category of crimes against them.[22] What was merely sad in the twelfth century may have been hideous in the sixteenth.

The manageable problems are difficult enough. It is at best premature to introduce such explanations for child abandonment as "Renaissance moral decline" or "courtly culture." The factual condition of children within a better understood society must be determined before such momentous moral problems can be faced.

The remainder of this article describes the children accepted into the foundling homes from the end of the fourteenth century until about 1455. This half century predates the great crisis in child care of the early sixteenth century, when over 900 children were being admitted each year to the Innocenti, when infanticide in a countryside stripped bare of child refuges became so common that the bishop had to start mass prosecutions of the guilty, and when starving children in great numbers roamed the streets of the city.[23] It shows the emerging problem, and some of the enduring dynamics of abandonment.

In 1419, the city decided to build the Innocenti because of the inadequacy of the two existing homes. Table 1 shows the matriculation into San Gallo during this period, and the effects of the opening of the Innocenti in 1445.

After a dip during the period 1404–1413, admissions to the hospital of San Gallo continued to increase even past the opening of the Innocenti. In 1377, San Gallo had only 38 children living with wet nurses.[24] In 1448 "a much larger number than usual" were being deposited, and San Gallo supported at that date 115 residing with *balie*, and 45 living in the hospital itself.[25] The

---

[20] Representative in this respect is A. Zanelli, *Le schiave orientali a Firenze nei secoli XIV e XV* (Florence, 1885).

[21] See I. Origo, "The Domestic Enemy: Eastern Slaves in Tuscany in the Fourteenth and Fifteenth Centuries," *Speculum* 30 (1955): 321–66. And see now C. Klapisch-Zuber, "Female Celibacy and Service in Florence in the Fifteenth Century," in her *Women, Family, and Ritual in Renaissance Florence* (Chicago, 1985), 132–64.

[22] Future legal scholarship may show that laws that did forbid infanticide and abortion considered them crimes against society rather than against individuals.

[23] For references to later developments, see my "Infanticide," p. 102.

[24] *ASF, Estimo* 338, fols. 10r–11v.

[25] *ASF, Prov.* 139, fols. 60r–v (24 May 1448).

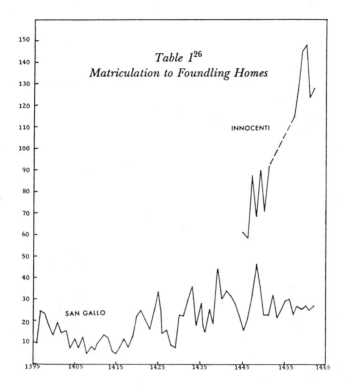

Table 1[26]
Matriculation to Foundling Homes

INNOCENTI

SAN GALLO

books of the Scala have not survived for this period, but other sources show that it too was supporting an increasing number of infants.[27] In 1319, three years after the hospital had opened, 60 infants were supported by the Scala.[28] In 1373 it was said that the citizens of Florence had "growing devotion" for the Scala, and by 1389 more than 130 children were residing with wet nurses.[29] In 1396 the hospital claimed it housed 150 nursing infants.[30] Writing after 1445, when the Innocenti was opened, a Florentine memorialist claimed that the Scala continually had 200 children or more residing with the *balie*.[31]

As early as 1395 both the Scala and San Gallo had petitioned the government for aid because of the *maxima quantitas puerorum* which they support-

---

[26] The table is based on *AIF*, II, 6–11 (*Balie e Bambini*), and *AIF*, XVI, 1–6.

[27] The only *Balie e Bambini* register surviving for the Scala is for the years 1510–1535, in *AIF*, III, 15.

[28] *ASF, Prov.* 16, fols. 47v–48r (26 March 1319).

[29] Ibid., 61, fols. 82v–83r (28 June 1373); 77, fols. 312r–314r (19 February 1388*sf*).

[30] Ibid., 85, fols. 160v–161v (25 August 1396). G. Bruscoli thinks this figure inflated; *Lo spedale di Santa Maria degl'Innocenti* (Florence, 1900), 20.

[31] *Archivio del Seminario Maggiore, Firenze, Codex Rustici*, fol. 55v. The post-1445 date is clear from the fact that besides the description of the Scala and San Gallo (fol. 79r), the author described the operation of the Innocenti (fols. 55v–56r). Recall that Traversari had used the figure 200 in referring to the Scala in 1435; see above, p. 75.

ed.[32] But Table 1 shows forcefully that the availability of a large new asylum quickly multiplied the number of children interned. Those supported by the older institutions had been only a fraction of the unwanted children. In its first eleven months, the Innocenti admitted more children than San Gallo had ever taken in a year.[33] Three years after opening, the Innocenti had already assigned more than 260 infants to wet nurses, and new children were entering every day.[34] By 1456, the number had increased again, and the home warned civil authorities that it might have to close for lack of funds to support such a population, and described the horrendous results that such an action would bring in its wake.[35]

What had happened to all these children before the new home opened? Had they simply been deserted in the streets, starved, or killed? Or had they been retained in the private homes of the city? To answer these and other questions, one must first know more about both the children and their parents—people who, as the city fathers so self-righteously described them, abandoned their offspring "against all nature."

The overwhelming majority of children who were brought to the foundling homes came directly from a particular residence. Depositions given to the hospitallers by bearers of the infants are not always reliable, since many of the porters had something to hide. Yet what they did reveal generally rings true. They occasionally said that the child had been found: a married couple asked to be made the godparents of the infant they had found;[36] a friar baptized an infant he found on the street for fear it would die;[37] pilgrims on their way to San Gallo for the indulgences brought *trovatelli* with them.[38] But these cases were unusual. With rare exception, even true foundlings were discovered in front of a shop, or upon an altar, or at the door of a country hospital.[39] Desertion to fortune, by a ditch or the river, was most uncommon.[40]

A few children came from the Misericordia, the asylum for lost children.

---

[32] *ASF, Prov.* 84, fols. 98v–100r (25 June 1395).

[33] It must be kept in mind that the comparable figures for the Scala are not known. If the *Codex Rustici* is correct, however, the matriculation to that home was maintained after the opening of the Innocenti.

[34] *ASF, Prov.* 139, fols. 46v–47v (29 April 1448).

[35] Ibid., 147, fols. 169v–171r (29 December 1456).

[36] *AIF*, XVI, 1, fol. 74r.

[37] Ibid., II, 9, *anno* 1432.

[38] Ibid., II, 6, fols. 91v, 95v (May, 1395).

[39] Of the 261 admissions to San Gallo in the period 1430–1439, for example, only one child was found in this way—in front of a shop. For a case of a child left on an altar, see *AIF*, XVI, 1, fol. 190v. I encountered only three cases of children being left at country hospitals, one at that of the Carthusian Certosa (ibid., fol. 42r); another at a hospital outside the city gate (*AIF*, II, 7, a. 1406); the third at a hospital in the town of Montelupo (ibid., a. 1411).

[40] Of the above 261 admissions to San Gallo, only three children were found in the street or by the river. The sample 1430–1439 is based on *AIF*, II, 9–10. For a rare case of children found in a ditch, see below, p. 82.

How many children went from there to the Scala we do not know; this hospital's records for the period are not extant. But between 1395 and 1463, only two two-year-old girls came to San Gallo from the Misericordia.[41] Of the first hundred admissions to the Innocenti, only three were brought by employees of the Misericordia, and two of the children's mothers were known to be slaves; the infants were not lost.[42] Obviously, parents who wanted their children to have a chance at life took them or had them taken to the foundling homes, or at least put them where the Misericordia would find them.

In early modern Germany, the porters of children to foundling homes formed a particular artisan group with set tariffs.[43] In Florence, however, this was not so. The bearers of the first 100 infants to the Innocenti were a mixed lot. They identified themselves as follows:

Table 2[44]
Porters of Foundlings to the Innocenti, 1455–1456

Relatives:				
Fathers	2			
Mothers	2			
Parents together	0			
Grandmother	2			
Grandfather	1	Total:	7	
Unrelated:				
Women	37			
Wet Nurses	6			
Men	14			
Boys or Youth	6			
Miscellaneous	9[45]			
			72	
Unknown and Unseen:	21		21	
		Total:	100	

In interpreting this table, two facts should be kept in mind. The period 1455–1456 was one of relative calm. During periods of war and famine, the number of *parents* bringing their children to the hospital increased dramatically. Second, many of the porters identified simply as women or boys or men were servants or friends of the parents. Two interesting results from the table

---

[41] *AIF*, II, 6, fols. 3r, 130v (1394, 1396).

[42] *AIF*, XVI, 1, fols. 17r, 26v, 30v. Unless otherwise noted, all tabulations dealing with the first 100 infants received in the Innocenti were made from *AIF*, XVI, 1 (*Registro de Fanciugli*).

[43] O. Werner, *The Unmarried Mother in German Literature* (New York, 1917), 7.

[44] See n. 42.

[45] This includes three couples, three slaves, two familiars (one of the Signoria), and a "person."

do, however, provide sure aids to understanding attitudes toward desertion. First, one-fifth of the bearers avoided being seen. Yet all but ten of those who personally delivered a child were willing to provide the authorities with information on the parents. Forty-nine of the carriers gave the mother's name or, if she were a slave, her owner's name. Fifty-one refused. Less than half as many gave the father's name (23). The other porters were either recalcitrant or unknowledgeable.

In general, then, the carriers exercised caution in identifying themselves and especially the fathers of the children. They displayed no overwhelming aversion, however, to being seen. The time of day when they deposited the children indicates this. Of 90 entrance times recorded for the same 100 first admissions to the Innocenti, approximately 51 fell between sunrise and sunset, with 39 children being left at the grate during the night. Still, only four of the latter were deposited in the four hours before dawn when the whole city slept.

During periods of relative stability, the children brought to the homes were predominantly of urban provenience. Thus in the decade 1404–1413 when only 92 children were admitted to San Gallo, only one child of the 20 whose provenience is known came with a private person from an area of the dominion away from the city and its walls; one other was brought in from a district hospital.[46] All the other children started to the home from within the city or hard on its walls.

The picture for 1430–1439 was very different. The Florentine district of the Casentino fell victim to treacherous mercenary bands and local princes.

> The whole land of the Casentino ... emptied itself of women and children. They bathed their skin with the tears which flowed from their eyes, and came toward the city with their tiny children, some hanging from the neck, some carried in their arms.... The great mass of the poor women with their children ... was received by the Florentines with open arms and paternal love....[47]

In this decade, 261 children entered San Gallo. Of the 83 places of origin recorded, 51 were from the city, but three-eighths of them (32) came from outside.[48] As might be expected, the proportion of children from the city and countryside in times of crisis depended on the location of the crisis.

No vital statistic regarding abandoned children remained unaffected by environmental conditions. Consider the ages of matriculants to San Gallo during the same two decades:

---

[46] The sample 1404–1413 is based on *AIF*, II, 7.

[47] G. Cavalcanti, *Istorie Fiorentine*, ed. G. Di Pino (Milan, 1944), 397f.

[48] At all times I have included among the rustics only those who assertedly brought their children from the country. The rural origin of the parents is not sufficient; they might have been city residents.

Table 3[49]
Stated Estimates of Children's Ages during Periods
of Low and High Admissions at San Gallo

	1404-1413		1430-1439			1404-1413	1430-1439
Days					Percentages of Total Ages Given		
1	41	(56.2%)	85	(36.2%)			
2	6	(8.2%)	18	(7.6%)			
3 to 6	3	(4.1%)	16	(6.8%)	Less than one week	68.5	50.6
Weeks							
1			4				
2	2		7				
2 to 3	2		3		1 to 3 weeks	5.5	6.
Months							
1	4		2				
2	5		9				
3	1		3				
4			2				
5	1		5				
6			3				
7			1				
8	2		2				
9			3				
10	1		1		1 to 10 months	19.2	13.2
Years							
1 to 1½	2		11				
1½ to 2			4				
2			11		1 to 2 years	2.7	11.1
3	1		16				
4			7				
5			6		3 to 5 years	1.4	12.3
6			4				
7	2		2				
8			4		6 to 8 years	2.7	4.3
9			2				
12			3		9 to 12	0	2.1
15			1		Adolescence	0	.4
Totals*	73		235				

*The total admissions for these two periods were: 1404–1413: 93; 1430–1439: 261.

[49] Based on *AIF*, 2, 9–10. Under "one day" are included those said to be just born. These figures are almost exclusively the estimates of hospital administrators and not of the porters of the children.

In periods of low admissions the hospitallers received almost exclusively children less than one year old. In fact, seven out of ten had just been born; one may assume that abandonment had been premeditated since they were abandoned immediately by their parents. This was a population of children who could not walk, and were still reliant on the breast for their nutrition. If those under three years of age are included in the total, fully 95.9% of the children entering were of pre-weaning age.

The situation during the 1430s was significantly different. True, one of every two children born was immediately abandoned; but a full 30.5% of those admitted were more than one year old, and almost one in five was beyond the normal age of weaning (ca. 2 years). Catastrophe brought into the hospital more children of higher age.

With the opening of the Innocenti in 1445, a division of labor took place with San Gallo, and perhaps the Scala. The new home installed a grate which limited the size of the infants who could be deposited. Older children were taken to San Gallo.[50] This fact explains why so few children beyond the age of weaning are found among those whose age was recorded when they entered the Innocenti. The hospitallers recorded an age estimate for only 52 of the first 360 admissions. Of this number only five were more than six months old, 16 more were between one and six months of age, while the remaining 31 were three weeks old or less. The great majority of children whose ages were not estimated may be assumed to have been newborn. Most were taken to the city baptistry the day after their admission, an indication that they were less than three weeks old.[51]

Under all conditions, more girls than boys entered the asylums. In the decade 1404–1413 the figure stood at 61.2%. In a majority of cases, consequently, parents waited till birth and then abandoned girls. The typical deserter was not a parent who had no room for any child of either sex, not consequently the wet nurse who *had* to sell her milk, not the prostitute, not the desperate unmarried mother. The reasons for the favor shown boys need no detailing. It might simply be mentioned that the boy stemming from the union of a citizen and a servant girl stood a better chance of being accepted into the home by the citizen's wife than did an infant girl.[52]

When catastrophe occurred, as it did in the 1430s in the countryside, the percentage of girls among those placed in the asylum increased, as did their age.

---

[50] Bruscoli noted that in 1483, San Gallo housed only older children (eighteen girls between sixteen and eighteen); see *Lo spedale*, 16. But an examination of earlier data shows that the division of labor was initiated in the first years of the Innocenti: On 15 May 1463, the scribe of San Gallo computed the number still alive of those who had entered since 11 November 1456. Intrapolating for the six calendar years 1457–1462, one finds that 134 of the 158 who had entered were alive and with wet nurses. This extraordinarily low death rate can be explained only by the children being older; *AIF*, II, 11, fols. 127v–129r.

[51] See below, p. 83.

[52] This would seem to at least partially explain the higher masculinity of richer families in Florence in 1427; see my "Infanticide," p. 39.

If they place [their twelve year old girl] with others as they are asked to do every day, it would end badly. And therefore I pray you for the love of God to accept her so that she may be conducted to honor, if it please God.

She would otherwise be harmed, and would become evil, as do the other young servant girls.[53]

Fully 66.3% of the matriculants to San Gallo in this decade were girls. In crisis the least valuable sex was most vulnerable.

Computing the sex ratios for the new asylum of the Innocenti, however, yields unexpected results. In the first 100 admissions to that home, only 54 females are counted, a marked difference from the rule at San Gallo, where the ratio was always above 61%. In the eight and a half years from its opening in 1445 until the end of August 1453, the Innocenti admitted 708 children; 58.9% were girls, 41.1% were boys.[54]

This statistically significant drop in femininity from previous levels must be viewed in conjunction with the fact, previously shown, that the opening of the Innocenti saw a quantum jump in the number of children received into foundling institutions. The new home did not pick up from the others. It ushered in a whole new experience. What explains these two sets of data? Excluding the possibility that San Gallo and the Innocenti preferred different sexes in admissions, and there being no evidence that the older hospitals had ever either refused children or sought out parents—either of which would have kept numbers down by endangering anonymity—one is led to the following hypothesis: the size of the Innocenti and the facilities it offered encouraged parents to abandon in greater numbers that sex which, in the more constricted foundling asylums of an earlier period, they had kept when they could: young males. Like other theses advanced in previous pages, this one could be tested by an examination of Innocenti records in successive decades.

The physical condition of the infants brought to the foundling homes was unexceptional: the children were hungry, perhaps, but in good physical condition. However, some terribly explicit descriptions of mutilated children can be found. Two sisters two and three years old, found in a ditch near the convent of San Marco, came into San Gallo in 1431 "almost out of their senses, for from the way they looked they had been mistreated."[55] But these were older infants. The same home also took in an occasional sick child, or one with physical handicaps who was unacceptable to any other hospital. But among the newborn children only one admission to San Gallo, a set of twins "very scrawny, because they were born before their time," mars the otherwise re-

---

[53] *AIF*, II, 9, a. 1433.

[54] "Si truova essere stati rechati in questa chasa fanciugli 708 tra maschi e ffemine e vera 291 maschi e 417 femmine, de quali sono morti insino a detto di 381 . . ." (*AIF*, XIV, 1, fol. 65r. [31 August 1453]).

[55] "Erano quasi ismemorate perche secondo che parevano erano state male tenute" (*AIF*, II, 9, a. 1431).

markable evidence that the abandoned children had not been mistreated.[56] The first 100 admissions to the Innocenti give a thoroughly representative picture. A month-old child had had smallpox. Four others had scarcely been born when brought to the Innocenti, two covered with blood, their umbilical cord not yet tied, another half dead, livid, and with his mouth full of mucous, and the last of the four with his umbilical cord hurriedly tied with a piece of shoemaker's thread.[57] In 95 of the 100 cases, the child arrived with trivial pieces of cloth its only dowry, but otherwise in acceptable physical condition.[58]

The first duty of the guardian who welcomed the innocent to its new home was to determine if it was baptized, for Christians believed that unbaptized innocents who perished were condemned to eternal perdition. If the infant arrived with a tiny sack of salt worn about its neck, the administrators knew that the child had not been baptized.[59] Otherwise they relied upon the deposition of the porters, or, when this was not forthcoming, upon their own estimates of age. At San Gallo the hospitallers assumed in such cases that a child estimated to be fifteen days old or less had not been baptized, while those over twenty days old were assumed to have received the sacrament. If they arrived in good condition, unbaptized children were sent on the following day to the communal font at San Giovanni, a half mile from the asylum of San Gallo, a third of a mile from the Innocenti. When assumed baptized because of their age, infants were simply named by the home and conditionally baptized. The foundling homes saw no reason to spend any more money on baptisms than necessary. "Because she was so old [ten months], we did not have her baptized in San Giovanni, but in the house, because we hope she had been baptized."[60]

Sometimes an infant arrived on the point of death. This was the one case

---

[56] "Lunedi a di decto mona Antonia di Nanni Berlinghieri da Lunari ci meno una fanciulla femina deta danni 4 o circa. Era inferma e disse che niuno spedale laveva voluta accettare. Disse cherra figliuola di Domenico di mona Pippa e disse che aveva nome Margherita"; ibid., fol. 118v (18 August 1432) ("Monday the said date madam Antonia di Nanni Berlinghieri da Lunari brought us a female girl about four years old. She was sick and she said that no hospital had wanted to accept her. She said she was the daughter of Domenico di mona Pippa and she said that her name was Margherita"). "Molti scriati perche erano nati innanzi al tempo, e sicondo che dissono, erano figliuoli di suor Nanna, monaca del munistero di San Baldassare"; ibid., 9, a. 1437. Mutes occasionally turned up. The father of one, "la quale e atratta sorda, ciecha, e mutola," had been executed (ibid., 7, a. 1413).

[57] The five cases are respectively at AIF, XVI, fols. 28r, 10r, 33v, 5r, and 44r, one Giorgio, who "avea leghato il belicho chonuno spaghetto" ("had tied the umbilical cord with a little string").

[58] That is, their physical condition was not remarked by the scribe. Cases where a child was placed dead through the grate are encountered only later; see for example AIF, XIV, nn. 119, 216, 281.

[59] "E recho a cholo il sale per sengnio non era batezato" (AIF, XVI, 1, fol. 44r). Such bits of salt were commonplace.

[60] A fifteen-day-old assumed unbaptized: AIF, II, 7, fol. 54v; a twenty-day-old assumed baptized: ibid., 6, fol. 101v. The quote is from ibid., 10, a. 1437.

where the universal church and the local baptistry permitted and even demanded immediate baptism by the nearest adult. The following entry gives the flavor of such an admission:

> She was put naked in the hole in the wall unbaptized, a newborn child all full of blood on the head and on the rest of her back. Her umbilical cord had not been tied, and we could neither see nor know who had brought her; he had fled away. The said girl had been born in that instant. She was brought on the second day of January, 1445, Sunday evening at four and a half hours of the night. Frate Mariano of the Servites and a companion were here, and Frate Mariano baptized her in the house, because it seemed to us that she would die. We did everything to warm her head and dry out all her parts. We had her umbilical cord tied and we washed away all the blood with warm white wine. On the following morning the third we had her baptized at San Giovanni with the aforementioned name [Smeralda].[61]

In a majority of the cases, the hospitallers either knew or assumed that the children had not been baptized. Using the first 100 admissions to the Innocenti as a sample, one finds that 68.3% of those whose vital statistics were given had not been baptized. More than two-thirds of the parents left this to the Innocenti.

It might seem surprising that parents endangered the children's souls after taking such good care of the children they abandoned. Reflection removes surprise. By diocesan and canon law laymen were prohibited from baptizing on their own except *in articulo mortis*.[62] Baptisms cost money, and for those desperate poor who abandoned their children, the ritual was beyond their means. Parents were also dissuaded from taking bastard infants to the city or rural font by shame, and for fear that their sin would become priestly and public knowledge. Had not Leonardi Bruni said that the Innocenti allowed Florentines to hide their blush from mortal men?[63] Florentines were certainly acquainted with the bad *exemplum* of the hospitaller who allowed the abandoned to die without baptism because of the expenses involved in their care.[64] But as the letters of harried parents show, and as the *spedalunghi* of the Innocenti and San Gallo were pleased to assert, the people of Florence

---

[61] *AIF*, XVI, 1, fol. 33v. Another case of emergency baptism was that of a premature girl whom the authorities named Innocente; ibid., fol. 37v.

[62] In the fourteenth century Florentine bishops learned that if too much leeway were given, laymen would avoid the priestly rite; see R. Trexler, *Synodal Law in Florence and Fiesole, 1306–1518* (Vatican City, 1971), 67. Following a decree of the Clementines, they restricted lay baptisms.

[63] "Oggi si và cercando di preparare dove essi abbin'occasione d'occultare, e tor dalle fronti loro quel rossore, il quale non sarà possibile nascondere, ne celare, per la colpa di fragilità contratta, nel cospetto dell'Altissimo Iddio" (Del Migliore, *Firenze Illustrata*, 308) ("Today one seeks to prepare a place where they can be hidden, and thus remove from [the citizens'] faces the blush of shame. It will not be possible to hide or conceal it, because of the guilt of fragility one has shown, from the eye of the high God").

[64] Salimbene De Adam, *Cronica*, ed. G. Scalia (Bari, 1966), 1:105.

had faith in the loving spiritual and temporal care which would be lavished on the innocents by their hospitals.[65] All in all, it was best to leave the baptism to the hospitals.

After the gateman had clarified the spiritual state of the infant, he was required to obtain from the porter as much information about the child as he could. Where and when had she been baptized, and by whom? What was the porter's name? The parents' names, domicile, and occupations? Where had the foundling been discovered? Did the bearer know why the child had been given up?[66] The administrator also carefully recorded all the pieces of clothing and other materials which were brought with the child, paying special attention to any "sign," such as an epistle or a particular symbol which would identify the provenience of the child.

This careful procedure served two purposes. Firstly, the identification of the child might aid the hospital in obtaining from the parents or guardians some stipend which would help alleviate the financial burden of the house.[67] Secondly, identifying marks such as a cross or a circle made it possible for parents to come to the hospital, pay the cost of upkeep, and reclaim their own child with no chance of mistake, a practice which the foundling homes were of course interested in fostering.[68] The conflict in the mind of the deserter can easily be imagined. A symbol could give away the father's identity, bringing him and his family to shame. Without a sign, however, there was no chance of reclaiming a child desperately wanted but, for the moment, financially or socially off limits.

Who were these fathers and mothers who yielded their offspring to the republic? The safest statement about them is one of the most difficult to tabulate: excluding admissions in times of personal or environmental (see below, Table 4) catastrophe, the majority of parents had conceived the child out of wedlock. In the first 100 entries to the Innocenti, for example, only one child can be definitely described as legitimate; his father had just died.[69] Not many other legitimate children could have been among this number. Thirty-four of the mothers were said to be slaves, their partners being various

---

[65] One of the reasons populations of the Innocenti and San Gallo were increasing, said their governors, was "quia etiam scitur quod ibi optime gubernantur" (*ASF, Prov.* 139, fols. 46v–47v [29 April 1448]) ("because it is known that they are optimally cared for there"). "Ex bona gubernatione que sit in presentiarum per dictum hospitale." (ibid., fols. 60r–v [24 May 1448]) ("due to the good care the said hospital gives those in it.").

[66] By law of 30 December 1451, the commune itself ordered the Innocenti to keep a book listing the first and middle names of all matriculated children, the day they were taken, and baptismal information (*ASF, Prov.*142, fols. 380v–382r).

[67] This stipend was adjusted according to the health of the child when it was returned; see below, p. 93.

[68] Examples of these symbols are recorded at *AIF,* XVI, 1, fol. 9r (a consecrated candle and a baptismal amulet minutely described; such amulets can be seen in many paintings of baptisms); see ibid., fol. 16v (an amulet); *AIF,* II, 9, *a.* 1435 (three rosaries of wood). Parents sometimes cautioned the hospitals not to yield the child except to someone bearing the "true sign"; see below.

[69] The father was a swordmaker (*AIF,* XVI, 1, fol. 40r).

freemen from Florence, and six other unions were declared illegal.[70]

Porters obviously did not hesitate to identify the mother when she was a slave, nor did they draw back from identifying her owner. They did so in 32 of the 34 cases in this sample. The results are illuminating. Only about half (15) of the owners were from the patriciate of Florence.[71] Another 14 were Florentines of professional or artisan status without outstanding names.[72] The remaining three owners were said to be foreigners.[73]

When it came to identifying the father of a slave's child, however, the porters were silent. Despite the strong presumption that the owners might be the fathers, in only one of the 34 cases did the porter say that a slave's child had been sired by a Florentine citizen: the mother of Mariano Manovelli brought the child and admitted that it had been fathered by her son.[74] The rules were almost absolute: the name of the father of a slave girl's child was taboo. These children were rarely reclaimed or subvented by their fathers.[75]

Many porters told the hospitallers that the father was a "buon cittadino" who would pay all costs, but such assertions were not taken too seriously by the authorities.[76] As often as not these identifications were forgivable deceptions by parents who could not keep the child, but wanted him or her to survive the hardships of life as an innocent. Assuming that children of "decent" parents were better cared for in the home, the parents naturally urged the porters to assert such dignified parentage. The administrators knew from ex-

---

[70] Two of the six fathers were foreigners; one was a soldier; one child had been born out of wedlock in the countryside; another resulted from a couple living together in Florence; one father secretly gave his name to the *spedalungo*.

[71] The families of the owners were the Ridolfi, Alberti, Boscoli, Parenti, Bardi, Cerretani, Panciatichi, Martelli, Pitti, Minerbetti, Soldani, Migi, Manelli, Pucci, and Altoviti. Of the slave-owners identified in the records of San Gallo, one holds more than passing interest: Cosimo de'Medici (*AIF*, II, 9, *a.*1437).

[72] These included Antonio di Taddeo, a *lanaiuolo* (*AIF*, XVI, 1, fol. 32v), the spicer Cambio di Giovanni (ibid., fol. 41r), and Maestro Simone, M. D. (ibid., fol. 51r).

[73] These included Francesco Contarini, "gentile huomo da Venezia," whose lover had given birth to her child in the house of Manno Temperanni (ibid., fol. 3v), and two Pisans.

[74] *AIF*, XVI, 1, fol. 22v. Subsequent entries in this volume do show an occasional Florentine patrician identified as the father of a slave's child: Vieri di Tommaso Corbinelli and a slave belonging to the lawyer Otto Niccolini, whose child entered 10 February 1447 and died one week later (ibid., fol. 72r); Baldassare del Rosso del Buondelmonte, whose child entered 22 February 1449 (ibid., fol. 170v). Riunigi degli Stozzi (ibid., fol. 172v); Francesco Manovelli (ibid., fol. 184r).

[75] Early exceptions were: the wife of Nerone di Nigi came to the Innocenti in 1445 and admitted that a child left anonymously belonged to her slave (*AIF*, XVI, 1, fol. 7v). Again, "Dipoi vene qui Bastiano di Meo di Piano di Ripoli della famiglia degli Azzi e disse era suo figliuolo" (ibid., fol. 13r) ("Then Bastiano di Meo di Piano di Ripoli, among the familiars of the Azzi, came here, and said it was his son"). Finally, Francesco de' Ginori and his wife came forward and recognized an anonymous child of a slave-girl as being of their nephew (ibid., fol. 22r). In a case at San Gallo, mona Giovanna, the wife of Jacopo Ardinghelli, confessed that the newborn child was the son of her husband and their slave Niccolina (*AIF*, II, 6, fol. 114v).

[76] This was very common at San Gallo in the 1430s. See for example ibid., 10, *a.* 1439 (twice). See also the letter quoted below, p. 25.

perience that such pretensions were practically never followed by either re-demption of the child or contribution to her welfare. When one porter re-fused all information except that the child's father was a rich citizen who would come to take her, the *spedalungo* departed from his practice of baptiz-ing according to the saint's day and christened this little girl "Richa."[77]

An examination of the data related to the children of slave girls shows that, almost without exception, parents considered slave parentage in itself suffi-cient justification for abandonment. Occasionally a shamed father hinted that he would have kept the child mothered by a slave but had to give it up "so as to avoid arguing with his wife," or because "his wife did not want to see it be-cause it was the child of their slave."[78] But in general, the anxiety attendant on abandonment which we shall encounter among other social groups was ab-sent among such fathers. The scribe's entry is free of second thoughts.

The one other group whose anonymity was unquestioningly preserved by the hospitallers were clerical parents. Hospitallers were themselves ecclesiasti-cal persons and interested in maintaining the reputation of the estate. Thus in 1412 the scribe of San Gallo wrote at two points:

> According to what she told me, [the newborn girl] came from a nun-nery, which I will not mention for reputation's sake.[79]

> A friar brought [the newborn girl] in a basket with which they go to beg bread, and secretly put her in the children's cottage. For reputation's sake I will not mention the order to which the friar belonged who brought her.[80]

With the exception of slave and clerical parentage, illegitimacy does not seem to have furnished sufficient moral or material justification for abandon-ment. Again and again signs of concern and shame appear in the separate pages devoted to each infant. In eleven of the first 100 cases of the Innocenti, the father sent along a note directed to the hospitaller. Most are scribbles ask-ing no more than mercy for the child. Others are full letters portraying the human qualities of their senders.

> Although I am poor, poverty or diffidence at being able to feed him is not the principal reason for sending him. Rather it is in the main the fear of scandal which could follow if such a thing were known. And to flee this, I have turned to Your Prudence. . . .[81]

> We were asked to raise the boy here, to flee great scandal and shame.[82]

---

[77] *AIF*, XVI, 1, fol. 78v.
[78] *AIF*, II, 9, *a.* 1437; ibid., 10, *a.* 1439.
[79] *AIF*, II, 7, *a.* 1412.
[80] Ibid.
[81] Ibid., 10, *a.* 1437.
[82] Ibid.

The illusions and hopes of desperate fathers are magnificently brought out in the following letter contained in a matriculation entry:

Wednesday on the said date, approximately before the third hour, a worker who did not want to say his name brought us a girl born at that moment. He brought with him a writing which speaks of a boy, but he who brought him brought a girl. And the tenor of the writing says as follows: "Jesus, 1429. *Rogo vos sicut charissime pater dominus prior*, that this boy-child be attended to by you, that he be given to a good wet nurse who has fresh milk. And if he could be placed [with a wet nurse] near the Casentino, I would be most thankful, for it would help for us to be near each other. But above all I pray you in love not to concede him to anyone except to one who shows you the true sign, for it is he who wants to pay you for every cost and be always obligated before God and the world. *Dominus vos custodiat ab omni malo. Die primo mensis Martii.*" And the said girl-child had salt with her as a sign that she was not baptized. We had her baptized and bestowed the name Alessandra.

The only other entry in this block is: "She died on the second day of June, 1430."[83]

Another father asked the local parish priest's indulgence for his act:

Tuesday night about midnight a boy-child of about two years old was left with us, and he carried writing that read as follows: "It is necessary to say a few words to you, honorable father. I commend this child to you in the name of the only God. Please baptize it and let his name be Matteo and Domenico. Ignore the fact that he brings so little with him, for in the future you will be reimbursed in such a way as to make you content, and before two months are up. And send him to the hospital of San Gallo and in God's name ask the lord prior to have good care taken of him and he will be well reimbursed, both for the cost of the wet nurse and every other thing. Be patient and do not be angered because you found him at your doorstep. And for God's sake, do not make any commotion! Carry him secretly [to San Gallo] and do not bother to keep this writing, which in time will be sought out. Dear Ser Domenico, I commend [the boy] to you. I have not been able to bring myself to write my name so that it will not be publicly known, because I do not want it to come into the hands of anyone. You are a great help. For God's sake, for God's sake, for God's sake, I commend [the boy] to you." We had him baptized and named him Matteo and Domenico.[84]

The entry gives no indication that the boy was ever further aided by his father.

---

[83] Ibid., 9, fol. 65v. The Latin phrases may indicate that the father was a member of the clergy.

[84] *Ibid.*, fol. 161v.

Invaluable as such missives are for penetrating the psychological make-up of a few fathers—I encountered no letters from mothers—they take one only so far. Illegitimacy was not in itself enough to extinguish moral compunction, the parental sense of obligation; these parents harbored guilt feelings and illusions. But so often in these letters, personal tragedy obscured the social forces—the disdain of neighbors, for example—which lay below expressions of individual guilt and shame. Some of the writers clearly wished that society were free enough to allow them to keep their creations at their sides, or they were wealthy enough to permit support. Their repeated assurances that in the future they would identify themselves symbolized the utopic freedom men and women postulate to give meaning to their acts. Like most humans then and since, however, they chose an illusion rather than resistance to the social order.

These social forces are seen at work with devastating earnestness in periods when war and famine ravaged the country. In the period 1430 to 1439, environmental conditions were so massively causative—the children were older, more often rustics and females, and legitimate—so dramatic, that a diligent and sensitive scribe at San Gallo took note of them often enough to make tabulation worthwhile. Table 4 summarizes the most specific reasons for abandonment given by carriers or parents during this decade.

Only the diligence of the scribe of San Gallo accounts for the extensive depositions which make this chart possible. None of the other early records of that hospital or of the Innocenti affords a statistical insight into the social motivations of parents. It is all the more important, therefore, that the anguish of familial tragedy and social injustice not be silenced by the historian's calculator. Here are examples of the reality behind the numbers:

War:
Because she had no bread to give her by reason of the war and the costs.

Because the father ... left in desperation and she did not know where, because they had lost or had had burned everything they had, and she was dying of hunger.

Because of hunger and war, since they had not harvested anything and she said Salvi was carried off to Siena, and she believed he would never return. For this reason she commended the girl to the hospital.[85]

She was brought in because of the war underway at Poppi; the mother could not feed her because, having lost everything she had, she had taken flight.[86]

---

[85] All three of these motivations were given in 1432 (*AIF*, II, 9). On the military operations around Barbialla, Avertina, Gello, Linari, and Colle, from whence these unfortunates came, see N. Machiavelli, *History of Florence* (New York, 1960), 178–79.

[86] *AIF*, II, 9, a. 1436.

Table 4[87]
Justification for Abandonment, San Gallo, 1430–1439

A. *Inability to support*
I.   War   11
II.   Poverty   17
III. Work requirements
      a. Servants   6
      b. Wet nurses   <u>3</u>   9
IV.   Family conditions
      a. Intact marriages
         1. Too many children   6
      b. No functioning parent
         1. Orphans   4
         2. Abandoned   2
         3. Father dead and mother remarried   2
         4. Father dead or missing and mother dying 2
         5. Wet nurse no longer paid   2
      c. Single parent
         1. Abandonment by husband   4
         2. Abandonment by wife   1
         3. Husband is widower   4
         4. Husband is disabled   1
         5. Husband is worthless   1
         6. Wife is widow   1
         7. Wife is beggar   <u>1</u>   31
B. *Societal Norms.*
I.   Clerical Parent
      a. Monk   1
      b. Friar   1
      c. Secular clerks   4
      d. Nuns   3
      e. Third order   <u>1</u>   10
II.   Fear of "scandal"   2
III. Wife refuses husband's bastard   <u>2</u>   4
C. *Mixed justifications of support and norms.*
I.   Slave-mothers   <u>23</u>
                                          Total: 105

Family Conditions:
Thursday on the said date, the weaver Antonio di Tommaso di Jacopo of the parish of San Felice in Piazza [of Florence] brought us four of his children both male and female, one of whom he said was named An-

[87] There were a total of 261 admissions during this period. For archival references, see n. 40.

drea, of six years, the second a girl he said was named Lisa and was five
years old, the third a girl he said was named Salvestra of four years old,
the fourth a boy he said was named Piero and Pagolo and was two years
old. He said that he gave them to the said hospital because the mother
has been dead some months and he has been sick for several months
with seven children, and that he has consumed everything he owns, and
so much so that he can no longer feed them. And thus he prays us that
for the love of God we should accept them. And we did that; they were
all scabby and sick because of the poor care.[88]

Work Conditions:
Because of poverty; through war she had lost everything she had. She
had to hire herself out as a servant.[89]

She could not feed her and she wanted to hire herself out as a wet
nurse to be able to live.[90]

Because she could not feed her and she neither knew how to nor could
she keep her with her, being the servant of others.

The father did not want to do anything. It was necessary for her to hire
out as a wet nurse if she wanted to live, because she was dying of
hunger.

Perhaps the 1430s were not a normal decade. Certainly Florentine society was
not the only one inhuman enough to force mothers to abandon their infant
children so they could sell their milk. But human beings do not experience
their lives *in specie saeculorum*. Seldom enough do the very words of the victims reach up to us. They should be grasped, the hundreds of similar letters
carefully examined for their imposing human and social content. They are especially valuable for students of Florence, that still magical, mythic city of cul-
tured burgher *insouciance*.

  With the opening of the Innocenti in 1445, parents needed to fear less for
the future of their child. The new asylum was spacious and uncrowded.
Males, the valuable sex, flowed into the Innocenti at a higher rate than before. The life of the innocents in these early years would at least be better
than the children could have enjoyed outside.
  Within a few years of opening, however, the Innocenti dashed such confidence. Conditions developed within the home which made it possible for children to die there as quickly, yes, even more frequently, than in general society. The parent in 1445 left his child with hope. The deserter of the end of
the century could wager he was consigning his child to death. An examination

---

[88] Ibid., 10, fol. 12r (30 January 1438).
[89] Ibid., 9, *a.* 1433; "Fante" is translated as servant, although it may have implied wet
nurse at times.
[90] The following quotations are from ibid., *a.* 1433, 1435, 1435.

of death expectancy in these first years initiates an attempt to understand the dynamics of foundling mortality.

Table 5[91]

Cumulative Death Expectancy of Entrants to Innocenti, 1445–1451 in Percentage of Entrants

Less than	1445	1446	1447	1448	1449	1450	1451
1 Year	26.2	23.7	29.9	53.6	43.3	47.9	57.6
2	29.5	28.8	45.0	59.4	52.2	53.5	
3	31.1	33.9	50.6	62.3	53.3		
4	32.8	42.4	58.6	62.3			
5	39.3	44.1	60.9				
6	42.6	44.1					
7	44.3						

Parents left an infant with the foundling home because they believed society had more resources to care for it than they. Surprisingly, the experience of the first two years at the Innocenti bore them out. The death rate in the new home was no greater than that in general society.[92] In a hospital of minimum crowding, and with a sufficient supply of *balie*, spared famine and pestilence, the first innocents had as good a chance as any children.[93] To this day bastards are about three times as likely to die in infancy as readily as legitimate children.[94] Thus the first two classes of Innocenti were "fortunate" indeed.

As long as incoming infants could quickly be moved out of the hospital to the wet nurses, the foundling system offered room for confidence. The monthly mortality rates show that infants' chances were poorest if they were in the hospital during the summer or with the rural wet nurses in late summer and early fall. The diseases of the summer and fall were more dangerous than the cold of winter. Under optimal conditions, the rural *balie* saved lives.

---

[91] Based on *AIF*, XIV, 1.

[92] Herlihy determined that around 1427 the death rate in the first year of life for the population of nearby Pistoia was 21%; *Medieval and Renaissance Pistoia* (New Haven, 1967), 283.

[93] In September, 1450, for example, the Innocenti scribe noted that a three-year-old had died at *balia* and a five-year-old in the hospital from plague. Clearly, infection from *morbo* was not yet a significant life-expectancy factor at the Innocenti (*AIF*, XIV, 1, nn. 14, 21).

[94] For Italian mortalities 1928–1930, see G. Chiassino and M. Natale, *Ricerche sulla mortalità infantile* (Rome, n.d.), 26f.

Table 6[95]
Month and Place of Death of Innocenti Foundlings,
12 March 1445 to 16 December 1452

	Total	Hospital	Wet Nurse
Jan.	15	3	11
Feb.	12	6	6
Mar.	14	5	9
Apr.	13	6	7
May	24	6	16
Jun.	28	18	9
Jul.	41	23	17
Aug.	50	29	21
Sep.	41	11	28
Oct.	34	9	25
Nov.	23	8	15
Dec.	27	9	17
	322	133 (42.5%)	181 (57.5%)

In early February, 1454, a scribe calculated that in slightly more than nine years, 395 of the 738 matriculants had died, 53.5% of the total.[96] Long-term operation was more sobering than initial optimism might have predicted. Overcrowding, with its potential for epidemic and crushing financial burden, was still only on the horizon, still only a minor factor in high mortality.[97] In these years, the great threat to life came from catastrophic events. Table 7 helps to locate the years and causes of these events.

From the death-expectancy figures in Table 5, the reader has already surmised that 1448 and 1451 were the years of catastrophe in the early operation of the Innocenti. Table 8 first shows where they died. In 1448 and 1449, for example, more than twice as many children died at wet nurse as at the hospital. Contrarily, in 1451 and 1452 many more children perished in the hospital than

[95] Based on AIF, XIV, 1, this table includes all deaths for which a month was available.
[96] AIF, XIV, 1, fol. 65v.
[97] For later materials, see Relazione storica-descritiva del regio spedale degli Innocenti (Brefotrofio) di Firenze (Florence, 1912), 41; L. Passerini, Notizie storiche dello spedale degl'Innocenti di Firenze (Florence, 1853), 33.

Table 7[98]
Place of Deaths of Innocenti Foundlings by Year, 1445 to 1452

| Died in the Year | | | Entered in the Year, Died before 1453 | |
Hospital	Wet Nurses		Hospital	Wet Nurses
5	6	1445	12	15
9	8	1446	9	16
10	17	1447	17	33
13	29	1448	12	30
15	48	1449	13	34
20	39	1450	15	23
34	19	1451	35	20
_26	_15	1452	_19	_10
132	181		132	181

with the rural wet nurses. Isolating the two classes of 1448 and 1451 to determine when within the first year of life mortality occurred will provide all the elements necessary to determine the cause of death.

Even without verification from other documents, these tables show that in 1448 children were going to wet nurses and dying of infectious disease. The class of 1451 never experienced the risk of epidemic; the hospital was not sending the arrivals to *balie*, and they died in the hospital. Comparing the 1451 rates of death in the early months of life to those of 1448, one sees that in 1451 roughly half of those who would die in the first year perished before they were two months old, as compared to 37.8% for the year 1448. The mortality of the class of 1448 was almost as high as that of 1451—pestilential epidemic could be as devastating as starvation. But death occurred more frequently among the wet nurses and at a later age.

External documentation confirms the evidence of the tables. In 1448 Tuscany and the whole of northern Italy were struck with the plague.[99] Entering the city in the fall, it apparently had no significant impact on the Innocenti, due probably to the low population density of the house. Elsewhere in Florence, however, its effects were substantial. Early in October, the government

[98] Based on *AIF*, XIV, 1.
[99] Alessandra Macinghi negli Strozzi, *Lettere di una gentildonnna fiorentina del secolo XVI ai figliuoli esuli*, ed. C. Guasti (Florence, 1877), 43.

Table 8[100]
Age and Place of Death Before the First Birthday,
Entrants of 1448 and 1451, Divided by Sex

| | 1448 | | | | | 1451 | | | | |
| | Hospital | | Wet Nurses | | % of 1-Year Mortalities | Hospital | | Wet Nurses | | % of 1-Year Mortalities |
	M	F	M	F		M	F	M	F	
Before										
1. *month*	4	2	1	1	21.6	8	5	1		27.4
2.	2		3	1	37.8	5	4		2	49.0
3.	1	1	1	3	54.1	3	2	2		62.7
4.				5	67.5	2		1	2	72.7
5.	2		1	2	81.1	1		2	1	80.4
6.					81.1	1				82.4
7.			2	3	94.6				3	88.2
8.			1		97.3			1	2	94.1
9.					97.3		1			96.1
10.					97.3					96.1
11.					97.3	1				98.0
12.	—	—	1	—	100.0	—	—	—	1	100.0
	9	3	10	15		21	12	7	11	

took steps to meet the threat.[101] Eleven people were said to have died on the twenty-ninth of the month. Five days later, the estimate was four or five per day.[102] In the friary of San Marco, five young Dominicans perished.[103] At the behest of the bishop, the Signoria ordered processions to implore God's mercy.[104] Through all of this, the Innocenti successfully isolated itself. It was in the countryside that the hospital's children suffered.

---

[100] Based on ibid.
[101] ASF, Prov.139, fols. 125r–126r (3 October 1448).
[102] Strozzi, Letter, 37, 43.
[103] Biblioteca Laurenziana, Biblioteca di San Marco, cod. 370 (Cronica del Convento).
[104] Strozzi, Letter, 43.

Since the census in the Innocenti was still fairly low—the density of later years made epidemic almost unavoidable—and since a significant part of the general society also put its children out to wet nurse, it may be that Innocenti mortality in 1448 was a microcosm of wider society. The same cannot be said for the deaths of 1451. Certainly there were parents in general society who stopped paying their privately hired wet nurses. But when the government did the same, catastrophe followed. In 1451 the commune simply stopped paying the Innocenti the interest due it on the hospital's investment in the public debt.[105] The result was famine. The children could not be put out to wet nurses, for the hospital could not pay their wages. Innocents were left to die.

Though the commune attempted in the 1450s to stabilize the income of the home so as to avoid repeating such a catastrophe, the steadily climbing resident census posed a continuing threat in later years. Other famines followed. In 1484 the hospitallers pleaded with the government for new subventions to avoid a replay of one just past. Of course, no contemporary chronicle mentions these disasters, but then, this was not the type of subject one talked about. Yet everyone knew. It was, said the governor of the asylum,

a thing which harms everyone, to be able to say that men as naturally mild and pious as is the Florentine *popolo* could, I do not say support, but narrate and hear [such a thing] without horror and fear.[106]

The future held many more tears, and great horrors. Florentine society's inability to reintegrate the graduates of the institute helped guarantee great warehouses of the unwanted, streets full of begging children, and recurring pestilence in the Innocenti. The increasing number of matriculants sent into the countryside caused major social dislocations and increased the mortality of rural as well as urban babies.

Could the commune of Florence have prevented this disaster while maintaining a system of open admissions to the Innocenti? In the nineteenth century the same type of question exercised the social planners of Europe. Did social welfare for infants create new problems without solving previous ones?[107] No complete response can yet be hazarded for the Florentine case, since so little is known about the causes of increased matriculations, the pay

---

[105] The Innocenti was actually struck by two communal attacks on its privileged tax status. In September, 1451, the commune laid a 25% gabelle upon any land passing from tax-supporting to charitable entities (ASF, *Prov.* 142, fols. 216v–217r [10 September 1451]). The archbishop finally forced the government to cancel the law under threat of excommunication; see R. Morçay, *Saint Antonin. Archevêque de Florence (1389–1459)* (Paris, 1914), 481f. Probably at about the same time, the government stopped paying interest on investment credits held by those not paying taxes. A law to that effect was passed in January, 1452; see the paraphrase of its contents in ASF, *Prov.* 161, fols. 271r–272r (12 March 1470). In 1456, the hospital still said it could not meet costs (ASF, *Prov.* 147, fols. 169v–171r [29 December]). In 1466 it admitted that the 456 wet nurses were refusing to serve because they were not being paid (ibid., 157, fols. 21v–22v [16 April]).

[106] Ibid., 174, fols. 157v–161r (18 Feb. 1483*sf*).

[107] Hügel, *Findelhäuser*, 395f.

arrangements of the *balie*, and many other factors. The present article does, however, provide certain information in this regard.

The prejudice against females was continuous; it was institutionalized in the operation of the Innocenti, and it was deadly.[108] The marked increase in total admissions to the homes after the Innocenti opened in 1445, coupled with increased masculinity, suggest that increased facilities stimulated parents' readiness to abandon. If the sex ratios at the Innocenti had turned out to be the same as at San Gallo, one could not present this view. But the increase in the favored sex's census may mean that some of the children swelling the rolls would otherwise have been kept in private homes. This tends to support the nineteenth-century "Protestant" argument that open-admissions foundling institutions, while they may have prevented some infanticide, actually stimulated the desertion of children from tolerable economic and social familial conditions.[109]

The deserters were not heartless or brutal. Children were in good physical condition when they were abandoned, and the depositions of parents show a keen sense of remorse at the loss of their children, excepting those of slaves and clergy. It remains to be seen whether the unprecedented desertions of the later part of the quattrocento and cinquecento were accompanied by an increasing indifference to the act. The paternal depositions of this period could provide an answer. They deserve careful study.

Alimentary, fiscal, and military catastrophes very significantly affected the vital statistics of the matriculants. Yet the loss of children was not completely beyond the control of members of the community. Contemporaries were quick to blame the wet nurses for malice. This paper shows that the commune itself, even in the early years when the financial burden was not crushing, deserted its children rather than its other responsibilities. Republican governments in turn only reflect the determination of citizens to deal with social problems. The attitude toward, if not the treatment of, the child, was not our own. Like women and slaves, infants' value—little enough to start with—rose and fell according to their social condition. In 1447, a father came forward to reclaim his child from the Innocenti. He paid only part of the cost which the hospital had incurred in caring for the child. The scribe explained why:

We let the rest go, because the boy was sick when we returned him.[110]

---

[108] Trexler, "Infanticide."

[109] Hügel, *Findelhäuser*, 395f.

[110] "El resto li lascio per dio, perchel fanciullo era malato quando lo riebbe" (*AIF*, XIV, 1, n. 148).

Infanticide in Florence:
New Sources and First Results

H OW MANY INFANTS, BORN AGAINST THEIR [MOTHERS'] WILL, ARE
thrown into the arms of fortune! Look at the hospitals! How
many more of them are killed before they sip mother's milk! How many
are given over to the forests, how many to the wild animals, and to the
birds! So many perish in these ways that, everything considered, the
least of [these women's] sins is having followed their appetite for
lechery.*

Male-dominated Western Christian society has traditionally associated infanticide with sexual or cultural inferiority. When it has reared its head within
Europe, child-killing has been regarded almost exclusively as a female crime,
the result of woman's inherent tendency to lechery, passion, and lack of responsibility. Infanticide was an unnatural act in a society whose soldiers and
merchants were busy exporting the idea that the individual human life is valuable. What man, a seventeenth-century writer asked, would eat his child? Only
women were capable of that.[1]

---

* G. Boccaccio, *Corbaccio*, in *Opere*, edited by C. Segre (Milan, 1966), 1212. I would
like to thank colleagues and friends who have helped me think about infanticide,
especially Sarah Blaffer Hrdy, Emily Coleman, the late David Herlihy, Christiane
Klapisch-Zuber, the late Thomas Krueger, Richard Mitchell, David Ransel, Patricia and
John Ruoff, and John Tedeschi. I am also grateful to the direction of the Newberry
Library for a grant-in-aid to pursue this research. This essay appeared previously in *History
of Childhood Quarterly* 1 (1973): 98–116.

[1] "Trovosi mai huomo tanto crudele, e che posto fra la pietà, e la fame, si divorasse il
proprio figliuolo?" (G. D. Tomagni, *Dell'eccellentia de l'huomo sopra quella de la donna* [Venice,
1565], fol. 129v). "Mulier," said a contemporary, "non est ad imaginem dei" (Johannes de
Nevizanis, *Silva Nuptialis* [Montferrat, 1524], fol. 22r). The silence of medieval sources on
such "shameful" matters as infanticide comes from the source itself. F. Van Der Meer noted
the unwillingness of the loquacious Augustine to address the problem of exposure and
infanticide from the pulpit (*Augustine the Bishop* [New York, 1961], 189).

Asian or so-called primitive societies' control of the infant population by such means was more comprehensible: they were godless and culturally inferior. Missionaries appealed to the shocked sensibilities of Europeans to raise money to buy Chinese infants so their souls and bodies could be saved. Ironically, the good people of Europe contributed to this cause at the very time when Europe could no longer ignore its own infanticide. In the eighteenth and nineteenth centuries, a very significant body of literature addressed itself to the widespread abandonment and murder of European children.[2] Missionary pleading and welfare concerns were like the proverbial two ships passing in the night, ignorant of each other. Despite all the evidence, it was as if infanticide in the West *could not be*.

The act was common among ancient Roman and Germanic forbears and, presumably, would have been difficult to suppress among the scattered populations of the Middle Ages. Its diffusion in the eighteenth century suggests that child-killing had been practiced in the intervening millennium. The folklore was there: old women who suffocated children;[3] ghost-children haunting their murderers,[4] the myth of the unwed mother who abandons or murders her child;[5] the good women who guarded the cribs.[6] In the high and late Middle Ages translucent projections of infanticide appeared in judicial motifs: the Jewish ritual murder trials and the prosecutions of witches. A prima facie case does, therefore, exist for continuity. Nevertheless, most scholars have been as ready to consider infanticide culturally alien as has the general population. Some writers think infanticide was rare in the Middle Ages because Christian ideas and laws were incompatible with it.[7] Tertullian and other church fathers had spoken against it. Constantine, Theodosius, and Justinian had codified prohibitions.

---

[2] Recent works with substantial bibliography on modern abandonment and infanticide are W. Langer, *Political and Social Upheaval, 1832–1852* (New York, 1969), 195f.; and his "Checks on Population Growth: 1750–1850," *Scientific American* (February 1972): 92–99; E. Shorter, "Illegitimacy, Sexual Revolution, and Social Change in Modern Europe," *The Journal of Interdisciplinary History* 2 (1971): 237–72. D. Bakan, *Slaughter of the Innocents* (San Francisco, 1971), provides some interesting insights into the psychology of infanticide and child-battering. On contemporary infanticide, see J. Léauté, ed., *Recherches sur l'infanticide (1955–1965)* (Paris, 1968).

[3] On the transmission of the classical *lamiae* (child-wreckers) to the Christian Middle Ages, see H. C. Lea, *Materials toward a History of Witchcraft*, 3 vols. (Philadelphia, 1939), 1:109–14, 172.

[4] J. Penlikäinen, *The Nordic Dead-Child Tradition* (Helsinki, 1968).

[5] Z. Kumer, *Balada o nevesti detomorilki* (Ljubljana, 1963).

[6] C. Ginzburg, *I benandanti* (Turin, 1966), 72, 90, 99, 101, 135, 140, 162.

[7] J. Noonan, *Contraception* (Cambridge, Mass., 1966), 85ff., contrasts Roman and Christian attitudes toward human life. F. S. Hügel, *Die Findelhäuser und das Findelwesen Europas* (Vienna, 1863). See also below, n. 9. Tertullian himself asserts how ineffective law and ideal could be: "The laws forbid infanticide but, of all the laws, there is not one eluded more easily or with more impunity" (cited in E. Semichon, *Histoire des enfants abandonnés depuis l'antiquité jusqu'à nos jours* [Paris, 1880], 292).

Germanic chieftains had stricken infanticide from the rights of free men.[8]

Infanticide's "reappearance" in the eighteenth century provided not a challenge to this view, but its confirmation. Eighteenth-century Europe was religiously divided and secular in its cultural tone. Infanticide, so runs this view, was, therefore, to be expected.[9] While recent scholarship has sought more prosaic factors to account for modern infanticide, few scholars have considered the possibility of substantial infanticide during the preceding centuries.

The present paper presents two pieces of quantifiable evidence which suggest that infanticide was a fact of life in the dominion of Florence during the quattrocento and cinquecento. It adds to a mosaic of studies on infanticide (in Nürnberg,[10] Nördlingen,[11] Paris and the Ile-de-France[12]) which will one day provide a better idea of the facts of infancy in Western society.

Widespread infanticide and abandonment of children were responsible for the spread of foundling homes in the late Middle Ages. It had been so during the early Carolingian period (in 787 the first foundling home was established in Milan because there were as many infanticides as there were infants born out of wedlock[13]); and it was thus at the end of the twelfth century: Innocent III instituted the hospital of the Santo Spirito in Rome because so many women were throwing their children into the Tiber.[14] Florence was no different. The earliest laws favored these asylums because men feared the alternative. Petitioning in 1294, a communal commission told the government that

---

[8] A precise chronology of the Roman laws on the subject is in Hügel, *Findelhäuser*, 7–13, 24–34. See also Noonan, *Contraception*, 20–29, 85f. In Iceland, there was significant opposition to abolishing infanticide at the time of the conversion to Christianity: *Njal's Saga*, ed. M. Magnusson and H. Pálsson (Baltimore, 1966), chap. 105, p. 226; Ari Thorgillson, *The Books of the Icelanders*, ed. H. Hermannson (Ithaca, 1930), 66f.

[9] "Dopo l'avvento del Cristianesimo, l'Infanticidio nelle sue diverse forme andò gradatamente diminuendo fino a quasi scomparire. Solo in questi ultimi tempi, con l'offuscarsi delle idee religiosi, esso ricompare più minaccioso; già nel 1905 il Surbled non temera di scrivere che più della metà dei bambini concepiti è vergognossamente sacrificata" ("Infanticidio," *Dizionario Ecclesiastico* [Turin, 1955]), 2:427 ("After the advent of Christianity, infanticide in its diverse forms slowly declined until it almost disappeared. Only in recent times, when religious ideas were obscured, did it again become menacing; already in 1905 Surbled did not hesitate to write that more than the half of conceived children are shamelessly sacrificed").

[10] H. Bode, "Die Kindestötung und ihre Bestrafung im Nürnberg des Mittelalters," *Archiv für Strafrecht und Strafprozess* 61 (1914): 430–81.

[11] A. Felber, *Unzucht und Kindsmord in der Rechtsprechung der freien Reichsstadt Nördlingen vom 15. bis 19. Jahrhundert* (Bonn, 1961), 94–99.

[12] Y.-B. Brissaud, "L'infanticide à la fin du moyen âge, ses motivations psychologiques et sa répression," *Revue historique de droit français et étranger* 50 (1972): 229–56. See E. Coleman's important article on population control in the lands of the abbey of St. Germain-des-Prés during the ninth century; "L'infanticide dans le Haut Moyen Age," *Annales E.S.C.* 29 (1974): 315–35; see also her "A Note on Medieval Peasant Demography," *Historical Methods Newsletter* 5 (1972): 53–58, and "Medieval Marriage Characteristics," *The Journal of Interdisciplinary History* 2 (1971): 205–19.

[13] A. Pertile, *Storia del diritto italiano* (Bologna, 1966), 5:586f. Also H. Bergues et al., *La prevention des naissances dans la famille* (Paris, 1960), 166.

[14] Hügel, *Findelhäuser*, 47.

the asylum of San Gallo was "utile and necessary to the salvation of the souls of the persons of the city and *contado* of Florence, and of the whole province of Tuscany ... to avoid the many crimes which were committed against infants, and also to sustain the poor."[15] A century and a half later, the rector of the new foundling institution of the Innocenti proclaimed that "if the receptacle of this hospital does not remain in operation, what will without doubt happen is that the majority of these children will be punished with death."[16] In 1484 the same institution warned of the infamy and "great inconveniences" which would result if the home were closed. "Many children would soon be found dead in the rivers, sewers, and ditches, unbaptized," and therefore condemned to an eternity without God.[17] Contemporaries viewed foundling homes as the answer to a major social problem.[18] The great size of the Innocenti (started in 1419, opened in 1445) reflected the scope of the problem which Boccaccio had described in withering terms almost a century before.

Wet-nursing, however, itself fed on death. The only good *balia* was one whose child had died and made her milk available. Thus a procurement agent of the late trecento complained: "It seems the world is emptied of [nurses], for not one is available. Their children, who were expected to die, have recovered."[19] The death of one child was good for another. In a happier vein, the proctor wrote: "I found [a woman] in the church square with fresh milk, two months [after giving birth]. ... And she promised that if her infant girl, who is on the brink of death, dies tonight, she will come [to me] after the burial."

Animal milk was not used in these times, but otherwise, foundling homes operated in much the same way in the Middle Ages as they did in the nineteenth century. Having arrived in the house, infants were promptly sent into the countryside with a wet nurse (*balia*) who cared for the infant as long as her supply of milk lasted.

These institutional *balie*, or their husbands (*balii*) entered into a contract with the hospital or foundling home much as the wet nurses did with private patrons in the city. Nursing reliability was absolutely critical, for any interruption of care meant the death of a helpless infant. From an early point, the commune took an interest in the nurses' behavior. In 1344, the wages and contractual obligations of wet nurses were under community supervision. By

---

[15] *Archivio di Stato, Firenze* (hereafter *ASF*), *Provvisioni* 4, fol. 8r (19 May 1294); printed in L. Passerini, *Storia degli stabilimenti di beneficienza e d'istruzione elementare della città di Firenze* (Florence, 1853), 935ff.

[16] "Nisi receptaculum eiusdem hospitalis vigeret, accideret procul dubio quod maior pars puerorum necis dispendio mulctaretur" (*ASF, Prov.* 147, fols. 169v–171r [29 December 1456]).

[17] "Le quali sanza baptesimo spesse volte et pe fiumi et per cloache et fosse sarebbono trovate morte, se no fussi suto tal luogho constituto," *ASF, Prov.* 174, fols. 157v–161r (18 February 1483 *stilus florentinus* [hereafter *sf*; modern calendar: *sc*]).

[18] In mid-nineteenth century, the relation between foundlings and infanticides was a standard evaluative formula (Hügel, *Findelhäuser*, 537ff.).

[19] I. Origo, *The Merchant of Prato* (New York, 1957), 214ff. I would like to thank Judith Ross for this reference.

1415 legislation forbade *balie* from relinquishing their charges before they were thirty months old. Violators were either fined or publicly whipped.[20]

Before mid-quattrocento and the opening of the Innocenti, however, there is no reliable method for judging wet nurses' performance. Some indication that the *balia*'s market for her product was good and that a new foundling institution was badly needed may be gained from the data in the Florentine Catasto of 1427. In the city at this date, at age 0, there were 114.60 boys per 100 girls, as compared to the 105 males of age 0 in a normal population. At age 1, there were 118.43, as compared to about 101 per 100 in a normal population. The disparity holds: at age 2: 119.28; 3: 119.50; 4: 119.42.[21] In the whole dominion, the ratio of males to females for those 0–4 years old was 119.72 per 100. The ratio for the rich was still more striking. Those assessed more than 400 florins had a ratio of 124.56.[22] Whatever the qualifications which might reduce such startling figures, it seems evident that the rural areas had proportionately fewer girls than the city, and that in both areas, the number of girls was abnormally low. In future decades the nunneries would absorb increasing numbers of unwanted girls from the more prosperous families of the city, and the Innocenti would care for large numbers of bastards of established families and for the legitimate children of the poor.[23]

A key index ascertaining the *balie*'s performance with infants after the Innocenti opened in 1445 is the death rate of children, distinguished by sex. Over the nine year period from the Asylum's opening until February 12, 1454, 41.1% of those entering were boys, and 58.9% girls.[24] The ratio for deaths till November 1452 slightly favored girls: 43.1% of total mortalities were boys, 56.9% were girls. The slightly lower death rate of girls in relation to their proportion of the

---

[20] G. Masi, ed., *Statutum bladii Reipublicae Florentinae* (1348) (Milan, 1934), 135f., 161f., 172. For the law forbidding unauthorized surrendering of the infants, see *Statuta populi et communis florentinae* (1415) (Fribourg, 1778), 2:267–70. See now C. Klapisch-Zuber, "Blood Parents and Milk Parents: Wet Nursing in Florence, 1300–1530," in her *Women, Family, and Ritual in Renaissance Italy* (Chicago, 1985), 132–64.

[21] David Herlihy was kind enough to send me these figures.

[22] This may be due to a greater willingness and ability of rich couples to keep a male bastard of one partner than a female one.

[23] Leonardo Bruni sought to convince the city fathers to build the Innocenti by arguing its practical utility in absorbing the illegitimate children of their sons and preserving family honor (F. Del Migliore, *Firenze città nobilissima illustrata* [Florence, 1684], 308). Perhaps some progress on that score is reflected in the incomplete baptismal records of San Giovanni, starting in mid-quattrocento, where the residents of Florence had their children baptized. The ratio is absolutely normal, about 104 males per 100 females (M. Lastri, *Ricerche sull'antica e moderna popolazione della città di Firenze per mezzo dei registri del battistero di S. Giovanni dal 1451 al 1774* [Florence, 1775]). For the higher ratios in the early sixteenth century, see below. See also C. Klapisch-Zuber, "L'enfance en Toscane au début du XVe siècle," in her *Women, Family, and Ritual*, 94–116.

[24] *Archivio degli Innocenti, Firenze* (hereafter *AIF*), 14, 1, fol. 65v.

population reflects their greater biological resiliency in the earlier years.[25]

Once a distinction is made between deaths in the hospital and at *balia*, however, a significant fact emerges. A disproportionate number of girls died with wet nurses and a surprisingly high number of boys perished in the hospital.

Table 1[26]
Deaths before the First Birthday, 1445 to 1452

	Hospital		Wet Nurses	
Entered In	M	F	M	F
1445	1	3	1	11
1446	5	2	2	5
1447	6	4	7	8
1448	9	3	10	15
1449	3	9	10	18
1450	2	11	10	11
1451	21	12	7	11
	47	44	47	79

During these years, 42% of those dying before their first birthday perished in the hospital, 58% with wet nurses. Of those dying in the hospital, only 43% were girls, even though they made up an average of 58.9% of the entrants. If one had predicted deaths commensurate with these entry ratios assuming an even distribution of sexes between hospital and wet nurses, 53.6 girls would have died rather than the 44 who did. The greater resistance to disease of girls in this first year might account in part for this disparity. But that same female resiliency and male vulnerability must have accompanied the two sexes into the countryside. Even if we postulate that girls should have died at the

[25] However, a comparison with some modern mortality rates in the first year shows that overall, too many females were dying.

	Overall	Males	Females
Sweden	15.4 per 1000	17.6	13.1
Italy	41.8	45.7	37.8
Spain	41.6	46.0	36.9
Greece	40.4	43.2	37.4

from "Infant Mortality," *Demographic Yearbook* 19 (1967): 292–347.
The comparable figures for all those Florentine Innocents dying before their first birthday between 1445 and 1452 are: 410.2; 432.3 males; 394.7 females.

[26] Based on *AIF*, 14, 1.

same rate as boys when with the wet nurses, however, the disparity remains: as against 74.2 predicted female deaths, 79 girls actually died.

The most evident cause of this phenomenon would be that a disproportionate number of girls were sent to *balie*. If, for example, infant boys made up a majority of those whose fathers either subvented the hospital or promised to redeem the child, or at least left some identifying mark encouraging hospital administrators to think that the child might be reclaimed, the hospitallers would have exercised more caution in assigning it to a wet nurse. While the matter does need further study, mid-quattrocento records make clear that the abandonment of boys more often led fathers to write explanatory and promissory letters than was the case with girls.[27]

According to this hypothesis, hospitallers would have had more reason to preserve the lives of boys than of girls, since to redeem a child, one had to pay the cost of upkeep. They could do this by assigning such boys to trusted wet nurses who resided in the asylum rather than outside the city. This would have resulted in boys being in the hospital in greater numbers and for longer periods than girls, keeping them under the eyes of administrators and close to doctors when the need arose. The reverse situation in the countryside would have made the girls placed in that setting more vulnerable.

This hypothesis could be tested by a painstaking analysis of the movement of the different sexes. If it is wrong and the sex distribution between hospital and countryside was even, then the explanation of the difference in death rates lies in preferential treatment of infant boys by the *balie*, rather than by the hospital.[28] Only the lawyer would want to distinguish in this situation between infanticide and malicious neglect. Disproportionately high death rates of female infants reflect either a societal or individual premeditation in the quality of care. The same prejudice evident in the abandonment of female infants to the foundling homes (ca. 60%) was at work in their care. Antifeminism was a matter of life and death.

In mid-quattrocento, the rate of admissions to the Innocenti had been between 50 and 100 children a year. The hospital was large, the matriculation small. By the early cinquecento much had changed. A large residual population of innocents over ten years of age now shared the premises with the in-

---

[27] Given the type of bookkeeping employed in the Innocenti, it would be quite involved to determine average percentages per sex in the Innocenti and at *balia*.

[28] The economics of the *balia* need careful study in order to explain when she would have found it necessary or in her interest to starve or kill a child. Pay was all-important. Within a few years of the Innocenti's opening, innocents died of starvation when pay was not forthcoming; ASF, Prov. 147, fols. 169v–171r (29 December 1456); ibid., 157, fols. 21v–22v (16 April 1466). Secondly, the supply of children was critical. In the eighteenth century, the Englishman J. Hanway refuted the argument that the wet nurses had no financial interest in poisoning infants: the supply from the parish wardens was unlimited. As for the officers, so for the nurses; it was easier to let the infants die than live (*Letters on the Importance of the Rising Generation of the Laboring Part of Our Fellow-Subjects* [London, 1767], 1:12f.). The same argument was rendered into poetry by Luigi Tansillo (fl. early cinquecento). If anything were refused the wet nurses, "Attendete veder le poppe asciutte" (*La Balia* [Vercelli, 1767], 23).

fants. Annual admissions had increased to about 500 infants.[29] In the 1520s, the city was plagued by hordes of abandoned children too old for admission to the Innocenti, too young for productive lives.[30] Worse, the older foundling institutions in the dominion of Florence were closing their doors, and no accessible child-refuge was available for thousands of destitute people in the countryside.[31] Finally, the period of the Italian Wars was one of almost intolerable military turmoil in the countryside. Is it purely fortuitous that in the early sixteenth century, the otherwise steady sex ratios in Florentine baptisms suddenly show a lack of girls?[32]

The child-politics of this period deserve a separate study. But even at this primitive state of our knowledge, it is not difficult to predict what will be found. The countryside was increasingly turned into a milk farm for the Innocenti. In the villages of Tuscany, this putting out system could only result in neglect and death for the innocents of Florence, the children of wet nurses,[33] and those for whom no refuge could be found in the countryside. It was common to abandon one child in order to sell milk to another.[34] Can it be doubted that the same circumstance stimulated young girls to seek pregnancy in order to sell their milk?[35]

In this setting around 1500 the bishop of Fiesole (Florentine Dominion), perhaps encouraged by the Innocenti and the government of Florence, issued a constitution setting fines and punishments for those involved in the suffoca-

---

[29] In 1530, 549 infants entered the Innocenti, and by 1539 the figure had skyrocketed to 961 (G. Bruscoli, *L'archivio del R. Spedale di Santa Maria degl'Innocenti di Firenze* [Florence, 1911], 11).

[30] B. Varchi, *Storia Fiorentina* (Florence, 1963), 1:433. Duke Cosimo I made serious efforts to deal with the plague of three- to ten-year-olds (Passerini, *Storia*, 800–809; A. D'Addario, *Aspetti della controriforma a Firenze* [Rome, 1972], 465–69).

[31] *ASF, Diplomatico, Spedale degli Innocenti*, 9 June 1513. In 1533, Cosimo ordered his rectors in the dominion to receive the foundlings in their hospitals and not send them to Florence (G. Bruscoli, *Lo spedale di Santa Maria degl'Innocenti di Firenze* [Florence, 1900], 50).

[32]

1451–1470	104.22 males per 100 females
1471–1490	103.93
1491–1510	104.89
1511–1530	**106.17**
1531–1550	104.31
1551–1570	104.38

S. Somogyi, "Sulla mascolinità delle nascite a Firenze dal 1451 al 1774," *Rivista italiana di demografia e statistica* 4 (1950): 465.

[33] Apparently, wet nurses were not permitted to sell their milk if they were nursing their own child. Thus, the infant of an Innocenti wet nurse must either have died or in turn been put out to another wet nurse, or been given to the foundling home. On the effects of nursing two infants, see T. Garzoni, *La piazza universale di tutte le professioni del mondo* (Venice, 1665), 614f.

[34] For examples, see *AIF*, 2, 9, (1433, 1435). These cases come from the justification records of the infant asylum of San Gallo.

[35] In 1857, Finnish authorities complained that in the villages where foundlings were sent, mortality was high, family life was disastrously affected, and young girls sought pregnancy to be able to nurse; "Vospitatel'nye doma," *Entsiklopedicheskii slovar* 7 (1892): 275–80. I owe this information to my erstwhile colleague David Ransel.

tion of infants. Further, his vicar issued a decree against those who kept infants in bed with them.[36] In the same year, the bishop began to absolve laymen from the excommunications they had incurred through the crime and sin of suffocation. In 1517 the Florentine synod spoke out against not only parents but "others" who suffocated children. Table 2 summarizes the absolutions from 1500 to 1540.[37]

A substantial number of infanticides were committed in the diocese of Fiesole; there are simply too many cases of infant mortality to suggest that most of them involved accidental, unintentional suffocations.[38] Almost all of the absolved parties were married couples. No unmarried females were judged by the vicar. A solid majority of infant deaths were female in all decades but the last, when male deaths predominated. The absolutions were highest in the 1530s, a period of almost continual civil war in the countryside. These few statements summarize what is certain. Beyond this lies uncertainty.

The sudden appearance of these absolutions for suffocation does not necessarily imply an increase in incidence. Other historians, seeing the beginnings of secular prosecution of infanticide at the end of the fifteenth century, have concluded that the crime was undergoing a dramatic upswing.[39] Readers of this article, seeing the congruence of the episcopal absolutions with the German evidence, might conclude the same. But at this point there is simply no evidence for this; prosecution and incidence of a crime are not necessarily related.

What is certain is that in late fifteenth- and sixteenth-century Europe, homicide against children was becoming a distinct crime. The criminous groups

---

[36] Earlier Fiesolan synodal reference to suffocations provided no financial penalty. Thus the episcopal constitution referred to in the following quote must be recent: "£ 1 et s. 8 convertendum secundum et prout disponit constitutio sinodalis de hoc loquens" (*Archivio Arcivescovile, Firenze (AAF)*, E. 18. 30, fol. 53r. [1 June 1500]). The vicarial decree: "Pro parte Antonii Roberti de Altovitis civis florentini, qualiter eius uxor peperit quendam puerum masculum quem ipse contra conformam edicti dicti vicarii huc usque tenueret in lecto, propter quod ipsa mulier et dictus Antonius eius vir sententiam excommunicationis noscuntur incurisse ipso facto ex forma ipsius edicti" (ibid., fol. 132v) ("For Antonio di Roberto degli Altoviti, citizen of Florence: that his wife gave birth to a male child and, against the order of the edict of the said vicar, kept him till now in a bed, because of which this woman and the said Antonio her husband are known to have incurred ipso facto, according to the rule of the said edict, the sentence of excommunication").

[37] The synodal modification is in R. Trexler, *Synodal Law in Florence and Fiesole, 1306–1518* (Vatican City, 1971), 127. The table is based on the *note causarum* of the see of Fiesole (*AAF*, E. XVII. 30), and *Archivio Vescovile, Fiesole (AVF)*, series XIV. III. A, regs. 52–53, 55, 58–59. The first volume, though in the Florentine curial archive, is of Fiesolan provenience. The see of Florence, for unknown reasons, did not regularly absolve suffocations. The only Florentine case I have found is in *AAF*, E. XVII. 34, fol. 12r (13 June 1503). The intermittent volumes in the Fiesolan series (54, 56, 57) are not part of the series in question, but erroneously mixed in.

[38] A. Thomson's *Barnkvävningen* (Uppsala, 1960) is the one book I know dealing entirely with suffocation. Thomson believes it would be hasty to consider the suffocations, subject of so much episcopal, papal, and secular concern in Scandinavia, as concealed homicides; see especially 207–15, 230f., 274.

[39] Felber, *Unzucht*, 95.

Table 2

Episcopal Absolution of Suffocation at Fiesole, 1500–1540, by Sex

Year	M	F	= Total
1500	5	& 2	= 7
1501	1	3	4
1502	0	0	0
1503	1	5	6
1504	2	7	9
1505	1	1	2
1506	0	0	0
1507	0	0	0
1508	1	0	1
1509	10	6	16
	21	24	
1510	4	& 4	= 8
1511	6	5	11
1512	6	6	12
1513	2	9	11
1514	2	0	2
1515	5	4	9
1516	2	1	3
1517	0	3	3
1518	1	2	3
1519	2	1	3
	30	35	
1520	0	& 0	= 0
1521	0	0	0
1522	4	8	12
1523	(3)	3)*	
1524	books missing		
1525	books missing		
1526	books missing		
1527	books missing		
1528	books missing		
1529	(8)	14)**	
	15	25	
1530	(3)	& 2)†	= ||
1531	5	3	8
1532	4	1	5
1533	5	4	9
1534	13	8	22 & 1§
1535	12	11	23
1536	7	9	16
1537	8	5	14 & 1§
1538	6	5	11
1539	9	8	17
1540	(2)	1)‡	
	74	57 & 2	

Totals: M: 140
        F: 141
Total: 281

* 1 January–20 February; ** 1 January–13 September; † 16 September–31 December; ‡ 1 January–30 July; § Sex unknown.

were two: the imperial and royal law attacked the unwed mother. If she had concealed pregnancy and birth, the death of her infant was presumptively infanticide.[40] The law of the church attacked witches. Infanticide was far and away the most common social crime imputed to the aged witches of Europe by the demonologists.[41]

Before this time, most of Europe was without the requisite legal means and, perhaps to some extent, the moral conviction to prosecute for infanticide, a word rarely used before the later sixteenth century.[42] It was also without the medical means to determine the cause of a newborn infant's death. Autopsies on infant corpses were unknown before the mid-seventeenth century.[43]

The law and conscience of Europe in the sixteenth century vented its force upon old women and unwed mothers. Little attention was given to married women and their spouses. How could one prove infanticide within the walls of the family home? Who would want to?[44] It was more reasonable to assume that witches passed through locked doors in the dead of night to suffocate infants than to believe that husband and wife, whether parents or *balii*, would do such a thing. The inquisitor of Como not only blamed witches for deaths at home. He blamed the high death rates of the foundlings on them

---

[40] Apparently the first law of this type is from Bamberg (J. Kohler and W. Scheel, eds., *Die Bambergische Halsgerichtsordnung* [1507] [Halle, 1902], arts. 43, 44, 156–58). With insignificant additions this was incorporated into the Caroline of Charles V (1521, 1529). There followed a French law on the subject (1556), a Lithuanian (1588), an English law (1623/24), and a Russian. See Kohler's comments on Bode, "Kindestötung," 481–84. *Litovskii statut 1588 goda*, ed. I. Lappo, vol. 2 (Kaunas, 1938), 11, 7; *Litovskii statut v Moskovskom perevode-redaktsii*, ed. I. Lappo, (Iur'ev, 1916), XI, 57. I owe the information on East European laws to Benjamin Uroff.

[41] The *Malleus Maleficarum* (1486) was important in establishing the nexus witchcraft-infanticide for subsequent demonologists. See part 1, question 1, chap. 13, questions 10, 11; part 2, question 2, chap. 1; part 3, question 34. The belief in the existence of child-killing old women was, of course, extremely old; see H. C. Lea, *Materials*, 1:109–37, 172. A slim article on the witchcraft-infanticide tie is M. Murray, "Child-Sacrifice among European Witches," *Man* 18 (1918): 60ff.

[42] Three of the foundation works of medical jurisprudence contain no mention of autopsy to determine the cause of infant death: F. Fedele, *De relationibus medicorum* (Palermo, 1602); Rodericus à Castro, *Medicus-Politicus* (Hamburg, 1614); P. Zacciae, *Questiones medico-legales* (Rome, 1621). The earliest works on the medical problem of infanticide appear in the late 1600s. See the extensive bibliography in "Infanticide," *Dictionnaire de Médecine* (Paris, 1837), 16:383–91. For some indication of the fantastic methods short of autopsy used in an earlier period, see *Aegidii Bossii patritii mediolanensis . . . tractatus varii, qui omnem fere criminalem materiam . . .* (Venice, 1574), fol. 155r. A still earlier (1475) case of determination of death in a two-and-a-half-year-old child is in "Simon of Trent," *The Jewish Encyclopedia* (New York, 1916), 11:374.

[43] In mid-seventeenth century an Italian was still urging that the killing of a child be called infanticide and not abortion; see *Vocabolario degli accademici della Crusca*, s.v. "Infanticidio."

[44] Parental love was presumptive evidence against infanticide. Thus Reginald Scot (1584), with only slight exaggeration, accused Bodin of teaching that no mother could be presumed guilty of killing her child unless she was assumed to be a witch (*The Discoverie of Witchcraft*, ed. M. Summers [Great Britain, 1930], bk. 2, chap. 5).

too.[45] To the modern, the witch craze and the terrible punishments inflicted on unwed mothers must appear in part as the projection onto marginalized elements of the community of a crime no longer psychically tolerable within the social and familial order.

There were, of course, recriminations against those couples who deserted their children, but little complaint that the family, the womb of the social whole, conspired against itself (parricide), or against the commonwealth (homicide). The unmarried mother whose child died was forced to go to any length to prove she had not been pregnant. If it was proved otherwise, she claimed that the child was stillborn. If that was disproved, she would state that the child suffocated or was accidentally overlain. The married couple, on the other hand, rarely needed to be concerned. With little or no risk, parents or wet nurses could claim accidental suffocation. Or they could indict old women. The peculiar merit of the episcopal absolutions of Fiesole is that they almost all involved married couples.

The legal foundations for absolutions were few: first, since early in the trecento the bishop of Fiesole, like his Florentine brother, had reserved to his curia absolutions of parental suffocations.[46] This meant that a penitent confessing to his priest that his child had suffocated or been suffocated—in the Latin, the active voice was always used—could not be absolved by that priest in the forum of conscience (forum poli) until the penitent had gone to the bishop's vicar to be absolved in the external forum of the curia (forum fori). As old as this reservation was, however, the note causarum or daily court diaries of the see of Fiesole (extant for the trecento and early quattrocento and again from 1495 on) record no absolutions until 1500.

Secondly, papal law and the episcopal constitutions of Florence excommunicated those parents, and after 1517, those third parties who kept infants in bed with them. This created levels of guilt and presumption. If the child died in bed the guilt, suspicion, and punishment were greater than if it died in a cradle.[47]

The third legal basis for absolution was that until the sixteenth century the secular forum could rarely prosecute infanticide, for it could not prove pre-

---

[45] Lea, Materials, 1:391f.

[46] The reservation of 1306 is in R. Trexler, Synodal Law, 207. In the Florentine episcopal constitutions of 1327, the death of a child under five "per negligentiam vel causam parentum" was a reserve, and a special rubric was dedicated to "those who kill children" (ibid., 64, 126f.). The texts are in C. Guasti and A. Gherardi, eds., I capitoli del comune di Firenze (Florence, 1893), 2:37, 46.

[47] "Nota che ogni donna che tiene e figliuoli piccini a lato la notte, atti a potere morire, il nimico di Dio dorme co lei" (Bernardino da Siena, Le prediche volgari inedite, ed. D. Pacetti [Siena, 1935], 67) ("Note that every woman who keeps little children at her side at night so that they are apt to be able to die has the enemy of God lying with her"). If a child died in bed with the parent, "grave guilt" was incurred. If it died in a crib, then there was no guilt, but nevertheless a penance; Niccolò dei Tudeschi, Lectura super quinque libros Decretalium (Basel, 1487), X.V.10.3. But in the late quattrocento, Angelo de Clavasio argued that those in extreme poverty could keep their infants in bed with them (Summa Angelica de casibus conscientiae [Venice, 1487], fol. 162r).

meditation (*dolus*). The process which led to concealed pregnancy being accepted as presumptive evidence of infanticide was slow;[48] in the period with which this paper deals, Florence had no such law. Like France and the Baltic countries, the city on the Arno simply left prosecution to church courts except in those unusual circumstances where infanticide was "atrocious," public, and scandalous, and where a suspect was present.[49] The forum of the church dealt with what the canonist Hostiensis called the ambiguity of duplicity.[50]

Finally, only canon law had a specific rubric "on those who kill children."[51] True, Roman law included specific single laws against infanticide (without using the word), but the law was equivocal at several points.[52] In any case, Florentine communal judges prosecuted only ex officio violations of the municipal law, and the Florentine statutes included no specific law against either abortion or infanticide.[53] Without forensic medicine, without a law of presumptive infanticide, and without municipal law, it was left to the church to defend the infant. And yet, if the Fiesolan registers are any guide, it did nothing for centuries. Infants had no natural defenders. Their death rarely provoked suits by third parties for damages and rarely affected testamentary dispositions.

What then accounts for the sudden activity around 1500: the new constitution, the vicar's decree, then the absolutions? The impetus may have come in part from the commune or from the Innocenti, which knew better than

---

[48] The new presumptions applied only to unwed mothers. The Roman law principle was that if premeditation (*dolus*) was doubted, child-homicide could not be prosecuted by that law; see Bonifazio de' Vitalani, *De maleficiis*, in *Tractatus diversi super maleficiis* (Venice, 1560), 341.

[49] For the French, Norman and Angevin tradition, see Brissaud, "L'infanticide," 246ff.; for Scandinavia, Thomson, *Barnkvävningen*, 210f. The prosecution of a nurse's accidental suffocation of another's child was *royal* right in England by the early twelfth century: "Si quis alterius puerum, qui vel ei conmissus sit ad educandum vel docendum, occidat vel dormiens opprimat, nichilominus reddat quam si virum adultum occidisset" (*Leges Henrici Primi*, ed. L. J. Downer [Oxford, 1972], 270 [88.7]) ("If anyone kills or while sleeping suffocates someone else's child who has been committed to him or her to rear or teach, he or she will be judged as if he or she had killed an adult male"). The known cases of Florentine communal prosecutions of infanticides are few enough; G. Brucker ed., *The Society of Renaissance Florence* (New York, 1971), 146 (1407) ; *Diario Fiorentino dal 1450 al 1516 di Luca Landucci*, ed., I. Del Badia (Florence, 1969), 267 (1503) ; *Chronicle of Antonio da San Gallo* (MS. Newberry Library, Case. 6A. 28, fol. 107v) (1544).

[50] *Summa Aurea* (Turin, 1963), X.V.10 (c. 1552).

[51] X.V.10. See also II. q. V.20 and X.V.38.7.

[52] D.25.3.4 (the one civil law reference to suffocating a newborn infant) ; D.48.9.1, 5, 9; C.9.16.8; C.9.17.1; I.6.18.5, 6.

[53] Very few towns had specific infanticide or abortion statutes before mid-cinquecento; see J. Kohler, *Studien aus dem Strafrecht. Das Strafrecht der Italienischen Statuten vom 12. bis zum 16. Jahrhundert* (Mannheim, 1896), 206, 333ff. Statute law, said the lawyers, was to be strictly construed, and "infans autem homo nondum est" ("an infant is not yet a person"); see this cavil in the civil law in mid-cinquecento in the gloss of the Codex by Denis Godefroy (1583), *Codicis Iustiniani ... libri 12* (Lyon, 1662), C.9.16.8 (p. 778).

anyone else which *balie* had repeated "misfortune" with their charges. A pain-staking comparison of the names of the absolved with the names of the wet nurses of the Innocenti could help to settle this point. Short of this, however, it is possible to determine in part the origins of the suffocated children through internal evidence.

The evidence suggests that the majority of the children were not the off-spring of the absolved. In general, it seems that the notaries specified when that was the case. Over the whole period, 23 sets of parents (from among 281 cases) were absolved of the suffocation of 14 girls and 9 boys. In the period 1531–1540, when the notaries' formula was most standardized, only 14 chil-dren, seven of each sex, from a total of 128 were said to be the children of the absolved. There are points in the documents which seem to question the assumption that most of the children originated elsewhere. In 1503, for exam-ple, all six deceased were listed as the children of the absolved, and five of the six were females.[54] Still, considering the clear distinction made in the canon and civil law between parricide and homicide, and the fact that the notarial form indicating parentage, "eorum filia," was in wide use elsewhere, one has to conclude that the majority of cases dealt with children who were not the offspring of the couples who sought absolution.

The only other specification in the documents as to the origins of the chil-dren was the occasional note that the child had been at wet nurse. In two cases, the absolved parties were serving as nurse for a private party. Thus a Lombard and his wife of Figline were absolved of suffocating the daughter of the Florentine Tommaso di Lorenzo de' Martelli—the one mention of a Flor-entine father.[55] A wet nurse and her husband were absolved of suffocating Angelia, the daughter of a man of Rubana.[56] In two other cases the suffoca-tors and their victims were definitely associated with the Innocenti: Donna Betta, a wet nurse in the Innocenti, was absolved of the suffocation of a fe-male innocent.[57] A couple from the village of Ponte Sogno was absolved of the suffocation of another girl.[58]

Presumably, the older the victim the better the chance he or she was a foundling, for parents tend to suffocate infants before they cry.[59] Thus the age of the infants might be of help in determining their origins. Unfortunate-ly, only in the early years, when the notarial formula was still uncanonized, do such odd notes as age and names of the decedents appear. Those for whom ages are noted are older: five different children were listed as either four, three, or two months old in the records for these early years, while not one was listed as newborn, and not one child was said to have died unbaptized. A further hint that the victims were not newborn infants can be found in the

---

[54] *AVF*, reg. 52.

[55] *AVF*, reg. 58, at date 4 March 1527*sf*.

[56] "Quam puellam tenebant ad alendam"; *AAF*, E.18.30, fol. 108r.

[57] *AVF*, reg. 58, at date 10 April 1529.

[58] *AVF*, reg. 59, fol. 470r.

[59] P. Brouardel, *L'infanticide* (Paris, 1897), 78, 83.

notes for the years 1504–1513, when the scribes made some attempt to distinguish between infants and children. Sixteen were called *infanti* or *infantule*; 52 others were designated *pueri* or *puelle*.[60]

The social origins of the absolved do not contradict the hypothesis that the absolved wives were mostly wet nurses. Some were so poor that the vicar excused them from the modest pecuniary penalty usually levied,[61] and only a rare couple had a family name. The recorded occupations were listed: Eleven were field laborers. One laborer worked with horses, another was called simply a laborer, and the thirteenth was a nuncio of the town of Turichio. With the exception of the three *balie* listed above, the women were identified only as wives, with the regular appellation "domina." Perhaps this latter derives from their nursing profession. It certainly cannot refer to their humble familial circumstances.

The absolutions give no further information on the provenience of the couples or the infants. Nor do they contain many specifics on the circumstances of death. In three cases, the vicar's inquiry into the question of premeditation made its way into the record, and those parties disclaimed an intent to suffocate. One child was suffocated by his parents in bed when they were not paying attention.[62] Another couple insisted that they suffocated their child "accidentally while sleeping, and without any consciousness on their part of killing."[63] The third couple stated that they were awake with the child at their side when he died; he had not suffocated.[64]

No mention was made in any case of medical consultation, let alone of surgical dissection. The vicar had no choice but to accept the penitents' denial of homicide, and mete out penance according to his judgment of guilt or negligence. To complicate matters, in one case he was prepared to waive the one safeguard which the church—not the commune or the civil law—had long insisted upon, the prohibition against infants being in bed with elders: the vicar licensed a Florentine couple to keep their child in bed with them, but bur-

---

[60] Apparently, this distinction between infant and child was similar to ours. But the word "infant" *legally* referred to anyone below seven years of age.

[61] "Rimissa pena pecuniaria propter paupertatem eorum . . ."; *AVF*, reg. 55, at dates 4 June 1519, and 29 January 1521*sf*.

[62] *AVF*, reg. 59, fol. 226r.

[63] "Ex improviso et inter somnos et absque aliqua eorum conscientia modo aliquo necandi dictum Pierum" (*AAF*, E. XVII. 34, fol. 12r). ("Accidentally and while dreaming and without any consciousness of killing the said Piero"). This is the one known case of absolution in the Florentine curia.

[64] "Asseruit eundem Antonium mortuum assio ipsis vigilantibus et non ex suffocatione. Ideo idem vicarius eos absolvit simpliciter et ita mandavit per se Nicolaum cappelanum Liccii admitti ad divina in ecclesia . . ."; *AVF*, reg. 59, fol. 149v ("He claimed that this Antonio died with them watching nearby, and not through suffocation. And therefore the said vicar absolved them simply and ordered Niccolò, chaplain of Liccio, to admit them to divine services in church").

dened their consciences in the event they did not use due caution.[65]

The place of death was mentioned only once, and it was a bed not a crib. Consequently, though the documents refer regularly to *absolutio a suffocatione*, it would seem that these cases of suffocation refer only to overlying in bed, a violation of canon and episcopal law, and do not include suffocation incurred in cribs. The active voice always used to describe the deaths (the absolved suffocated the child) would also seem to indicate death by overlying, rather than asphyxiation by the covers.

Accidents did happen, and to guard children, Florentine craftsmen of the cinquecento built a contraption called an *arcuccio*, or little arch, which fitted over a crib and prevented the covers from smothering the child. The crib itself had a semicircular hole on the side through which the nurse could breast-feed the infant. The advantage was that the child could be kept in bed alongside the nurse with no danger of suffocation from nurse or covers.[66]

The existence of the *arcuccio* suggests that it filled a need for nurses concerned about suffocation. Yet one should not jump to the conclusion that accidental death, and not premeditation, was the problem solved by the *arcuccio*. It is possible that nurses used them to avoid the suspicion of the authorities, who wanted to deprive suspected nurses of the excuse of accident as well as to protect children. At a later time, nurses were required to keep their charges in these boxes, *under pain of excommunication*.[67] In an age when medical jurisprudence concerning infanticide was still unreliable, the *arcuccio* became another mechanism used by the ecclesiastical authority—not the duchy of Florence—to permit the presumption of infanticide.

These absolutions raise two final questions. First, what was gained by bringing these couples before the episcopal court? After all, the sentence of an ecclesiastical court could not involve the shedding of blood, and there is absolutely no evidence that any of the couples were handed over to the secular courts. In fact, the bishop's absolution (*absolutio in foro fori*) seems to have amounted to a guarantee against prosecution in the secular forum.[68] The

---

[65] "Et insuper dedit et concessit licentiam eidem Antonio [Altoviti] et uxori sue predictum dictum infantem in lecto usque ad tempus non prohibetur retinendi, non obstantibus ... conscientiam eorum nisi diligentia debita usa fuerit onerando. Propterea commisit absolutionem in foro poli, quia ipse eum absolvit in foro fori"; (*AAF*, E. XVII. 30, fol. 132v) ("And he further gave and conceded license to this Antonio and to his wife that they were not prohibited from keeping the said infant in their bed, despite ... burdening their conscience if due care was not used. Therefore he ordered they be absolved in the forum of conscience, because he absolved him in the external forum"). For a papal license to a foundling home to ignore this law, see G. F. Viviani, *L'assistenza agli "esposti" nella provincia di Verona (1426–1969)* (Verona, 1969), 122f. (1548).

[66] The first reference to the *arcuccio* I have encountered is in Giovanbattista Gelli's *I Capricci del Bottaio*, written before 1548 (*Dizionario ... Crusca*, s.v.). A picture of it is in Thomson, *Barnkvävningen*, 219.

[67] In 1732, the Royal Society of London was informed of this fact; *Philosophical Transactions of the Royal Society of London* 7 (1732): 528.

[68] For an analysis which equates forum fori with the judicial forum (ecclesiastical or secular) as against the *forum poli* (the sacramental forum of conscience), see Jo. de Nevizanis, *Silva Nuptialis*, fols. 14r–v.

curia did not benefit financially from the absolutions. What then was gained?

The answer lies in the penance itself. In roughly half the cases, absolved couples paid not only a sum of money to a specific charitable organization, but were sentenced to a public penance as well.[69] Usually this involved standing in front of the parish church on the next Sunday or holy day with candle in hand, showing a crib as an emblem of their sin, and wailing their repentance.[70] They remained there from the first bell until the Introitus, during the time local people arrived for mass. The penalty was difficult to avoid, for the parish priest was permitted to complete the absolution *in foro poli* only upon couples' fulfillment of the public penance. Such a procedure involved the humiliation of the couples and of their older children, many of whom had been implicated in the suffocations and been absolved. The purpose of the curial actions was to discipline the faithful by exposing them to the ostracism and humiliation of fellow villagers. The striking widescale use of public penance in an age when, according to all authorities, its use had all but disappeared, is but another indication of the seriousness with which infanticide was viewed by authorities.[71]

Finally, it may be asked if these documents show the extent of infanticide in the dominion of Florence. Unfortunately, they simply indicate that infanticide against one's own and against other children was common. The trouble lies in the lack of identification of the couples. If the majority of the cases involved traditional reserve procedures, in which the original impetus came from a confession to a parish priest, then these absolutions must refer to only a fraction of the actual number of crimes. Few of the faithful would have spontaneously confessed to a dutiful priest a crime which could involve a trip to Florence and public humiliation. A significant number of the absolved, roughly one-tenth, definitely were parents of the suffocated children and

---

[69] Fifty-seven of 128 cases between 1531 and 1540 included public penance. Some others were to be "the usual," others were left up to the parish priest, and some were limited to financial penalties.

[70] "Permaneant ante hostium ecclesie predicte cum cunabula et candela aciensa una die domenica vel festiva, a primo sono campane usque ad introitum emisse. Et hoc iniuncto eis pro modo culpe penitentia salutari" (*AVF*, reg. 59, fol. 152v) ("They are to remain before the door of the said church with crib and lit candle for one Sunday or feast day, from the first bell until the introitus has been intoned. They are enjoined to do this as a form of salutary punishment of their guilt"). Also "plerando eorum delictum" (ibid., fol. 74v) ("deploring their crime"). On the use of public penance for suffocation in Scandinavia, see Thomson, *Barnkvävningen*, 233ff.

[71] In 1553, Duke Cosimo I gave the *operai* of the Innocenti the right to prosecute the *balie* except in atrocious cases meriting capital punishment, when competence was reserved to the ducal judges. The motivation: "Spesse volte è occorso et occorre che per le balie o balii di epsi [puttini] et molti altri anchora si sono commesse et commettono varie et diverse fraude et inganni circa li detti putti, in danno et dishonore di detto spedale et preiuditio d'altre persone"; D'Addario, *Aspetti*, 1469f. ("It has happened and still does happen that these [children's] wet nurses or their husbands and many others have committed and do commit various and diverse frauds and deceptions on the said infants, to the damage and dishonor of the said hospital and to the prejudice of other persons"). Perhaps this ducal order is a continuation of the same struggle against unexplained infant deaths of which the episcopal absolutions were a first part.

probably were absolved by this route. If on the other hand the government and Innocenti were fostering prosecution of specific wet nurses, the absolutions would be no guide at all to the extent of the problem. In that case, the only sure statement would be that the government believed that many of the Innocenti's *balie* were doing away with the foundlings. Either way, the nature of these documents will never allow a statistical measure of infanticide. This must be left to analysis of census data, and family reconstructions.[72]

For all their excruciating uncertainty, these documents retain great value. It is perfectly true that genuine accidental suffocations may be included among them. If the suspicion that suffocations were often premeditated was widespread, so too was the belief among doctors that such suspicions were often unfounded, and that faulty pediatric procedures were to blame in many cases.[73] It is just as possible that the physiologically unexplained "crib deaths" of today may have had their counterpart in the past. And of course, one may not ignore the recent evidence that foundlings suffer from "emotional dwarfism," and that such factors may explain their pronounced death rates.[74]

Still, the evidence of extensive infanticide cannot be gainsaid: the significant number of identified *parents* under suspicion (including in one year those alleged responsible for the suffocations of five girls and one boy); the sudden appearance of the episcopal procedure along with the new episcopal regulations; the change in the Florentine rubric on parents killing children to cover third parties; and finally the number of children involved.

In the early years of the Innocenti, the fact that too many girls were dying at *balia* led us to conclude that evidence of sexist attitudes did not end with the greater incidence of abandonment of girls; a still higher percentage of girls died with wet nurses. In three of the four decades covered by the cinquecento absolutions for suffocation, a clear majority of girls died. Perhaps it can be shown that the latter and the former superfemininity merely reflected the greater number of girls at *balia*, but, as I have stressed, that would simply avoid the problem. In law, in the family, and in the foundling home, European society preferred boys. This meant more deaths for infant girls. It preferred adults to infants. The infants died at a frightening pace. How many died of prejudice, of hunger, of disease?

To the charge that public begging damaged the honor of the community, sixteenth-century Franciscans argued that if beggars were removed from the streets, they would be forgotten. Worse, they said, the very heart of charity, the individual contact of two unequal human beings, would be annihilated. The Franciscans lost. Modern Western society has ever since been zealous in hiding inequality from the public eye, whether it be that of the destitute poor, women, or the perished child who only in dreams and tales returns to haunt the guilty. (Societal *cannibalism* was not fit even to contemplate.)

---

[72] See Coleman, "Infanticide."

[73] S. Pinaeus, *De virginitatis notis, gravitate, et partu* (1579), (Lyon, 1650), 16f.

[74] L. I. Gardner, "Deprivation Dwarfism," *Scientific American* (July, 1972): 76.

The reason for concealing inequality lies in a fundamental ambivalence between two central ideological postulates of modern Western man. Beyond all questions of the distribution of property, the effects of plague, drought, and common human desperation, the West for centuries has assumed that its main cultural values were on the one side reason, calculation, order, balance, and harmony, on the other the sacredness of each individual life. For as many centuries, the family has been viewed as the source of balance *and* the seat of unlimited generativity. The two are at odds. As Malthus saw, something or someone must consume a generativity that threatens order. If fifteenth-century parents could not support the new infant without starving themselves or their older children, they had to act. Charity, said the medieval lawyers in touching on the problem, begins at home.

Ritual in Florence:
Adolescence and Salvation
in the Renaissance[*]

R ECENT INTEREST IN THE DEVELOPMENT OF THE MODERN FAMILY AND THE modern concept of childhood and youth was largely sparked by the seminal work of Philippe Ariès.[1] In his view, the modern child produced the modern family. The new child was himself the result of pedagogical innovations and aristocratic sensibilities which, over a long period of time, drifted down to the middle and lower classes from the leisure class, and to society at large from the schools. Late medieval and early modern teachers had perceived that children and youth learned different disciplines best at certain ages, and this specification of curriculum led in the seventeenth century to the discovery of child psychology. The child was no longer an "idiot" whose parents waited for him to grow up, but a particular human being with behavioral modes valuable in themselves, which could rightly be enjoyed by the parents. Around this new creature grew the family, a unit for the child's protection and self-expression.

This paper contributes to the growing literature that is attempting to elaborate upon Ariès's views of this evolution from medieval to modern familial and generational institutions.[2] It is specifically about urban Florence, with emphasis not on private aristocratic or patrician sensibilities, but on the crea-

[*] This essay appeared previously in *The Pursuit of Holiness in Late Medieval and Renaissance Religion*, ed. C. Trinkaus with H. Oberman (Leiden, 1974), 200–64. I am especially grateful to my erstwhile research assistant Jane Goldberg, and to Rab Hatfield, for their help.

[1] P. Ariès, *Centuries of Childhood* (New York, 1965).

[2] See especially D. Hunt, *Parents and Children in History. The Psychology of Family Life in Early Modern France* (New York, 1970); N. Davis, "The Reasons of Misrule: Youth Groups and Charivaris in Sixteenth-Century France," *Past and Present*, no. 50 (1971): 55f., 61f.; J. Thirsh, "The Family," *Past and Present*, 27 (1964): 116–22; R. Goldthwaite, *Private Wealth in Renaissance Florence: A Study of Four Families* (Princeton, 1968), 234–75.

tion of social instrumentalities–confraternities for boys–aimed at socializing the adolescents of Florence.[3]

The canon Delaruelle asked in 1963 if the boys' confraternities of the quattrocento were the first such groups specifically intended for youth.[4] The answer seems to be affirmative. Why did such sponsored pious groups appear in Italy at the beginning of the Renaissance? What were their goals? How did they evolve? What was their relation to the religious and educational currents of the period?

We will see that adolescents emerged in the quattrocento as the male "saviors" of society, a role which traditionally had been reserved to monasteries and governments. The youth were incorporated as the monasteries declined. How did organized religious and other integrative activities bridge the gap from a traditional society in which incorporated holy men had functioned as the ritual saviors of society to the new society in which an age group would fill the same role?

In northern Europe, the fifteenth century witnessed an ever-heightened attempt to bring students into colleges and subject them to greater discipline. One of the spurs to this enclosure of young students was the influential sermons of Gerson on the rearing of the young. Like other moralists and educators of the fifteenth century, he saw the problem of unruly students as part of the general indocility of the young.[5] In Italy as well, new pedagogical directions were contemporary with attempts to harness young people as a whole.

The traditional youth groups of medieval Europe did not lend themselves to social planning. Their main purpose was diversion, achieved through such means as parody, masquerades, dances, and other forms of festive "nonsense." In the small communities of Europe, such *badie* or *charivaris* could

---

[3] Goldthwaite (*Private Wealth*, 293–303) has provided a bibliography of recent works on Italian familial history. See also the study by R. Starn, "Francesco Guicciardini and His Brothers," in *Renaissance Studies in Honor of Hans Baron*, ed. A. Molho and J. A. Tedeschi (Dekalb, 1971), 409–44. C. Bec, *Les marchands écrivains. Affaires et humanisme à Florence 1375–1434* (Paris, 1967) provides the best analysis of family sensibilities in Florence during this period. See now O. Niccoli, "Le Compagnie di Bambini nell'Italia del Rinascimento," *Rivista Storica Italiana* 101 (1989): 346–74.

[4] E. Delaruelle, "La vie religieuse dans les pays de langue française à la fin du XVᵉ siècle," in *Colloque d'histoire religieuse* (Grenoble, 1963), 14. In all the following, I adhere to the most common quattrocento usages of the following terms: infancy is until the child speaks; childhood (*puerizia* or *fanciulezza*) is until about twelve or thirteen, the age of puberty; adolescence (an *adolescente* or *giovanetto* and sometimes *fanciullo*) is from about thirteen to twenty-five; youth (*iuvenis* or *giovane*) is from twenty-five to forty, after which point I speak of the adult or *uomo fatto*. "Young people" is meant to convey a generality for those under thirty. This admittedly anachronistic procedure has the advantage of mirroring contemporaries' formal conception of ages, and prevents textual misunderstandings. On the question of these formal age differentiations, see Ariès, *Centuries*, 18–25; I. Del Lungo, *Dino Compagni e la sua cronica* (Florence, 1879), 1:1100f; D. Herlihy, "Vieillir à Florence au Quattrocento," *Annales E.S.C.* 24 (1969): 1339. A variant series of ages is offered by the Florentine humanist Matteo Palmieri in E. Garin, ed., *L'educazione umanistica in Italia* (Bari, 1949), 114.

[5] E. Delaruelle, et al., *L'Église au temps du Grand Schisme et de la crise conciliaire (1378–1449)* (*Fliche et Martin*, 14, part 2) (Paris, 1964), 845ff.

function as a type of social control element enforcing accepted village norms.[6] But in the cities they often proved more conducive to disorder than to burgher piety. The Florentine evidence suggests that the modern youth club, distinguished in the early period by its pious and deliberate pedagogic thrust, was an urban creation at odds with the old communal or rural gang.

Youth had long played a major role in Florentine festive brigades, groups organized to provide both amusement and visual pleasure. Giovanni Villani's descriptions of the brigades of the outgoing duecento and early trecento can be summarized in the following fashion:[7] the groups were occasional, organized mainly for the festivities of May Day. They were competitive, with brigades from different sections of the city vying with each other to please the citizenry. They were financed by rich families. While young people may have predominated (Villani speaks of brigades of *gentili giovani* in the 1290s),[8] participation does not seem to have been limited to them. Villani would have us believe that in the good old days, the brigades were composed of noble youth, while in his own latter days, grown *artefici* and *popolo minuto* walked the streets as play emperors, dukes, and the like.[9] This too obvious dichotomy between past purity and present decline is dubious. I should imagine that the traditional brigade of this and later times was composed of a few rich youth (and some not so young) financed by their fathers, who in turn mobilized groups of lower-class young people and adults.[10] In any case, Villani and other trecento chroniclers made no clear and lasting distinction between men (*uomini*) and youth (*giovani*) in describing the leisure-time institutions of

---

[6] N. Davis, "Charivaris," 55 et passim. The Italian counterparts to the French charivaris were concentrated in rural northwestern Italy; see G. C. Pola Falletti Villafalletto, *Associazioni giovanili e feste antiche*, vol. 1 (Milan, 1939), and the same author's *La juventus attraverso i secoli* (Monza, 1953).

[7] I draw my summary from *Croniche di Giovanni, Matteo e Filippo Villani*, vol. 1 (Trieste, 1857), bk. VII, chap. 89 (1283); VII, 132 (1289); VIII, 70 (1304); X, 219 (1333); XII, 8 (1343).

[8] Ibid., VII, 132.

[9] Compare Villani's characterization of the 1283 brigade as "la più nobile e nominata che mai fosse nella città di Firenze e Toscana" ("the most noble and renowned of Florence and Tuscany there ever was") with that of 1343 during the dictatorship of Walter of Brienne: "Fu movitura e con sentimento del duca per recarsi l'amore del popolo minuto, per quella isforzata vanità" ("It was instigated by and with the sentiment of the duke's forced vanity, so as to win the love of the *popolo minuto*") (ibid., VII, 89; XII, 8.)

[10] The historian Cambi, for example, described a carnival in 1499 where there were "raghunati assai duomini tutti plebei, el forte, benchè e' Messeri alchuni fussino fanciulli da bene per segnio"; I. a San Luigi, ed., *Delizie degli eruditi toscani*. vol. 20 (1785), 136 ("gathered a lot of men, all or mostly lower class, although for show, some of their lords were well off children"). An example of old leadership is provided by Doffo Spini, who led the group of Compagnacci against Savonarola. He was fifty years old. His approximately nine associates from the nobility, called *I Vecchi*, had a group of some 300 *giovani* at their beck, "i più scoretti della città" (J. Schnitzer, ed., *Quellen und Forschungen zur Geschichte Savonarolas III: Bartolommeo Cerretani* [Munich, 1904], 54f.; P. Villari and E. Casanova [eds.], *Scelta di prediche e scritti di fra Girolamo Savonarola* [Florence, 1898], 481) ("the most unruly of the city").

Florence. This lack of differentiation continued until the latter part of the trecento.[11]

Children and adolescents at school do not seem to have been corporatively organized. At all educational levels—schools for reading and writing (ca. seven through twelve years old), through those for arithmetic (ca. twelve through fourteen), to those of Latin grammar (ca. fourteen to eighteen years old)— town students visited their lecturers and returned home each evening.[12] We have no basis for speculating as to the degree of solidarity school associations may have engendered. Debenedetti has shown that the school masters had organized,[13] but nothing suggests that the school was the institutional base for any youthful social activity in Florence.

In these early centuries, therefore, there was no extra-familial group instrumentality for the stated purpose of indoctrinating young people in religious and other social values. The typical trecento school of the master certainly imparted these values de facto; many of the instructors were clerks and priests, and the textbooks for reading and writing had a strong ethical content. Yet instruction in social piety was not formalized.[14]

Parents who sought such training for their sons outside the home had little choice. Florence's monasteries and friaries do not seem to have allowed externs to attend their schools, for here in Florence, as elsewhere in Europe, the

---

[11] From then on, the *brigate* were by definition *de' giovani*; see for example the Alberti and Castellani brigades of 1386 in which *giovani* were wonderfully dressed; *Biblioteca Nazionale, Firenze* [hereafter *BNF*], *Fondo Panciatichi* 158, fol. 150r; almost all of the numerous brigades described by Bartolommeo Del Corazza in his *ricordi* were of *giovani* (G. O. Corazzini, ed., "Diario Fiorentino di Bartolommeo Del Corazza, anni 1405–1438," *Archivio Storico Italiano* [hereafter *ASI*], ser. 5, 14 [1894], 243f., 254, 255, 276). In religious processions, however, the lack of distinction continued for some time. In his famous first description of a *festa* of S. Giovanni Battista (about 1405), for example, Goro Dati speaks of "compagnie d'uomini secolari" wearing angels' dress (C. Guasti, *Le feste di San Giovanni Battista in Firenze* [Florence, 1884], 5). The first mention of young people participating as a distinct unit in a religious procession would seem to be Del Corazza's description of the entry of Martin V into Florence in 1419, when "gioveni, de' maggiori della terra e più politi" ("youth, from among the most important and polite of the area") accompanied the Corpus Christi (see Del Corazza, "Diario," 257, 271–74, 285, 292f).

[12] See the summary in R. Davidsohn, *Storia di Firenze*, 8 vols. (Florence, 1956–68), 7:211–23.

[13] S. Debenedetti, "Sui più antichi *doctores puerorum* a Firenze," *Studi Medievali* 2 (1906–7): 338–42. Unfortunately, question of manners and piety are excluded from P. Grendler's recent, rich *Schooling in Renaissance Italy* (Baltimore, 1989).

[14] Davidsohn and Debenedetti seem to have assumed that lay schools had uniformly lay teachers, which was certainly not the case. What was missing was formal religious instruction within the school's framework. Informally, in the Christian age any teacher, lay or ecclesiastical, imparted religious norms: "Nam pueri religiosi nascuntur, atque educantur, et in religione firmissimi permanent, quousque in adolescentia ratio excitetur ..." (M. Ficino, *Opera Omnia* [Turin, 1962], 1:4) ("For boys are born and raised religious, and remain firmly religious until in adolescence they excercise reason"). In 1514, the Council of the Lateran V ordered school masters to teach the catechism to children, and forbade them to teach anything else on feast days other than "religion and good manners" (P. Tacchi Venturi, *Storia della compagnia di Gesú in Italia* [Rome, 1950], 1:339f.).

tendency was to limit these conventual schools to those who had vocational intentions.

The only possibility in Florence of an education that would insure training for secular youth in piety as well as in grammar came through the existing adult confraternity system. At the end of the duecento two of these sodalities maintained schools at the churches where they met. Details are sketchy, but it seems that instruction was provided by religious persons, and that the best students, upon terminating their courses, had preferential but nonobligatory access to the religious life.[15] Apart from these distant forerunners of the boys' confraternities of the quattrocento, no pious group specifically for young people has left its trace in the Florentine records. Fleeting as their appearance is, these confraternal *scuole* provided the only instrument outside the family for an education which would not neglect religious acculturation.[16]

In the trecento there were no lay sodalities statutorily limited to *giovani* or *fanciulli*.[17] Confraternities were for *uomini* or *donne* or both. They were organized into *laudesi*, indoor groups for singing church music, and the *disciplinati* or flagellants, characterized by stern internal discipline and by their participation in outdoor processions.[18] These confraternities increased during the quattrocento, and became more diversified in type. Companies bearing "standards" or baldachins appeared at the end of the trecento, and in early quattrocento the so-called "night companies" made their debut. With the traditional *laudesi* and *disciplinati*, the new companies of the standards and the

---

[15] The necrology of the Dominican friary of Santa Maria Novella relates that Fra Uguccio di fu Lapo Morelli (d. 1301) before he entered the order, was "a teneris annis cum multa devotione cum aliis pueris nostre Societatis Beate Virginis" (R. Davidsohn, *Forschungen zur Geschichte von Florenz* [Berlin, 1908], 4:430) ("from tender years among our boys of our confraternity of the Blessed Virgin with much devotion"). For both this society and the one at the collegiate church of S. Lorenzo, see also Davidsohn, *Storia*, 7:225f. Fathers may have used these societies as a means of insuring the future of their sons in an overpopulated society. For confraternities created to guarantee members' daughters' entrance into a nunnery, see *Archivo di Stato, Firenze* (hereafter *ASF*), *R. Diritto*, 4892, fols. 293r–297r (1516).

[16] Parental concerns on this score had spurred the development of the college within the northern European university, and the expansion of the oblate system within the Mendicant orders; see J. R. H. Moorman, *The Grey Friars in Cambridge, 1225–1538* (Cambridge, 1952), 104–11.

[17] Richa's assumption that a company of *fanciulli* had existed in the friary of San Marco since the outgoing thirteenth century is incorrect (G. Richa, *Notizie istoriche delle chiese fiorentine*, 10 vols. [Florence, 1754–62], 5:329–31). See also G. M. Monti, *Le Confraternite Medievali dell'Alta e Media Italia* [Florence, 1927], 1:149–90. Writing about 1405, the Dominican reformer Giovanni Dominici made no mention of pious organizations for children or youth in his pedagogic recommendations to parents (G. Dominici, *On the Education of Children*, ed. A. Coté, [Washington, 1927]).

[18] In 1419, "Flagellants and *laudesi*" were still used to describe the range of lay confraternities; see *ASF, Provvisioni*, 109, fols. 160v–162r (19 October 1419). In the Diary of Del Corazza, the "compagnie cogli stendardi" which took part in processions were the same as the "compagnie de' battuti" or "di discipline" (Del Corazza, "Diario," 242, 249, 279f.).

night companies formed a rich web of secular sodalities into which poured a large number of Florentine citizens and *artefici*. The articulation of fraternities into age groups was a part of this wider confraternal organization. While several scholars have recognized the growing importance of the confraternities in Florentine cultural life during the quattrocento, the creation of special confraternities for young people has not caught their attention.[19] A description of their origins and development will focus attention upon this particular institution.

Our first evidence of a confraternity specified by age is contained in a petition of 1396 directed to the Signoria of Florence by the captains of the "venerable and devout" society of San Matteo, which met in the Augustinian church of Santo Spirito. Made up of "honest and devout youth," the society was growing rapidly. It asked for and received annual alms of the type normally given to ecclesiastical entities by the *Mercanzia* and guild consuls.[20] It was the first non-ecclesiastical group to receive such funds. Once the first of these groups of *iuvenes* was established, others quickly followed.[21]

The process of age delineation continued, and soon the first companies for adolescents appeared on the scene. The oldest may be that of the Nativity (also called "of the Archangel Raphael"), established in 1410 by a goldsmith. It met for some years in the hospital of the Scala.[22] A second company, that

---

[19] Monti has attempted to quantify the secular trend, and in terms of numbers of confraternities founded, the quattrocento is indeed remarkable. But a full-length study of the Florentine confraternities will be necessary before we know how many people were involved, the average life span of the foundations, and what classes of the population were involved in them. Important articles on the cultural significance of the confraternities are: P. O. Kristeller, "Lay Religious Traditions and Florentine Platonism," in his *Studies in Renaissance Thought and Letters* (Rome, 1956), 99–122; E. Garin, "Desideri di riforma nell'oratoria del quattrocento," now in his *La cultura filosofica del Rinascimento Italiano* (Florence, 1961), 166–82; R. Hatfield, "The Compagnia De 'Magi," *Journal of the Warburg and Courtauld Institutes* 33 (1970): 107–61. For the constitutions and matriculation of one company of flagellants, see O. Marinelli, ed., "La Compagnia di Disciplinati di S. Domenico in Firenze," *Bolletino della deputazione di storia patria per l'Umbria*, ser. 1, vol. 66 (1969): 211–40.

[20] "Per devotos iuvenes et honestos dicta societas creata fuit," *ASF, Prov.* 85, fols. 247r–248r (8 December 1396).

[21] Among the subsequent companies of *iuvenes* was that of S. Michele Archangelo, meeting in the Servite church, and "recently made" when its *capitoli* were approved by the bishop on 23 November 1420; *ASF, Notarile antecosiminiano* S 672 (1417–21), at the date. In 1419 the commune approved a payment for candles to "certain societies of youth" participating in the celebration of S. Giovanni Battista; *ASF, Prov.* 109, fols. 49v–50r (12 June). It is unclear whether these latter groups were pious or festive.

[22] Del Migliore in recording this information in his *Zibaldone* said that it aimed at teaching Christian doctrine to *giovanetti*. I have been unable to find any verification for the traditional assertion that this and the other boys' confraternities were called "confraternities of [Christian] Doctrine." It will become clear in what follows that no reference is made to catechetical training in any of the quattrocento records of these companies. For the early wanderings of the company, whose statutes of 1468 are extant, see Monti, *Confraternite*, 1:183. When the famous *cartolaio* Vespasiano da Bisticci was "di non molta età," (born 1421), he was encouraged to join the company of *fanciulli* of ser Antonio di Mariano. Ser Antonio was the custodian of this company (see below, n. 53); *Vita di uomini*

of San Niccolò del Ceppo, purportedly transferred to the Ceppo from Oltrar-
no in 1417. Morçay tells us that it had earlier been a *scuola di lezione*.[23] A
third company, that of the Purification, is said to have issued from the over-
crowded company of the Nativity in 1427.[24] The documentation for the
institution of these first three companies remains inconclusive. With the establishment of the company or *scuola* of *giovanetti* of San Giovanni Vangelista
in the same year, we finally enter upon firm ground. Both its *capitoli* and the
episcopal approval are extant.[25]

By 1435, a Florentine prelate could refer to "several" societies of boys or
children in the city.[26] Their rapid growth generated quick demands for their
limitation. An important papal bull of 24 June 1442[27] shows the custodians
of four such Florentine companies for boys complaining to the pope about
this needless multiplication. One reason for this proliferation, they said, was
that the boys themselves were creating new clubs, and removing their custodians at will. Eugenius in his letter recognized the existence of four groups for
pueri: S. Giovanni Vangelista, S. Niccolò, the Nativity, and the confraternity of
the Purification. Acceding to the recommendation of the four custodians, the
pope set up a commission composed of the custodians of these confraternities, the abbot of the newly reformed *Badia Fiorentina*, and the prior of the
Observant Dominican house of San Marco.[28] Without the advice and consent of a majority of these six men, no new groups could be created; the re-
moval of custodians by the boys could not be legal; and elections to vacant
custodianships could not be formalized. The pope recognized the archbishop's traditional right to approve such creations and elections. Unlike

illustri del secolo XV (Florence, 1938), 145 (*Vita* of the cardinal Albergati, d. 1443).

[23] The same author cites no evidence for his assertion that its statutes were approved
by the archbishop in 1450 (R. Morçay, *Saint Antonin. Archevêque de Florence (1389-1459)*
[Paris, 1914], 91). In the document cited at n. 29, it is called a *societas adolescentium*. The
confraternity's history is thoroughly confused because there was at least one and perhaps
two other confraternities *del Ceppo*; see L. Passerini, *Storia degli Stabilimenti di Beneficenze
di Firenze* (Florence, 1853), 188; L. Santoni, *Raccolta di notizie storiche riguardanti le chiese
dell'arci-diogesi di Firenze* (Florence, 1847), 96; E. and W. Paatz, *Die Kirchen von Florenz*, 6
vols. (Frankfurt, 1940-54), 2:97-100, 4:292-95.

[24] The group's *capitoli* were approved by the archbishop on 3 April 1448 (Monti,
Confraternite, 1:184, citing Del Migliore's *Zibaldone*, cited above). On 29 June 1444, the
company or *scuola* of *fanciulli* was given possession of its new quarters around S. Marco
(Morçay, *Antonin*, 473f.). It retained them until 1506 (Hatfield, "Magi," 127).

[25] Membership was limited to those between thirteen and twenty-four years of age.
Copies of the *capitoli* and archepiscopal approval of 2 July 1427 may be found in the
BNF, Cl. 31, cod. 11, fols. 8v-9r, and in the *ASF, Not. antecos*. J 7 (1417-27), at the date
2 July 1427. Morçay erroneously identifies this company with one founded in 1388
(*Antonin*, 91). Despite its statutory age limits, in the document cited at n. 29 below it is
called variously a *societas puerorum et iuvenum* and a *societas . . . puerorum et adolescentium*.

[26] See below, 62.

[27] Printed in C. C. Calzolai, *Frate Antonino Pierozzi* (Rome, 1960), 83f.

[28] The abbot of the *Badia* was the Portuguese reformer Gomez da Silva (see G. Bat-
teli, *L'abate don Gomez Ferreira da Silva e i Portoghesi a Firenze nella prima metà del quattrocento* [Rome, 1940]). The prior of San Marco at the time was the saintly Antonino
Pierozzi.

many another legislated body, the commission established by Eugenius did function. In 1453, we find it consenting to the boys' election of the custodian of a fifth confraternity, that of the *iuvenes et adolescentes* of Sant' Antonio da Padova, meeting in the monastery and church of San Giorgio.[29] According to D'Ancona, this company was founded in 1441.[30] There may have been more than five such groups in the city at this time. This document shows only that the four mentioned in Eugenius's bull were controlling elections in at least one other club.

One of the important provisions of Eugenius's bull of 1442 was that it forbade any group of boys besides the original four and those approved by the commission to call itself a "society" and to take part in public processions dressed in white. Various boys' groups were obviously competing for processional posts. Despite Eugenius's guidelines, this tension continued and the San Giovanni celebration of 1453 was marred by confusion.[31] Therefore, in 1454 the commune asked the archbishop for a list of clerical entities and lay confraternities authorized to participate in the Patron's procession. Antonino's response listed seven confraternities of *fanciulli*. Of the five we have mentioned previously, four are directly listed in this document, while the fifth is probably included, but under a variant name. The company of Santa Brigida listed by Antonino is scarcely known. According to Del Migliore, the last of the seven, that named after Bernardino of Siena, was founded in 1451, the year after the saint's canonization.[32]

After this point, it is difficult to follow the institutional development of the boys' clubs. Their particular relation to the great movement of *fanciulli* under Savonarola, for example, remains to be clarified. In Benedetto Varchi's time, about 1530, there were nine boys' confraternities in the city.[33] Thus from mid-quattrocento to mid-cinquecento a net gain of only two groups had been made.

In the year 1435, the Camaldolan general and scholar Ambrogio Traversari addressed Pope Eugenius on the subject of boys' confraternities. To learn

---

[29] S. Orlandi, *S. Antonino* (Florence, 1960), 2:313–16. In this document its membership is said to include *iuvenes et adolescentulos*. The "nominatio et deputatio" by the forty-four members took place on 31 March 1453; the assent by the commission and the archiepiscopal approval followed on 1 June 1453.

[30] A. D'Ancona, *Origini del teatro italiano* (Turin, 1891), 1:406. The group's *ordinamenti* of 1466 are extant (Monti, *Confraternite*, 1:186).

[31] For one aspect of this confusion, see *ASF, Prov.* 145, fols. 86v–87r (19 June 1454).

[32] "Regole di frati come vanno a processione secondo la nota del vescovo Antonino come mi dette Baccio Falsamonstra" (*ASF, Signoria e Balia, Carte di Corredi* 45, fol. 18v) ("The Mendicant Religions: their order in processions, according to the note of bishop Antonino, given me by Baccio Falsamonstra"). The document bears no date. But according to an unsubstantiated remark of Gori, Antonino drew this up in 1454 (P. Gori, *Le feste fiorentine attraverso i secoli. Le feste per San Giovanni* [Florence, 1926], 20f.). For the company of S. Brigida, see Paatz, *Kirchen*, 1:406f. The company of S. Bernardino met in the Franciscan church of Santa Croce. Its *capitoli* were written in 1471 (Monti, *Confraternite*, 1:186, citing the Del Migliore *Zibaldone*).

[33] B. Varchi, *Storia Fiorentina* (Florence, 1963), 1:591 (bk. IX, chap. 36).

something of the organization and social position of these groups, we can do no better than to start by citing his remarks:

> Hear now something equally pious, most Holy Father. Our city has several societies of noble, middle-class, and poor boys [*puerorum*]. At the head of each is a faithful, grave, religious, and God-fearing man who rears these [boys] and who, in secular dress, drills the recruits for the militia of the Eternal King. Following their rule, they observe continence in everything. They flee from inane spectacles and all games, and they abstain also from the idle talk [of the games and spectacles]. They confess more frequently, and take communion often. And while during the remaining days of the week they exercise their individual trade under the supervision of their relatives, on Sundays and feast days they all meet at a designated place where they give themselves over to the praise of God [*divinis laudibus*] and use their time for worthwhile colloquies. When however they have left their childhood years behind, they transfer to another group where older people meet, and continue in similar works. Many of them, once they have tasted the goodness of innocence, enter the religious life.[34]

In another letter on the same subject, Traversari gives us more information on their position and social utility. Speaking of one such *scuola*, he says:

> The leaders of the city are repeatedly pleased to send their sons to be nourished in this school and to be educated in this school of Christian virtue. In it nothing impious is learned, nothing other than good habits are imbibed ... [Through this training] they often remain innocent amidst the obscene railery of criminals ... On Sundays and feast days, when greater license for lasciviousness is usurped, they gather together, and after salubrious admonitions, they either recite the psalms or sing hymns together. And if perhaps someone has occasionally or lightly violated the rules, penance is meted out and the crime is confessed. Formed and indoctrinated in this way, they return to their parents' homes and, the parents being presented with such a specimen of religion, the boys [contribute] through example and incitement to the good morality of the family ... [If the boys] decide to remain laymen, they retain the taste of supernal grace which they received in their tender years. To whatever magistracies of the city they are elected, they cultivate justice before all else.[35]

The main purpose of these confraternities or schools was obviously to remove the boys from the chaos and spontaneity of the street, and to provide a leisure-time activity under competent direction which would aid the forma-

---

[34] A. Traversari, *Latinae Epistolae* ... , ed. L. Mehus, (Florence, 1759), 2:40.

[35] Ibid., 134 (printed in E. Garin, ed., *Il pensiero pedagogico dello umanesimo* [Florence, 1958], 304). Both of these letters were written in 1435.

tion of a pious character.[36] Separation of age groups was one of the means used to achieve this character. In itself the division according to ages reflected only the corporate mentality of the time: children were of a different sect than youth, youth than grown men.[37] Such a division did not assume that youthful piety was to be reached through activities different from those of the men's confraternities. In fact, one of the striking aspects of these clubs is the markedly adult character of their internal group practices. The decision to create corporations of young people was new; the legal instruments for doing so were old. The *capitoli* of the new groups followed the classical associative formulas for grown men. The boys of the Vangelista were to be between thirteen and twenty-four years of age. These adolescents proclaimed in their constitutions, however, that it was they who had decided to organize. It was these boys who "made the constitutions," choosing the goals and methods of their group.[38]

The similarity to adult modes was more than merely legal. The youngsters effectively controlled by vote all the offices of the confraternity. From their midst the *fanciulli* of the Vangelista elected their governor (second in command in the confraternity) and his two counsellors. Together with the guardian of the confraternity, these three boy-officers then elected the boy-*infermieri* who would act as masters of the novices.[39]

The *confratelli* also had a determinant voice in the election of the adult men who were attached to the groups. The confessors, for example, were directly elected by the boys from a list of four candidates submitted to them by their adult custodians or guardians, as they were sometimes called. As for this latter official, there are traces in the *capitoli* of a desire to prevent the boys from removing him at will: If on his death-bed the guardian revealed to the group's confessor his choice of a successor, that choice was to be honored. Still, the boys themselves retained the greatest authority. Each year the confessors, together with the three boys serving as governor and counsellors, were to reaffirm the guardian.[40] We have seen that before 1442, the boys exercised these rights to the fullest, dismissing their guardians at will and instituting new groups when they encountered opposition. Eugenius's decision to appoint a commission of grown men to advise and consent was a small step

---

[36] Vespasiano da Bisticci tells us, for example, that as children Piero and Donato Acciaiuoli entered a company of *giovani* with their tutor "to flee youth to whom good manners were foreign. . . . All this was done to form well the habit of virtue" (*Vite*, 355 [*Vita* of Donato Acciaiuoli]). The Vangelista, like an adult sodality, outlawed gambling, whoring, and blasphemy (*BNF, Cl.* 31, cod. 11, fols. 3v–4r [chap. 3]).

[37] "When he became older," for example, Donato Acciaiuoli moved from the company of youth to the night company of S. Girolamo (*Vite*, 355). In earlier times an occasional adult confraternity seems to have had *pueri* or *adolescentes* attached to it in some capacity; see above, n. 15, and the 1278 *capitoli* of the adult company of S. Egidio, where *fanciulli* above fourteen or fifteen might be admitted (Monti, *Confraternite*, 2:153).

[38] "Vogliendo dunque alcune divote persone deta danni tredici in quattuordici et non piu cominciare et dare principio al bene operare . . ." (*BNF, Cl.* 31, cod. 11, fols. 2r–3r).

[39] Ibid., fols. 5r–v.

[40] Ibid., ff., 4r–5r.

toward controlling organizations which, despite their youthful membership, retained the democratic associative principles common to the corporations of their fathers.[41]

The internal activities of the clubs, as they are revealed in the *capitoli* of the Vangelista, were as adult as their election procedures, not significantly different from the traditional activities of the non-flagellant men's confraternities. They met on the first and third Sundays of each month and on all Sundays of Advent and Lent. On Holy Thursday the guardian washed the feet of the boys, a traditional confraternal practice. The boys were to confess once a month to the group's confessor, take communion together on the feast of the Evangelist, and attend mass every morning "or at least try to see the body of Christ."[42] As in the confraternities of the *uomini fatti* the brothers suffered correction by the guardian when they violated the *capitoli*. Finally, novices were accepted in typical adult fashion: voted upon during the second meeting of their novitiate, they were formally installed during the third gathering, dressed in white and singing the *Veni Creator* and *Te Deum*.[43]

At their inception, then, the boys' confraternities were democratic in their operation and adult in their practices. These "schools of virtues"[44] were not, however, without controls imposed by elders. Internal control was fostered in the Company of the Purification by allowing only the older boys to vote on certain affairs,[45] a custom found also in a Pistoian confraternity of *fanciulli* in 1516.[46] A more important control element was the dependence of the boys' groups on confraternities of *uomini fatti*. Thus the Purification was under the protection of the men's confraternity of S. Girolamo.[47] The Vangel-

---

[41] For an overview of the long process by which university students were stripped of their medieval corporate privileges, see E. Durkheim, *L'évolution pédagogique en France* (Paris, 1938), 1:146–56. Compare the long battle of the Dominican students at Padua to retain their traditional rights in L. Gargin, ed., *Lo studio teologico e la biblioteca dei Domenicani a Padova nel tre e quattrocento* (Padua, 1971), 16f., 19–36.

[42] *BNF*, Cl. 31, cod. 11, fols. 3r–v.

[43] Ibid., fols. 5r–6v.

[44] See above, 62. The Pistoian boys' confraternity of the Purità, founded in 1516, also referred to itself as such (P. Vigo, ed., *Una confraternità di giovanetti pistoiesi a principio del secolo XVI* [Bologna, 1887], 45).

[45] Decision made by "guardianus societatis puerorum purificationis beate Marie seu Sancti Marci, una cum gubernatore et consiliariis et pueris natu maioribus" (Florence, *Biblioteca Laurenziana*, Fondo *Biblioteca di San Marco*, cod. 370: *Chronica conventus Sancti Marci de Florentia*, fol. 17r [1496]) ("the guardian of the confraternity of the boys of the purification of holy Mary, or of St. Mark, at one with the governor and counsellors and with the older boys").

[46] Vigo, *Confraternità . . . pistoiesi*, 60.

[47] The 1543 acts cited above (n. 29) refers to "Pierus Mariani, custos societatis . . . [*sic*] que congregatur apud hospitale Sancti Mathei seu dictum *l'ospedale di Lelmo* de Florentia." This is without doubt the Purificazione, as a comparison of the papal bull of 1442 with the 1453 document makes clear. Del Migliore had read an old document in the archive of San Marco on the night company of San Girolamo, "ad quem protectio et cura dicte societatis [dei fanciulli della purificazione alias di S. Marco] spectat" (F. Del Migliore, *Firenze Citta' Nobilissima Illustrata* [Florence, 1684], 256) ("to whom belongs the protection and care of the said society").

ista had a similar relation to the adult confraternity of S. Paolo.[48] And the boys' group of S. Bastiano was fathered by the men's company of S. Jacopo, which decided to alleviate its overgrowth by "making two companies in one body, one company of the men of the night of S. Jacopo and S. Giovanni Gualberto, the other of *fanciulli* under the title of the glorious martyr S. Bastiano."[49] The Pistoian boys of the Company of Purity gathered in the same meeting place as the *uomini* of S. Matteo, and the prior of that company approved the boys' election of a guardian.[50]

A further element of control by elders and parents may be mentioned, but without the documentation one would like. The guardians of these boys' confraternities may have come from the companies of *uomini fatti* and formed an elite of pious laymen. The guardian of the confraternity of the Vangelista, for example, was at the same time one of the twelve Buonomini, a prestigious confraternity created in 1442 to aid the shamed poor of good family.[51] The original home of this same boys' group was donated to it by another member of the Buonomini.[52] Further, in one short period, three members of one family headed confraternities: Piero succeeded his father Mariano as guardian of the Purification, while ser Antonio di Mariano governed the company of the Nativity.[53] Further research may show that a relatively small group of citizens was the motivating force behind much of the drive to organize the boys.[54]

The firmest control exercised by adults was, however, not institutional at

[48] See *ASF, Comp. Relig. Soppr.* 1579, containing information on relations between the companies. I owe this information to the kindness of Rab Hatfield.

[49] This information comes from a memorial of the parent company's cinquecento historian, who says that it took place in 1460; cited in Richa, *Notizie*, 10:352ff. In the process of founding the Pistoian boys' confraternity of the Purità, the men's sodality of S. Matteo assigned two of its *giovani* to the Purità to provide guidance (Vigo, *Confraternità ... pistoiesi*, 6).

[50] Ibid., 6, 50.

[51] This was Jacopo di Biagio dell'Ancisa, *cimatore* or tailor's cutter, custodian in 1453 (on the Buonomini, see my "Charity and the Defense of Urban Elites in the Italian Communes," in F. Jaher, ed., *The Rich, the Well-Born and the Powerful. Elites and Upper Classes in History* [Urbana, 1973], 64–109).

[52] Luigi d'Urbano di messer Francesco Bruni bought the property of S. Trinità Vecchia from the Gesuati in 1438 and then donated it to the Vangelista in 1441 (Monti, *Confraternite*, 1:188). On Bruni, see Trexler, "Charity," 89.

[53] A document cited by Morçay records that in favoring the Purification, Cosimo de' Medici "tutte le partite di per se pagò et tolse per la compagnia di Mariano" (Morçay, *Antonin*, 474) ("himself took and paid all the debts for Mariano's confraternity"). Thus in 1444 one Mariano must have been guardian. It may be assumed that Piero di Mariano, the guardian in 1453, was his son, and that ser Antonio di Mariano was another son. It will be recalled that the Nativity fathered the Purification (see above, p. 60).

[54] Ser Alessio di Matteo Pelli, notary who acted as Cosimo's procurator in handing over the Purificazione's new quarters in 1444, was also a member of the Buonomini; see Morçay, *Antonin*, 474. On Pelli, see Trexler, "Charity," 89. According to a tradition that goes back to Del Migliore, but which I have not been able to document, the original Buonomini came from the membership of the night company of S. Girolamo (Del Migliore, *Firenze ... Illustrata*, 256).

all, but through monetary support. As we shall see, the boys' activities were costly, and financial support came from lay benefactors. We know next to nothing about Florentines' attitudes toward having their children in these companies. On the one hand they wanted their boys to receive pious instruction, while on the other the majority probably did not want their children so exposed to clerical ways as to develop a vocation for the religious life. Duecento adult confraternities may have supported schools so as to channel surplus sons into the religious life, but with population at a much lower level, the average middle and upper class Florentine of the quattrocento wanted a pious son, but not a religious one. A father might be forced to place a surplus daughter in a nunnery; a son could be emancipated.[55] The religious vocation desirable to a Camaldolan monk like Traversari was not so attractive to the average father,[56] and the Savonarolan period was marked by parental recriminations against the reformer who had won their sons to the religious life. The same values hindered increased membership in the Pistoian confraternity of the Purità. When three boys chose a life of religion in 1517, parents reacted by withdrawing their sons—and their financial support—from the group.[57]

. Lay leadership of these confraternities was an evident attempt to prevent boys from being seduced into the religious life. Who then were these guardians and, just as important, who were the boys who matriculated in the companies of the *fanciulli*? As limited as our information presently is, and as misleading as matriculation lists can be in assessing the tone of social groups, some limited overview of their social composition may be offered.

The guardians were small shopkeepers rather than civic leaders. In 1453 one carried the title "ser"; he may have been a notary. One guardian was a dyer, another a shoemaker, while a third was a small wool master. This shopkeeper leadership seems to have been preserved in subsequent years.[58] True, in 1483 the guardian of the Purification was a *dominus* Domenico di Stefano, and in 1495 one ser Chiaro di Giovanni.[59] Yet in the 1490s the guardian of the company of the Vangelista was a brass worker named Cristofano di Miniato. The fact that in 1491 this confraternity performed a *sacra rappresentazione* written by Lorenzo de' Medici and that Lorenzo's twelve-year-old son Giuliano was the *messere* of the boys during this time, did not necessitate a change

---

[55] On this problem, see below, 68.

[56] See Traversari's enthusiasm for the confraternities as generators of vocations above, 62.

[57] "Imperochè molti per timore haveano che non andassino alla sancta religione, da propri padri e madri hebbeno comandamento che non andassero all decta compagnia, nè al convento di San Domenico si appellassino . . ." (Vigo, *Confraternità . . . pistoiesi*, 59 [see also 64f.]).

[58] The founder of the Nativity, it will be remembered, was a goldworker (see above, 59). In 1453, the custodians or guardians of five companies were Antonio di Paolo, *tintore* (del Ceppo) Onofrio di Filippo di Bartolommeo, *calzaiuolo* (S. Antonio da Padova); Jacopo di Biagio, *cimatore* (Vangelista); Ser Antonio di Mariano (Nativity) and his brother Piero di Mariano (Orlandi, *S. Antonino*, 2:314f.).

[59] Richa, *Notizie*, 5:330f.

in the social quality of the group's leadership.[60] None of the known guardians of these groups during the quattrocento played any discernible role in government, and none was of significant financial standing in Florence.[61]

What of the boys serving under such "decent" but relatively humble citizens? A perusal of the matriculation of the company of S. Antonio da Padova in 1453 reveals that its forty-four members were predominantly of artisan background.[62] Of those whose occupations are listed, six were shoemakers, as was the guardian of the group. There were four flax dressers, three mercers, and two each of barbers, goldsmiths, silk merchants, and thread sellers, plus an assortment of five other artisans. The only crafts listed which pertained to the major guilds were the mercers and silk merchants (*setaiuoli*) (the others were minor guildsmen).

Those without occupational designations included one patrician, a Gianfigliazzi, three members of the Salvetti and Da Filicaia families, and two sons of notaries or priests. The last eight matriculants also have no given occupation. They were probably too young for such a designation.

Since the company of S. Antonio was for "adolescents and youth," the average age of the matriculated was probably higher than the clubs strictly for adolescents. Its social makeup was probably quite similar to the others: sons of honest burghers, plus a sprinkling of patricians exercising much influence among their *confratelli*.

We have sketched the creation and growth of the new boys' confraternities, said something of their internal organization and activities, and tried to relate them to a wider picture of confraternal diversification within the city of Florence. Before proceeding any further, however, it is necessary to mention the creation of another type of confraternal organization during the quattrocento. I refer to the foundation of two important *scuole* under mixed secular-ecclesiastical direction located in the cathedral church and in the Medici parish church of San Lorenzo. While there certainly were differences between these *schole clericorum* and those of the secular *fanciulli*, these were less important than the commonality of certain of their aims and practices.

The *schola puerorum ordinandorum* was instituted in the cathedral of Florence in 1436 through the joint efforts of Pope Eugenius IV and the commune.[63] Acting for the commune, the Florentine wool guild matched an in-

---

[60] See below, n. 107.

[61] I could trace none of them in the Catasto lists of 1427 published in L. Martines, *The Social World of the Florentine Humanists* (Florence, 1963), appendices.

[62] *ASF, Not. antecos.* B 386 (1453–54), fol. 10v. Rab Hatfield was kind enough to transcribe this matriculation for me.

[63] This sketch is based on two bulls of Eugenius IV printed in J. Lami, *Sanctae Ecclesiae Florentinae Monumenta* (Florence, 1758), 2:1147ff. (23 March 1436), and 1465f. (4 October 1441). The first of these has been reprinted in A. Seay, "The 15th-Century Cappella at Santa Maria del Fiore in Florence," *Journal of the American Musicological Society* 11 (1958): 45–55. The bull of 1441 may also be found in F. A. D'Accone, "A Documentary History of Music at the Florentine Cathedral and Baptistry during the Fifteenth Century," (Ph.D. diss., Harvard Univ., 1960), 2:6f. A list of the known masters of the *Scuola* is found in Richa, *Notizie*, 6:105f. On the background to the Eugenian investment, see J. Kirshner,

vestment by the pope in the communal funded debt, and the perpetual interest from this sum was to finance the salaries of a master of plainchant and grammar and thirty-three student-clerks. The master was to be a priest erudite in both fields; the boys were to be natives of the dioceses of Florence and Fiesole, and at the time of their entrance to be between ten and fifteen years old.

This *scuola* was for externs; like the boys of the confraternities, these clerks lived at home or in rented quarters. Two occasions brought them to the seat of the *scuola*. The first was for instruction in song and grammar, the second and more important was for participation in cathedral ritual. The stated purpose of the *scuola* was to meet the increased needs of the enlarged cathedral for singers and altar boys through grammatical and voice instruction.[64] The ritual expected of the boys was extensive; it involved a procession from their school to the cathedral and their presence in church "at all times of all days on which it happens that masses and canonical hours and other divine offices are celebrated in the said church."

Eugenius seems to have intended not only to augment the solemnity of divine services, but to create a seminary-type institution which would produce diocesan priests of assured competence and experience. Each boy received a stipend of nine florins a year for the ten years of his membership in the *scuola*. It was assumed that when the boy reached canonical age he would take Holy Orders (from about twenty-two for subdiaconal orders to twenty-five for sacerdotal orders). If at any time the boy gave up his intention, or if at the age of twenty-five he had not taken the Holy Orders, he was required to return all the salary he had received during his years in the *scuola*.[65]

The arrangement was an attractive one. A father could enter his boy, receive the income from the *scuola*, and at worst pay back the sum (without interest) if he withdrew the boy at twenty-two or twenty-three. For this the boy received free instruction—we will see later what some of that was. Very importantly, the *scuola* bound him to a regular attendance at divine services and consumed his time during Sundays and feast-days, when divine services were almost continual. The scheme was so successful that just six years after its foundation, Eugenius had to restrict the number of boys being sent to the school, while at the same time correcting an already apparent abuse: it is evident that fathers and tutors were using the school to procure the stipend, in-

---

"Papa Eugenio IV e il Monte Comune," *ASI* 127 (1969), especially 354.

[64] "Dictam ecclesiam in clericorum in cantu et grammatica peritorum numero adaugere" (Lami, *Monumenta*, 2:1147). The institution of this school preceded by only two days the consecration of the rebuilt cathedral. For Eugenius's encouragement of such *scuole* in other cathedrals, see D'Accone, "History," 1: 96.

[65] "Et quod quilibet puerorum praedictorum cum pervenerit ad aetatem, per quam secundum canones possit ad sacros ordines promoveri, ex tunc teneatur et debeat ad ipsos ordines se facere promoveri. Si quis autem antequam ad sacros ordines promotus fuerit, vel ad annum vigesimum quintum, ut praemittitur, pervenerit, a proposito clericatus duxerit divertendum, volumus, ac praesentium tenore statuimus, ut talis, ut praemittitur, divertens, quicquid perceperit ex huiusmodi scholastriae emolumentis, ipsis consulibus refundere teneatur" (Lami, *Monumenta*, 2:1148).

struction, and discipline, and then withdrawing the young people to avoid sacred orders.[66]

Certainly the founders' intentions were not the same as those who promoted the confraternities of boys. The former aimed at insuring a supply of priests and a decorous divine service. For example, the twelve clerks in the *scuola* founded by Cosimo de' Medici at San Lorenzo in 1458 were being referred to as "novices" at the beginning of the cinquecento. Further, it would seem that scientific instruction was given in these clerical *scuole*; by 1441, the pope had to arrange the hierarchical position of other masters who had attached themselves to the cathedral school.[67] Yet the similarities to the confraternities are many. In both, boys from puberty to twenty-four or -five were being organized under masters or guardians. Both involved the boys in pious activities, especially on Sundays and feast days. The church *scuole* as well as the confraternities fostered social piety. At San Lorenzo, the boys were to be instructed not only in plainchant and grammar, but in piety and ecclesiastical

---

[66] "Magistro ... inhibemus, ne ultra numerum triginta trium praedictorum clericorum, ac aliorum viginti, qui tamen omnes ecclesiae cum superpellicetis deserviant, non possit alios aliter recipere aut retinere ... Si quis autem cuiuscumque status ... existat, qui aliguem de clericis dicti collegii sine licentia praefati episcopi, et dilectorum filiorum consulum artis lane Florentinae, qui pro tempore fuerint, abstraxerit, seu removerit, quidquid salarii nomine clericus ipse receperit, restituere memorato collegio teneatur ... , ad quod etiam clericus ipse obligatus existat; et nihilominus, qui huiusmodi clericos abstraxerint, et qui eos retinuerint, poenam ipso facto excommunicationis incurrant, a qua non possint, nisi huiusmodi salario restituto, absolvi" (ibid., 1465) ("We prohibit the master from accepting or retaining others beyond the number of thirty-three of the said clerks, or twenty others, who, nevertheless, all must serve in church with their own habits. ... If however someone of whatever status ... is found, who has taken away or removed any of the clerks of the said college without the said bishop's license and that of the delectable sons, the consuls of the Florentine wool guild, he is required to restitute to the said college ... , and the said clerk also remains thus obliged; and beyond same, whoever removes and keeps any of the clerks, incurs the penalty ipso facto of excommunication, from which he cannot be absolved without a restitution of the said salary").

[67] The Lorenzan designation is contained in a protocol of 1520 against a master who "negligentemente faceva quello se li apparteneva circa il dar letioni, et costumi alli nostri novitii et cherici, per cui la nostra scuola al tutto era guasta et corrotta" (D. Moreni, *Memorie storiche ... S. Lorenzo. Continuazione* [Florence, 1816], 1:64f.) ("He to whom it fell to give lessons and customs to our novices and clerks has been negligent, and because of this our school was completely ruined and corrupted"); see also 63, where the boys are referred to simply as "novices" [1510]. The Eugenian reform: "Quod si scholasticum memoratum virum in grammatica et cantu peritum eligi contigerit, utrumque officium grammaticam et cantum docendi exercere possit, prout in praefatis literis nostris continetur. Si autem in altera dumtaxat peritus esset, possit alius eligi, qui alteri facultati satisfaciat" (Lami, *Monumenta*, 2:1465) ("If it happens that the said scholar with a specialty in teaching grammar and song is elected, he can hold the grammar and song teaching offices, as is said in our said letters. If however he is said to specialize in just one, then someone else may be elected who will fulfill the other discipline"). Despite these seeming references to a scholastic curriculum, I have been unable to find any quattrocento evidence that the cathedral school was related to the Florentine University, or at all subject to the communal officials of the *Studio*. According to Davidsohn, however, the theological college of that *Studio* was called after 1495 the *Collegio Eugeniano* (Davidsohn, *Storia*, 7:279).

discipline; they were to receive not only lessons, but good habits.[68] As we shall also see, the church schools developed thespian activities similar to those of the confraternities. The organization and development of boys' groups in Florence during the quattrocento remains the prime social fact. The *scuole* of the young clerks were definitely part of that phenomenon.

Adolescent groups were not originally conceived as different from the confraternities of the *uomini fatti*. What of their historical development? Did they evolve in a fashion distinct from the groups their fathers belonged to? Were activities developed which were thought more suitable to their tender years?

To provide an answer, we divide their activities into four categories:

1. internal activities of the traditional type, called "practices of the old law" by one confraternal writer of the early cinquecento;[69]

2. oratorical activities;

3. processional activities;

4. *sacre rappresentazioni* and other dramatic presentations.

We possess no information on the more traditional activities of the Florentine boys' groups during the quattrocento, and that includes those of the Savonarolan period. Yet if we examine the *ricordi* of the Pistoian confraternity of the Purità (1516–1517), we see that little had changed in their indoor activities: correction, self-accusation, confession, individual prayer, and the "external cult" of the group *laudi*.[70] The only peculiarity of the boys' domestic activity was in their "corporal exercises." It will be remembered that the boys had been organized to avoid the lasciviousness of carnival and other feasts, and it seems that in order to accomplish this, the boys were kept together for most of those days. The guardians and confessors of the companies realized that spiritual exercises could not hold the boys' attention throughout the day. They were just as aware that some of the boys would yearn for the customary street diversions on feast days. Consequently, the boys elected or were assigned a *messere* from among their midst—as was the custom of the typical street or carnival gang—who was responsible for supervising his colleagues in dignified physical diversions such as games of ball. This *messere* further provided the boys with meals, an expense and responsibility usually assumed by the governors of adult confraternities. In such a fashion "decent" sport or diversion was encouraged, and the boys could "come through Carnival without horrendous sin."[71] The inability of young

---

[68] "Non solum docere bonos mores, et grammaticam pueros sive clericos, sed etiam eos imbuat arte canendi, intelligendo de cantu, qui vulgo dicitur fermo" (Moreni, *Memorie*, 1:67 [1528]). For Cosimo's intentions, see ibid., 54.

[69] Vigo, *Confraternità . . . pistoiesi*, 23f.

[70] Conspicuously missing from this most extensive description of a Tuscan boys' group is any mention of catechetical or doctrinal training. Tacchi Venturi conjectured that a "libretto della dottrina christiana, la quale è utile et molto necessario che li puti pizoli et zovenzelle limpara per sapene . . .," included among Antonino's works and printed at Venice in 1473, was written for the boys of the Purification (Tacchi Venturi, *Storia della compagnia di Gesù*, 1:337f.).

[71] Vigo, *Confraternità . . . pistoiesi*, 49–69.

people to concentrate over a sustained period of time was the rationale for these amusements; and to this extent the particular proclivities of the young were recognized. Yet such innocuous games were viewed here—as to some extent they were by humanistic pedagogues—as concessions to the weaknesses of the young, rather than as creative activities. The games were there to permit a quick return to the adult practices they were cultivating.[72]

The orations delivered in these confraternities were typical of confraternal life as a whole. Those still accessible to modern scholars were delivered before at least eight different confraternities. Five of these were of *uomini fatti*, while the other three were read in the boys' confraternities of S. Niccolò (del Ceppo), S. Antonio da Padova, and the Nativity.[73] Our limited evidence suggests that the orations to the boys were given by boys, and not by grown men.[74]

Many of the boys in these groups could not understand the humanistic Latin of their speakers. But this would not detract from the edification offered the boys by such fine examples of maturity. In these centuries, Latin awed rather than bored. Besides, dignified bearing and gestures as much as the words marked the successful speaker. Here is the reaction to a sermon delivered to the Pistoian confraternity of the Purità by a boy of childish years, standing before a scaled down rostrum and addressing his brothers:

> [He] explained the meaning of the words "company," "fraternity," and "purity," and to what end [the company] had been instituted and many other things, exhorting purity of conscience and right, honest, and virtuous living in these early years [of life.] He pronounced the said sermon not with artificial gestures, but with ones taught by God, [and] with such grace that he reduced many of the bystanders to tears and to great devotion.[75]

The processional and dramatic activities of the boys' groups were as innovative as the "practices of the old law" and the orations were traditional.[76] In discussing these creative activities, I shall first consider their processional activities devoid of any dramatic or narrative content, and reserve my com-

---

[72] It is significant that not only the ball games, but the *rappresentazioni* or sacred plays which the Pistoian group performed were considered "external" activities, while sacramental reception and individual prayer were internal (ibid., 23f., 58, 68f.). See also below, 221.

[73] This information is culled from a list in A. Bandini, *Specimen Literaturae Florentinae Saeculi XV* (Florence, 1751), 2:160ff. See also on the orations Kristeller, *Studies*, 105f.; Garin, *Cultura filosofica*, 167, 178f.; Hatfield, "Magi," 128-35.

[74] The budding humanist Giovanni Nesi (born 1456), for example, delivered one oration to the rectors of S. Niccolò at the age of sixteen. At eighteen, he addressed the boys of S. Antonio da Padova, and then between the ages of nineteen and twenty-two this "adolescent" spoke three times to the Nativity (Bandini, *Specimen*, 2:160ff.).

[75] Vigo, *Confraternità ... pistoiesi*, 40f.

[76] As early as 1305, a Sienese confraternity required its lay director to deliver a sermon to his successor (Kristeller, *Studies*, 104).

ments on their dramatic and semi-dramatic activities, whether in procession or at rest, for a later point.

Secular confraternities played an increasingly important role in Florentine processions during the quattrocento, and it is against this background of a growing secular imprint on public religious expression that the boys' new role must be understood. In the celebrations attending the conquest of Pisa (1406), for example, twenty companies marched in the procession. In the following year, there were twenty-two.[77] In 1454, Archbishop Antonino authorized seven companies of *fanciulli*, thirty-seven flagellant companies from the city, and thirty-six from the *contado*.[78] In early cinquecento, a memorialist recommended to the political authority that all the companies of *fanciulli* be permitted to march in the general procession on the eve of S. Giovanni, but only twelve to sixteen of the men's companies, "so as not to tire" the spectators.[79] A few years later, Varchi tells us that there were thirty-eight flagellant companies which marched in processions.[80]

The growing importance of the companies in these processions came at the expense of two competing images: the political representation of the city by the procession of its geo-political subdivisions or *gonfaloni*, and the representation of the clergy. These remained, of course, but with the growing elaborateness of the *feste*, it was the secular companies which benefitted most.

Certainly the propitiatory processions of the commune in crisis remained more traditional, with the clergy in a prominent position in front, and "the people" in back. The indiscriminate mixing of different social classes in these crisis processions stood in the strongest contrast to the representation of political order in the celebratory procession.[81] But increasingly the order em-

---

[77] These companies were called "compagnie cogli stendardi" or simply "stendardi" (Del Corazza, "Diario," 242, 245).

[78] See 61 above.

[79] C. Guasti, ed., *Le feste di San Giovanni Battista in Firenze* (Florence, 1884), 27.

[80] Varchi, *Storia*, IX, 36.

[81] On "clamare," as this propitiative organization was called, see C. Torrente, *Las Procesiones Sagradas* (Washington, 1932), 6f.; G. Meersseman, "Disciplinati e penitenti nel duecento," in *Il Movimento dei Disciplinati nel settimo centenario dal suo inizio* (Perugia, 1962), 68. Chroniclers in Florence liked to refer to an undifferentiated mass of people following the clergy in these propitiative processions, but a closer look suggests that they were ordered according to sex and age group, if not by political organization: "Ricordo che giovedi a di 16 dottobre 1455 comminciano a farsi le processioni solenni per impetrare la vitoria divina contro al turco, e 4 giorni cioe ogni di a uno quartiere sempre multiplico il popolo. E da prima e fanciulli e fanciulle, poi in ultimo le donne assai vestite di bianco, cioe con camice sopra e panni, e uno + rossa nel petto" (*ASF, Carte Strozziane* II, XVI bis, fol. 21r [*Libro di Francesco di Tommaso di Francesco Giovanni*]). ("I record that on Thursday 16 October 1455, the solemn processions to impetrate divine victory against the Turk began, for four days, that is, one per quarter. Attendance multiplied continually. First [came] the boys and girls, then behind them the women quite dressed up in white, that is, with a blouse and cloth, and a red cross on their breast"). On processional orders, see below, 109f.; also Trexler, "Ritual Behavior in Renaissance Florence: The Setting," *Medievalia et Humanistica* 4 (1973): 125–44.

phasized in the latter type was more the cumulation of private groups than the public or political structure.

Accompanying this increase in secular participation and the privatization of representation was the juvenescence of all the groups represented. We see it in the desire to have *giovani* representing Florence in its embassies to foreign lands.[82] At home, *giovani* rather than *uomini fatti* came to represent each of their families in the *gonfaloni* which assembled for the offering to S. Giovanni and the accompaniment of the Corpus Christi.[83] By 1419 it was richly dressed *giovani*, "the most polished" in the land, who surrounded the sacred host.[84] The confraternities of *uomini fatti* at the beginning of the quattrocento started to incorporate numbers of *fanciulli* into their processional ranks. Goro Dati tells us (1405) that the "companies of secular men" in the S. Giovanni procession had angels dressed in white amongst them, and from this point on angels formed a standard part of celebratory processions.[85] In 1428 another chronicler was dazzled by youthful pages bedecked with rich clothing, through which shone "their angelic faces."[86] Soon it would be companies of boys, and not single children, who would present the image of innocence to the Florentine populace.

From Pope Eugenius's letter of 1442 regulating the four original companies, we may assume that the groups were already taking part in public processions. Our first documented evidence, however, comes from 1454. Of the seven companies which Archbishop Antonino approved, the humanist Matteo Palmieri in his description of that year's S. Giovanni procession names three as having taken part.[87] He seems in fact to be describing four: About thirty members of the confraternities of Jacopo di Biagio (the Vangelista) and of Nofri di Filippo (S. Antonio da Padova) paraded together just after the cathedral clerks (the *Scuola Eugeniana?*) and immediately before the float representing S. Michele Archangelo. Following this float came an equal number of boys from "the company of Antonio and Piero di Mariano" (probably the Nativity governed by ser Antonio di Mariano, and the Purification headed by his

---

[82] A law of 30 April 1498 required that in order "to learn about statecraft," a *giovane cittadino* fiorentino danni 24 in 40 "was to play a full part in every embassy sent abroad" (*ASF, Prov.* 189, fols. 17v–18v). See also F. Guicciardini, *The History of Florence* (New York, 1970), 150.

[83] See *ASF, Prov.* 129, fols. 214r–v (22 December 1438); ibid. 132, fols. 151v–153r (9 August 1441).

[84] "Giovani, de' maggiori della terra e più politi" (Del Corazza, "Diario," 257; see also 271–74).

[85] Dati is cited in Guasti, *Feste*, 2. I suspect that the habit of placing young people in front of an adult group was by no means new; for an example of the duecento, see Davidsohn, *Forschungen*, 4:432 (a procession in a cloister). But the importance of and attention given young angels clearly increases in the quattrocento.

[86] Hatfield, "Magi," 146.

[87] Cited in Guasti, *Feste*, 21.

brother Piero).[88] These were followed in the procession by a long line of floats or *edifizi*, each probably sponsored by a different company. The incorporated boys were by now the public image of youth in the life of the city, asexual innocents reflecting the institutionalization of secular innocence: "The *fanciulli*," reads a report from 1455, "were all dressed in white with the red cross on their shoulders, [and] went singing and psalmonizing with great melody." Here were the seeds of the great Savonarolan processions of the 1490s.[89] Yet the Florentines do not seem to have recognized the new role played by the young in their processions. Not until the advent of the great Dominican are we again informed of the boys' groups' participation in procession.

We turn now to the most complex and fascinating aspect of boys' confraternal life in the quattrocento: their dramatic and representational endeavors. These are well known, for they have attracted the attention of historians of drama. Our interest is more social in nature. A new relationship between Christian ritual and social order can be traced in these adolescent dramatic presentations. In them is mirrored a new pedagogy of social acculturation. As the statues started to move in late trecento and early quattrocento, as the representations of Jesus and his mother and the saints came to be played by real people, the faces were those of children and young people. When the bourgeois of Florence saw their everyday concerns and ideals represented in theater, it was an adolescent voice and face which reflected those values.[90] Before analyzing this important socio-cultural fact more closely, however, let us summarize the scanty information on the confraternities' dramatic activities.

Children and young people first emerge in representational roles under the aegis of confraternities of *uomini fatti*. In the period between the 1370s and the 1420s, these groups had gradually substituted live representatives of the sacred statues and paintings which had been and long remained an important part of representations of sacred history. The chronicler Pietrobuoni emphasized that in the representation of the Assumption in the church of the Carmine in 1422 "a living man instead of *misser domenedio* [went] to heaven."[91] A few years later the same chronicler tells us that the Compagnia de' Magi in its processional public presentation of the story of the Magi included an infant Christ played by a three-year-old *fanciullo*, Francesco d'Andruccio de' Ricasoli. In one hand the child held a goldfinch; "with the other he did things so spontaneously natural that a man of forty could not have done them

---

[88] It is interesting that these boys' companies, which Palmieri generically called "compagnie de' fanciulli di disciplina," were the only ones in the procession whose names he gave; see ibid., 22.

[89] *BNF, Conv. Rel. Soppr.* C–4–895 (Priorista of Paolo di Matteo Pietrobuoni), fol. 170v. For another description of the same procession, see above, n. 81; for the Savonarolan processions, see below, 109f.

[90] See the remarks on adolescents as actors in the often suggestive book of C. Molinari, *Spettacoli fiorentini del quattrocento* (Venice, 1961), 63, 69.

[91] "Eando uno huomo vivo invecie di misser domenedio in cielo" (*BNF, Conv. Rel. Soppr.* C–4–895, fol. 107r [21 May 1422]).

better."[92] Already in this report of 1428 we trace the amazement so common to the Florentines of the quattrocento on finding that young people, in this case a child scarcely removed from the breast, could be taught to artfully simulate "natural behavior" by careful indoctrination. Perhaps hard adult experience was not necessary before men learned to formalize their behavior.

Sometime before mid-century the boys' clubs first became responsible for their own presentations. Palmieri's description of S. Giovanni's celebration in 1454 seems to contain the first evidence that a boys' sodality was solely responsible for a representation. The *edifizio* of St. Michael which separated the four clubs in that parade may have been produced by the Vangelista, for this angel was one of the patron saints of the confraternity.[93] Another scholar has suggested that the float of the Nativity in the same procession was probably presented by the boys' group of the same name.[94] These identifications are based on the principle that each confraternity honored its patron saint or titulary name.[95] In subsequent processions, the boys' groups continued to play their role along with the companies of adults in providing the public with instruction, devotion, and amusement.

There is some evidence that in most of these early processional productions, children played children's parts and adults—or at least grown youth—played the adult roles. Cosimo de' Medici is only the best known of many adults who represented sacred figures in the quattrocento *spettacoli.*[96] Even in the indoor *rappresentazioni* viewed by prelates attending the Council of Florence (1439), the visitor's eye was not caught by children performing adult roles, but by a verisimilitude which "made the *giovani* look just as [the sacred personages] do in the pictures."[97]

All of the representational roles mentioned up to this point were of figures in sacred history. Florentines had learned that the young could be taught to play the young of sacred myth, to ape their pictorial representations through clothes, and their godly innocence through perfected gestures. All of this was amazing to contemporaries; they could not help but be pleased at these manifestations of youthful piety and gravity. Yet there was more to come. Florentine processions, wonderful mirrors that they are of the dreams, fancies, and

---

[92] "Uno fanciullo di circha a tre anni fasciato e lle mani isvolte; in sull'una [fu] uno calderugio vivo, et coll'atra faceva cose pronte naturali che huomo di quaranta anni meglio non avarebbe fatto. Iddio pareva in quel corpo del fanciullo Francesco d'Andruccio da'Richasoli" (cited in Hatfield, "Magi," 146).

[93] The confraternity honored him "perche il di di santo Michele del mese di Maggio si ragiono di dare principio alla nostra squola . . ." (*BNF, Cl.* 31, cod. 11, fols. 7v–8r) ("because it was on St. Michael's day in the month of May that one contemplated starting our school").

[94] Hatfield, "Magi," 114.

[95] Cf. for example Dati (1405) speaking of the lay companies "facendo bellissime rappresentazioni di que' Santi e di quelle reliquie a cui onore la fanno"; cited in Guasti, *Feste,* 5 ("doing very beautiful representations of those saints and those relics whom they honor").

[96] Cosimo paraded in more than one *festa* of the Magi (Hatfield, "Magi," 136f.).

[97] See the two descriptions printed in D'Ancona, *Origini,* 1:246–53.

ideals of the society, yielded in 1468 a description of *social imitation* stunning in its forthrightness, one showing that the boys were learning to be not gods and saints, but the very alter egos of their fathers: grave yet innocent, just but unspoiled, heroic but sexless. The description is of a Magi processional festival:

> Thus, as the appointed time arrived, all involved convened in the square of the city. They had represented as well all the optimates and leaders of the city, as if Herod had sent these in the capacity of legates in order that they might escort [the embassy of the Magi] to the king; the conformity of which representation of the citizens to real citizens was so great that it hardly would seem believable. For they had so carved their faces and countenances in masks that they might scarcely be distinguishable from the real. And their very sons had put on their clothes, which they then used, and they had learned all of their gestures, copying each and every one of their actions and habits in an admirable way. It was truly lovely for the real citizens who had convened at the public buildings to look upon their very selves feigned, with as much beauty and processional pomp as the regal magnificence and the most ample senate of the city, which they would proudly conduct before them.[98]

Social ideals emerge from a play within a play. The sons involved were surely physically mature—the Magi was not a confraternity of *fanciulli*.[99] Still, the important element in this illusion was its reflection of a societal search for the reproduction of the father or older generation, to be realized by instruction in acting while the sons were still young. The method was a perfected ritualization of the gestures of their fathers. The father represented in this festival was not the private figure, with all his weaknesses and dark sides, but rather a normative elder, decked out in his own mask of senatorial splendor, the perfect father of official Medicean culture: grave and opulent, theatrical, and individual in his personal idiosyncrasies.[100] Is it not striking to find in this complex urban culture a ceremony of rite of passage so similar to that

---

[98] This was written by the Dominican Giovanni di Carlo, and is translated in Hatfield, "Magi," 116. Note this passage by the humanist pedagogue Vergerio: "Quanto a ciò bellissima è la costumanza practicata fin dall'antico in Roma, dove la gioventù conduceva i senatori, chiamati i padri, nella curia . . . e alla fine in folla li reconduceva alle loro case" (Garin, *L'educazione*, 64, referring to Valerius Maximus) ("How beautiful in this regard is the custom dating from Roman antiquity, where the youth conducted the senators, called the fathers, into the curia . . . and at the end en masse conducted them back to their houses").

[99] Fra Giovanni di Carlo was apparently referring to its members when he spoke of "socia quedam iuventus" performing the Magi ca. 1466–69. On the internal organization of this important company, see Hatfield, "Magi," 119–28.

[100] This essentially private image preserved the luster of public dignity, since the "actors" were members of the city councils. Note also that the Signoria of Florence joined the march of the Magi, and thus became a part of the representation, "not indeed as Florentine citizens," said Fra Giovanni di Carlo, "but wholly as their images and shadows" (Hatfield, "Magi," 117).

found in so-called primitive cultures? This festive practice and the solemn rite of exclusion at age twenty-four from the company of the Vangelista—both carried out at an age of social rather than biological maturity—point to a new *social* function of secular Christian ritual, the recreation in that society of a group both infinitely better than, yet the same as, the dominant social class. The monastic life had once monopolized that role for this male society. Now it was to be taken over by the boys. The Thespian muse in the hands of the young was more than mere make-believe. It regenerated social norms and gave hopes of a New Age—fathered by the Old.

We will return to this problem. For now we must conclude our review of the activities of the boys' companies by examining their fixed dramatic productions. During the quattrocento, boys' groups performed both sacred plays and classical comedies. In all probability the so-called *sacre rappresentazioni* came first; the first known performance was in 1449.[101] Based on biblical or hagiographical stories, and performed in and around churches and cloisters, they included all the basic elements of theater: a script, a musical score for the *laudi* included in them, scenery, and the bare bones of dramatic action. Rossi has pointed out how markedly Old Testamental and Evangelical the surviving Florentine plays are: a heavy emphasis on social and familial order characterizes one after the other.[102] Isaac, boy that he is, submitted himself to his father, Abraham, and to God with all the mature deliberation of a grown man:

> Quanto è ignorante, cieco, stolto e pazo
> Chi va cercando fuor di Dio, letizia!
> Qual cosa è più bestial ch' esser ragazo
> Del mondo, e del dimon pien di tristizia![103]

> How stupid, blind, proud and mad
> Is he who seeks happiness apart from God!
> What is more bestial than to be a worldly boy,
> Wretched, and belonging to the deamon.

A prostrate Ishmael and Agar plead for God's forgiveness:

---

[101] In that year the "Abramo ed Isac" of Feo Belcari was performed in the Cistercian church of S. Maria Maddalena (D'Ancona, *Origini*, 1:260). According to V. Rossi, the earliest datable text of a *sacra rappresentazione* is the "Rappresentazione del dì del giudizio" by Feo Belcari, with additions of Antonio di Meglio (d. 1448). "Beato Bernardino" is one of the actors, and this dates its composition after the friar's death (d. 1444), but its performance probably after his canonization (1450). Rossi opts for the period 1444–1448 (*Il Quattrocento* [Milan, 1964], 282; see now N. Newbigin, ed., *Nuovo Corpus di Sacre Rappresentationi fiorentine del Quattrocento* (Bologna, 1983).

[102] Rossi, *Il Quattrocento*, 283. Molinari has made the point that at least three Florentine *sacre rappresentazioni* on the theme of the Prodigal Son were written during the quattrocento (Molinari, *Spettacoli*, 77).

[103] "Abramo ed Isac" by Feo Belcari; see A. D'Ancona, ed., *Sacre Rappresentazioni dei secoli XIV, XV e XVI* (hereafter *SR*), 3 vols. (Florence, 1872), 1:55.

Signor, dal quale noi siam stati creati,
Che, senza te, nessun saria,
E se noi meritammo esser cacciati
E d'aver d'un po' d'acqua carestia,
Per la tua grazia siamo or liberati,
Onde a te laude e gloria sempre sia,
Qui ci starem, Signor, fin che a te piace;
Chè guerra è senza te, teco ogni pace.[104]

Oh lord who created us,
For without you there would be nothing,
And if we deserve to be chased
And to want for a drop of water,
By your grace we now are freed,
Thus praise and glory always be to you,
Lord. Here we stand until you wish otherwise;
For without you there is war; with you, peace.

Upon which another boy throws himself at the feet of his earthly father and says:

O caro padre mio,
    Io sono uno Ishmael:
E come a Dio quel,
    A voi chiego perdono;
E se tal stato sono
    Ch'io merti esser cacciato,
Datemi, se v'è grato,
    Come a lui acque e pane.[105]

Oh my dear father:
    I am an Ishmael
And just as I from God,
    So from you I ask pardon;
And if I have been so
    As to merit being repulsed,
Give me, if it pleases you,
    Water and wine, as was given Him.

Historians of Italian drama have long assumed that the *sacre rappresentazioni* of the quattrocento were performed by adolescent confraternities. The evidence for young actors is convincing: several of the plays start with apologies

---

[104] "Abramo e Agar," anonymous (ibid., 36f.). In the title of a 1556 Florentine edition of this play, one reads: "E prima per annunziazione è un padre con duoi figliuoli, un buono e un cattivo, per esempio universale de'padri e de'figliuoli" (ibid., 2) ("And first for annunciation there is a father with two sons, one good and one bad, as a universal example for fathers and sons").

[105] Ibid., 37.

for infelicities because "we are only *fanciulli*."[106] The protestations in themselves might persuade one that it was the confraternities of boys that, from the start, undertook the performance of the *rappresentazioni*. Still, our available evidence is slim: although we know of two such plays written in the 1440s, one of which was performed, it is not until 1491 that we have proof that a company of boys—the Vangelista—performed a *sacra rappresentazione*.[107] In the same year, we are informed that a group of young monks performed "The Judgment of Solomon" in a Florentine monastery.[108] At this time, the young novices at San Marco were also performing *sacre rappresentazioni*.[109] Perhaps the young novice nuns and girls boarded in the nunneries were already performing the *rappresentazioni* before audiences of older nuns and an interested public.[110]

Thus it is not certain that secular *confratelli* were the first performers of these sacred plays. It may turn out that the impulse for these *rappresentazioni* came from ecclesiastical institutions seeking to educate their novices *and boarders* (those not fully committed to the religious life) through dramatic representations.[111]

---

[106] For a selection of such apologies, see D'Ancona, *Origini*, 1:401–5.

[107] "Ricordo fo come, a' di xxi di dicenbre mcccclxxxx Piero mio fratello ed io Bartolomeo faciemo l'entrata, questo dì sopradetto, nella conpagnia de'fanciugli di santo Giovanni evangelista.... El carnasciale sequente fu messere di detta conpagnia Giuliano di Lorenzo di Piero di Cosimo de' Medici ...; e feciesi detta festa el secondo di quaresima, di detto anno.... E la sopradetta festa fu la rappresentazione di santo Giovanni e Pagolo" (from the *ricordanze* of Bartolommeo Masi, cited in H. A. Mathes, "On the Date of Lorenzo's *Sacra Rappresentazione di San Giovanni e Paolo*. February 17, 1491," *Aevum* 25 [1851], 324–29; Masi's exit from the company in 1507 is printed in Monti, *Confraternite*, 1:190) ("I record how on December 21, 1490, my brother Piero and I, Bartolomeo, entered on this same day into the boys' confraternity of St. John the Evangelist.... The following carnival the lord of the said confraternity was Lorenzo di Piero di Cosimo de' Medici.... And the said feast was the representation of Sts. John and Paul").

[108] The author was a priest. One of the young monks played the courtesan with too much conviction, which was remembered in later years by Pope Leo X; see G. B. Picotti, *La jeunesse de Léon X* (Paris, 1931), 29.

[109] Speaking of Savonarola's relations to the young friars, the biographer refers to "li spettacoli delle rappresentationi, le quali in tanto odio erano venute che tutti li suoi figliuoli, per persuasione del servo di Dio, giurorno di mai più fare o aiutare" (P. Ginori Conti, ed. attrib., *La vita del beato Ieronimo Savonarola* [Florence, 1937], 46; also see ibid., 90, where they swear never to "dire o dectare" the same). For evidence that the Carmelite and Servite friars made and accompanied *edifizi* in the S. Giovanni procession of 1514, see Giovanni Cambi, *Istoria*, in *Delizie*, 22:45.

[110] D'Ancona, *Origini*, 1:404; 2:157–72.

[111] As has long been realized, the salutations of "padri e fratelli" ("fathers and brothers") in the prologues of many *sacre rappresentazioni* could refer to abbots and fellow monks or friars. Or consider this prologue to the anonymous "Re Superbo," from L. Banfi, ed., *Sacre Rappresentazioni del Quattrocento* (Turin, 1963), 471:

> A laude e gloria sia del buon Iesù
> e di San Bernardino predicatore,
> che presti a' servi suoi tanta virtù
> che mostriamo un esempio d'un signore
> il qual superbo più ch'ogni altro fu ...
> To the praise and glory of good Jesus
> and of the preacher St. Bernardino,

It has been almost a century since Isidoro Del Lungo discovered the
strongest evidence for this hypothesis: it happens that the first identifiable
group which we know to have performed a play in quattrocento Florence was
not composed of laymen at all, but of clergy—the clerks of the *Scuola Eugeniana!*[112] Del Lungo was so surprised that clerks were studying Terence
and, as he thought, performing the pagan's works in churches, that he missed
the larger social significance of his find: clerks of the church *scuole* were at
one with lay adolescent groups in filling a social need for youthful piety
demonstrated through acting.

The correspondence in which Del Lungo made his discovery contains
some invaluable information on the attitude of a boys' teacher toward youthful dramatic representations. From a letter to Lorenzo de' Medici from Piero
Domizi, the master of the cathedral school, we know that in August 1476, the
clerks were prepared to perform a play called *Licinia*, perhaps written by the
master himself. The church of Ognissanti was one of the projected performance sites. The letter makes clear that the clerks were competing with other
dramatic groups for the attention of Medici.[113] A second letter shows that
Lorenzo had attended a performance by the clerks in Ognissanti during the
Florentine year 1477 (25 March 1477–24 March 1478). It is implied that the
play was the master's own. Medici's visit had so inspired the master that he
was now determined to prepare more comedies for presentation. Still, the
priest was concerned about his students' welfare, and felt it necessary to ask
for Lorenzo's mature advice:

> Terence is certainly a divine poet, and Donatus has rendered him more
> divine. If only all these things were not read to the clerks! How very dif-
> ficult it is to censor the reading so that [the boys] do not imbide pas-
> sionate habits, since especially the wit of boys is so perceptive. By the
> choice of God it is necessary that I supervise their discipline on Sun-
> days. To do this I have written a serious little work in which I admonish
> [them] to develop those foundations of the life of adolescents from
> which exactly the cult of God is formed; [that] there is not much con-
> stancy in the man who considers divine percepts only in retrospect;

> so that he will give his servants enough virtue
> so we can show an example of a lord
> who was more proud than any other . . .

This sounds to me as if it were recited by Franciscan novices or fellow friars. For a
variant interpretation, see D'Ancona, *Origini*, 1:405.

[112] Both of the relevant articles of Del Lungo were reprinted in his *Florentia. Uomini
e cose del quattrocento* (Florence, 1897), 357–87.

[113] "Il perchè oggi eravamo in ordine, se voi degniate d' udire e vostri cherici insieme
col maestro: essi ve ne priegono, acciò che noi non siàno più schacciati degli altri.
Volendo verremo costì chè siamo pochi: se none, degnate d'essere contento che la nostra
Licinia si reciti in vostro nome . . ." (ibid., 382 [letter of 19 August 1476]) ("which is why
we have come together today, on the chance you would listen to your clerks and their
master: they pray you this, so that we will no longer be disgraced by the other [groups].
If you wish, we will come there, for we are few. Otherwise, deign to allow us to recite our
Licinia in your name . . .").

[that] he is happy who leads a good life, and many other such things.[114]

The master-priest sent his little play to Medici with the implicit recommendation that Lorenzo, in the interest of the boys' spiritual health, favor the performance of this Christian text rather than a pagan one. There is some reason to believe that Domizi was genuinely concerned. He was probably the author of a Latin comedy on the conversion of St. Augustine, known to have been performed in Ferrara in 1494.[115] Furthermore, there was bitter opposition to the budding revivals of pagan theater in Florence, and we may imagine that training clerks in Terence provoked the especial ire of the "little hooded [friars] with feet of wood."[116]

Domizi, however, was competing with another group of boy-clerks for the favor of the city's lord; Del Lungo was probably right in supposing that this competition came from the church of San Lorenzo, whose *scuola* of clerks was in all probability responsible for the production in 1488 of Plautus's *Menaechmi*.[117]

The long development which we have traced had seemingly reached its culmination. Boy-clerks and lay adolescents alike entertained the lord of the city and an admiring clientele with impressive regularity. The boys had something to teach, and they in turn shone in the brilliance of Lorenzo's sun. One young angel recorded his participation as a member of the Vangelista in the performance of Lorenzo de' Medici's *San Giovanni e Paolo*:

> Lorenzo de' Medici was there to see the said *festa* . . . along with many other upstanding men and such a crowd that it was a marvelous thing. And all the boys of the company stood on the stage, especially those who were wearing linen clothes. Piero and I, Bartolommeo, were among those to stand there.[118]

And another play began with one of these angels stepping forward and saying:

> Cari, diletti padri, e frate' nostri
> Noi vi preghiam per l'amor del Signore
> Poichè siate adunati in questi chiostri,
> State divoti e non fate romore:
> Le fatiche son nostre, e' piacer vostri
> E ogni cosa ci fa far l'amore:
> No' v'abbiam ragunati in questi poggi
> Per fuggir le pazie che si fanno oggi.[119]

---

[114] Ibid., 383.

[115] Tiraboschi recorded "una commedia latina in versi iambici sulla conversione di Sant'Agostino, scritta da Pietro Domizio sacerdote" (ibid., 385).

[116] This was Poliziano's description of the opponents (ibid., 361).

[117] Ibid., 379. Reumont discovered from a letter that a performance took place on 12 May 1488, and published this information in *ASI*, ser. 3, 20 (1874), 190–91.

[118] Cited in Mathes, "On the Date of . . . *San Giovanni e Paolo*," 325f.

[119] In the anonymous "Giuseppe Figliuolo di Giacobbe" (D'Ancona, *SR*, 1:62f.).

Dear delectable fathers, and our brothers,
We pray you for the love of the lord,
Since we are brought together in these cloisters,
Be devout and don't make noise:
The effort is ours, the pleasure yours
And everything is done to create love:
We have joined together on these hills
To avoid the madnesses that are done today.

We have now concluded a summation of the activities of boys' confraternities during the quattrocento. Starting with typical adult practices, they developed thespian activity peculiar to them and to the semi-ecclesiastical *scuole* of at least two Florentine churches. In the cinquecento at least two of the sodalities evolved into philodramatic institutions.[120] But in the same century, professional adult actors appeared, and the relationship between adolescence and acting lost much of its earlier sociocultural significance. The golden age of these youthful dramatic productions had been contemporary with a spate of new pedagogical thinking. I shall argue that there was a strict tie between the two. With the decline of the one went that of the other.

In the preceding hundred years, however, some exciting social innovations had been tried. Fathers had come to recognize the potential of adolescence, whether their sons were in the confraternities, *scuole* of the secular churches, or in the houses of the Mendicants. By corporate segregation from public life, biologically mature adolescents could be indoctrinated and taught to act out the ideal and even the seamy daily needs, thoughts, and gestures of their elders, male or female, without losing their innocence. The social institutionalization of adolescence could not only end street crime and moral perversion of the sons of citizens, it could create a society that embodied all the norms of the present, all the gestures of the elders, but that would be in a New Age of justice and gravity. The century had been astonished by the educability of the new generation, and had been quick to parade its institutions of innocent gravity. The success of Savonarola sealed the conviction that the young were the salvation of the world, that without an institutionally indoctrinated adolescence, only a revolution of the corrupt could await a sinful society.

I turn now to an analysis of the nexus education-ritual-acting, as it has emerged in this review of juvenile activities.

The ritual protection of the city of Florence had traditionally been entrusted to four social groups. The priests performed divine services. The monastic element, theoretically living apart from the world, protected the city through communal ritual and saintly life. The government, in procession, periodically

---

[120] These were the Nativity and the confraternity of S. Niccolò del Ceppo (D'Ancona, *Origini*, 1:405). On the evolution of the Vangelista, see ibid., 412. On the later Nativity, see now K. Eisenbichler, "Plays at the Archangel Raphael's," *Fifteenth-Century Studies* 13 (1988): 519–34.

renewed the contract of the *popolo* with God, his mother, and the saints. An additional but less important element in this ritual schema was the confraternal system of lay men and women, who prayed together for the good of the city. Consequently, to placate God, the city relied not only on purity (the monastic element), but upon the ritual mechanics of sinners (priests, governmental members, *confratelli*). It was not wholly reliant on the Donatistic efficacy of its monks and nuns; the *saeculum* as well was capable through the mechanics of its ritual of influencing the divine will.[121]

This ritual schema may be conveniently divided between outdoor and indoor activities. The procession was the typical outdoor ritual. Its ideal had always been order: a lineally designed spectacle of intermeshing parts, all moving together at a steady rate. In it no particular person was distinguishable, for it had no biographical or narrative element. Its purpose was rather to display the assembled political or social order. Within the church, monastery, or confraternal oratory, however, commemorative ritual had an important place, the washing of feet, the mass, flagellation, etc., all recalling the life of the various peoples of Christian tradition.

Adolescents, children, and youth had played no specific part in this traditional ritual pattern. In the fifteenth century, they enriched Florentine ritual experience by their new, organized, presence. What had been the precedents for child and adolescent ritual? What was the immediate background to their emergence as a ritual element? And what prospects did the new importance of adolescent ritual offer the city of Florence?

Traditionally, young people filled no social role until they had left behind their childishness and adolescence. Society was for *iuvenes* and adults, and until one reached the mid-twenties one was a private being, whose training in social piety was entrusted to the mother and to the master grammarian. It is in the handbooks for these teachers that we find the guidelines for traditional practices of socialization and acculturation. The Dominican Giovanni Dominici painted a charming picture of how the young person should be schooled in respect for religion, the anchor of all values:

> The first regulation is to have pictures of saintly children or young virgins in the home, in which your child, still in swaddling clothes, may take delight and thereby may be gladdened by acts and signs pleasing to childhood.... Make of such pictures a sort of temple in the house....[122]

But make a little altar or two in the house, dedicated to the Savior whose feast is every Sunday. You may have three or four different colored little vestments, and he and the other children may be sacristans, showing them how on all feasts they should variously adorn this chapel. They may ... have in place the little bell and run to ring it at all hours as is done in the church. They may be dressed in surplices as acolytes,

---

[121] For an elaboration of the above sketch, see my "Ritual Behavior in Renaissance Florence: The Setting," 125–44.

[122] G. Dominici, *Education of Children*, 34f.

sing as well as they know how, play at saying Mass, and be brought to
the church sometimes and shown how real priests do it, that they may
imitate them. Teach them to preach after they have heard preaching
several times in the church ..., you and the family remaining seated
while they speak from above, not laughing but commending and re-
warding them when they have imitated the spiritual office. Pardon them
punishment due when they take refuge at the altar and, kneeling down,
ask as a favor from Jesus that you will not strike them, so that they may
early accustom themselves to have recourse to the True God in their
troubles and demand grace from Him who alone can give it.[123]

The schoolmaster's pious responsibilites are brought out well in the statutes of a rural school in Piedmont:

Item. He has promised to preserve these students in the fear and love
of Christ and with good habits, so that they will be reverent, obedient,
humble, dignified, and not say turpitudes or other bad words, nor be
mendacious, especially to their parents. Item. He has promised to lec-
ture on some devout and spiritual authorities on feast days after mass
and vespers, and to lead them two by two to church and order them so
as to insure that the students remain still, dignified and devout, penitent
and alert.[124]

Florentines liked to be told that in the good old days, children had been
brought up in this fashion.[125] Even if they had been, however, the fact was
that once the child reached twelve or fourteen, the age of puberty and of
some discretion, no social institutions had ever existed to take over the familial training in socialization.[126] At the very age when motherly authority
waned, and fatherly attention emerged, the boy found that he could exercise
his will alone.[127] True, the young novice in the religious order spent his
first year in a regimen of acculturation, and the brigades in Florence offered
another type of training in sublimation, but neither of these choices was attractive. The religious life—whether deservedly or not—was in disrepute, and
the brigades were scarcely the place to learn respect for elders. Bands of boys
were to the domestic quiet of the city what foreign mercenaries were to diplomatic tranquility.
    The immediate cause of the intense interest in boys as social beings was a

---

[123] Ibid., 42f.

[124] Garin, *Pensiero*, xxv.

[125] See the sermon of Savonarola on this subject, abstracted by L. Scremin, "Savonarola educatore e la psicologia sessuale," *Genesis. Rassegna di studi sessuali ed eugenica* 12
(1932): 91f.

[126] As mentioned above, some confraternities of adults accepted boys from about this
age on; training of the young was, however, no part of their intended work; see above, n.
37.

[127] On this turning point, see Dominici, *Education of Children*, 44, and Matteo Palmieri,
cited in Garin, *L'educazione*, 114.

crisis in the structure of the Florentine family. Men were marrying extremely late, while an alarmingly high percentage of young girls was entering the nunneries.[128] The results of these trends were both demographic—an increase in the passive population and a consequent increase in family extinctions—[129] and moral—an assumed increase in extramarital hetero- and homosexual activity[130] and an assumed decline in youthful reverence for elders. What was responsible for the late male marriages and for the monasticization of the females? The following is not a sufficient answer, but it does present elements which throw light on the problem of the family.

Dowries rose rapidly throughout the quattrocento. This in itself causes an increase in the number of nuns, and it was not uncommon that the father had to consign several, if not all but one, of his daughters of the religious life. There was a second reason for the increase in female religious. Because of the late marriage age of males, mothers often found themselves widowed with several children.[131] The girls could be placed in a religious habit more easily than in a marriage bed. Mothers readily chose this course, and they were encouraged in this by the testamental dispositions of their dead spouses, which commonly made a religious life possible for their daughters, but the married life unaffordable.[132]

Males were encouraged by humanistic and other moralists to marry late, and this climate of opinion made it all the easier to accommodate the demographic and financial impracticality of early marriages.[133] Firstly, the pool

---

[128] In an important article on the subject, David Herlihy reports an average age of 39.75 years for the fathers of 1005 infants born in Florence in twelve months of 1426–27, and an average age of 34 for males reported marrying in 1427–28; for the necessary refinements of this characterization, see his "Vieillir à Florence," 1340f., 1344, 1346. During the quattrocento, the percentage of the female population of the city in the convents rose from approximately 2.5% to approximately 13%; see my "Le célibat à la fin du Moyen Age: Les Religieuses de Florence," *Annales E.S.C.*, 26 (1972): 1337.

[129] Our evidence on family extinction is indirect. Certainly there was great concern about the problem, and communal steps to meet it. See A. Molho, *Florentine Public Finances in the Early Renaissance* (Cambridge, Mass., 1971), 138, 176. Alberti wrote his books on families partly because so many were dying out (*I Libri della Famiglia* [Turin, 1969], prologue, and 128–32).

[130] This was the opinion of contemporary chroniclers, but it had also been that of countless commentators from the beginning of the commune. All of the demographic indices do suggest that conditions were ripe for an increase. Herlihy has shown that of the males between eighteen and thirty–two years of age, in his sample of 4,456 males, only a quarter were or had certainly been married (Herlihy, "Vieillir à Florence," 1348). The consequent importance of the orphans' institution in Florence during the quattrocento was not surprising. Bernardino explained the ubiquity of homosexual behavior from men's desire to avoid generating children (Scremin, "Savonarola educatore," 93).

[131] Herlihy, "Vieillir à Florence," 1342.

[132] The normal procedure for the straitened father was to leave enough to dower his daughters in a nunnery, but not for marriage.

[133] The pedagogue Vegio recommended that men marry at thirty-six, while others suggested thirty (Herlihy, "Vieillir à Florence," 1346). Archbishop Antonino believed that in his day "nimis cito contrahunt matrimonium ...," but saw the moral quandary: "sed si differunt perpetrant innumera mala"; cited in Scremin, "Savonarola educatore," 89.

of eligible females from one's own social level was declining. Secondly, the
father's early death usually meant that his business was sold or died with him,
for the orphaned boys were often too young to assume these responsibilities.
Thirdly, the estate of the deceased father was often dissipated in the absence
of a party capable of defending its interest. Poor boys and girls! Their plight
formed such a clearly defined societal image in the quattrocento that The Orphaned Boys and The Girls Forced to Enter the Nunnery were among the social corporations which appeared before the crowds during Carnival.[134]

The moral component of this dilemma was no less severe. David Herlihy
has demonstrated how reliant Florentine society became upon mothers for
the acculturation and education not just of children, but of adolescents and
youth as well. Yet how limited were their legal and moral resources for the
task! And for a male-dominated society, what a disgrace. With his daughters
in the nunnery and his sons—if sons there were—unmarried, many a Florentine father died convinced that his name died with him. Worse, many lived
too long, only to see that name besmudged by the activities of unmarried
sons who wasted their limited substance in the lascivious company of a
brigada. What was to become of a society whose regeneration rested so
heavily upon the weak, sensual, shoulders of the female sex? Such were the
self-righteous notions of this deeply patriarchal society.

It is not surprising that prevailing opinion held the family to be a poor
place to rear the male members of the next generation.[135] The continual
warnings of the humanistic pedagogues to preserve the children from the
baleful influences of women have as their Florentine background a factual situation in which, to an alarming extent, the mother was the only person available to rear them.

The threat to masculinity was not something one talked about in polite
company. When Bernardino of Siena insisted upon the subject of homosexuality in a sermon in his home town, shamed parents started to leave, and the
preacher railed at their shame and over-sensitive ears.[136] Despite the reti-
cence of contemporaries, however, the problem of boyish effeminacy left its
traces. A traditionalist like Dominici and even a progressive pedagogue like

---

("they contract marriage too rapidly"; "but if they defer, they perpetrate innumerable
evils"). Savonarola recommended marriage for men at thirty-five or -six (J. Schnitzer,
Savonarola [Milan, 1931], 2:324).

[134] Herlihy, "Vieillir à Florence," 1342, 1348.

[135] Vergerio praised the practice of some peoples of sending their sons abroad or at
least away from the immediate family. This removed the sons from the indulgence of
parents, and the boys pursued their studies with greater alacrity when away from home
(Garin, *L'educazione*, 66). Vergerio wrote: "And even if in regard to educating sons much
is left to education in the home, still some things are usually ordained by law. I am of the
opinion they all ought to be, for a well behaved youth is of the highest importance to the
commonweal" (Garin, *L'educazione*, 61). For Gregorio Correr's view, see Garin, *Pensiero*,
707f. Although several writers thought parental indulgence an almost insuperable obsta-
cle, no one argued that the family *could* not be a fit place for youngsters' maturation, but
that it *was* not.

[136] Cited in Scremin, "Savonarola educatore," 95.

Maffeo Vegio da Lodi warned against females who gave boys names "which smack of femininity."[137] Bernardino chastized his female listeners most forcefully:

> O woman who has a son already a little man, make him look pretty, dress him up so that he is pleasing. . . . Do you know what he is? There's no danger, you know, you don't have to put anything on him. He is a male. If he were feminine you wouldn't do such things, because she would get pregnant. Because the boy doesn't get pregnant, you're content to do what you do. . . .[138]

Children were scarcely five when, dandified by their mothers, they were first titillated by their own flesh, left exposed to suit the sensual tastes of mother and father.[139] Fathers were commonly considered poor examples for their progeny. From childhood sons frequented the obscene banquets of their fathers, lived in houses with lewd pictures, heard the name of the Lord blasphemed.[140] Under the care of a sensual mother and an indulgent father, little could be expected. Boys from well-to-do families who grew up in virtue were a miracle to the pedagogue Pier Paolo Vergerio[141], and Vincent Ferrer was convinced that all boys had lost their virginity by the time they reached age fifteen.[142] Was it not better to remove children from their families, even send them abroad, to escape such bad influence? Vergerio was not the only humanist to think so.[143] The crisis of the family was rooted in demographic and financial fact and in a climate of opinion. Its result was double: the ideological vaunting of the Roman family and the creation of new institutions to supplement and supplant the existing social institutions for the socialization and acculturation of children and adolescents. For rich patron types, this meant humanistic schooling; for other elements of the middle class and for the resident scions of the rich on Sundays and holy days, the confraternity. The two were united in their cause and in much of their method. Let us glance briefly at the humanist boarding school to discover those points at which it reflected the familial and social preoccupations just sketched, and those at which it bore an affinity to the Florentine boys' confraternity.

Rarely in the history of Western education have teachers been so idealized by their students as they were by the "graduate" of the schools of humanistic master-teachers. A substantial literature sprang up vaunting the person and methods of a master like Vittorino da Feltre, written by students who were

---

[137] Garin, *Pensiero*, 177.

[138] Cited in Scremin, "Savonarola educatore," 96. For the opinions of other Italian preachers on the extent of homosexual behavior, see ibid., 89.

[139] Ibid., 92, citing Savonarola.

[140] See, e.g., Gregorio Correr as cited in Garin, *Pensiero*, 707 (for Savonarola's description, see Scremin, "Savonarola educatore," 92).

[141] Garin, *L'educazione*, 66.

[142] Scremin, "Savonarola educatore," 989.

[143] See above, n. 135.

glad to call themselves the creatures of such an outstanding pedagogue.[144]
These writers were not so much creating an intellectual paternity as describing the teacher and his approach to young people. In listing the master's students, as he often did, the panegyrist was not so much recalling the friends he
had made at school—there is practically no indication of strong ties of friend-
ship between students—as he was guilding the crown of the pedagogue by
mentioning the princes and scholars who had sat at the feet of the master.
These students found both a father and a mother in their master, and their
parents found an invaluable servant. While in fact pedagogues like Guarino
were shamelessly obsequious toward their patrons, in the mythology of humanism the teachers were the equals of men of power, calling princes their
brothers, raised equal to the papal chair by respectful pontiffs.[145]

The figure of Vittorino da Feltre sums up the qualities of the humanist educator. He combined the best features of the contemporary notion of the
mother—individual attention to the specific personality of each student, warm-
ness and understanding—with those of the ideal father—sternness, encouragement to perform, wisdom, dispassion, a lack of sexuality and other forms of
luxury. He cried repeatedly, yet produced students who did not.[146] He flag-
ellated daily, but his students did not.[147] He was of course a virgin who
watched over the health of his charges "just as much as parents do with their
children."[148] The humanistic school was a type of family, with an indispens-
able moral legislator at its head, a lay abbot, or, if one likes, an ideal Prince
of a small absolutist territory.

To the extent that humanistic education had a political goal at all, its aim
was to produce good princes from the sons of princes, and good servants of
the prince from the other students. These latter made good functionaries, but
not equal participants in an acerbic civil life. In fact, Alberti believed that the
failure of the teacher to repress voluptuousness was a cause of treason, while
others warned of rebellion and insubordination among the incorrectly
educated.[149] Vergerio felt the new education must dissipate the native egali-

---

[144] See the still fundamental work by W. H. Woodward, *Vittorino da Feltre and other
Humanist Educators* (Cambridge, 1897), 1–95. For the more recent literature, see Garin,
Pensiero, 736. An example of a creature of Vittorino can be found ibid., 623. For exam-
ples of Guarino's and Vittorino's flattery, see ibid., 335–37, 613f.

[145] For one account of Vittorino before the pope, see Garin, *Pensiero*, 623.

[146] Ibid., 613, 641.

[147] Ibid., 519, 629.

[148] Ibid., 541, 693, 695, 702. For Francesco da Castiglione's comparison of Vittorino
to the ascetic Antonino, see ibid., 549. On the humanist school as family, see Sassuolo da
Prato's enthusiasm, ibid., 517.

[149] "La voluptá. Questa in sé conduce i tradimenti inverso la patria, produce eversioni
della repubblicha, di qui sono i colloqui coll'inimici" (cited in Garin, *L'educazione*, 150)
("Voluptuousness. This in itself leads to treason toward the fatherland, produces the
destruction of the republic, from here come conversations with enemies"). "Quos si
contra nimia cum licentia educaverint, ne mirentur postea si delicatiori licentiorique vitae
assuefacti dent se ignaviae et socordiae, coinquinent se omni labe turpidinis, fiant eis
rebelles, si tanquam equi indomiti—quod sacra docent verba [*Eccl.* 30.8]—evadant duri et
praecipires ..." (Vegio cited in Garin, *Pensiero*, 178). ("Those on the contrary who are

tarianism of the young. They had to learn that they were not the same as the *cattivi* and lay aside their readiness to believe others were suffering unjustly.[150] Because they had never worked for a living, the young were too ready to be generous, and had to learn measure: "The man who has accumulated with his own sweat is not so ready to squander his property."[151]

Vivacious students, those quick to play and associate with their fellows, were sought out by the educator.[152] They had to come free and remain free, not servile in their attitude to the Prince, but straightforward and honest: Quick-witted, alert, sparkling, learned, spirited; courtly, honestly obsequious, "good citizens," humanistic technocrats, realistic, worthy emissaries of a not necessarily enlightened bearer of power.

The success of the school rested on its segregation from the outside world. This in turn depended on adequate financing. Through parental support and, if necessary, the charity of the teacher, the student must have no worries

---

educated with too much license, don't be surprised if later, accustomed to a more delicate and licentious life, they give themselves over to ignobility and neglect, get involved in every type of turpitude, become rebels, if like unbroken horses, in the words of the bible [Eccl. 30.8], they avoid what is hard and dangerous . . ."). A close study should be made of the meaning of "buon vivere civile" in the pedagogic texts. Was the ideal a professional and bureaucratic, or a political *vivere*? It is certainly true that finished students were meant to "ornament" public places and in that sense there was a definite choice of the "active life" in most pedagogic writings; for examples of training to speak well in councils, see ibid., 526. Still, I could find little evidence of a desire *to increase political participation through correct education* (for an exception, see ibid., 188), but repeated suggestions that a good education for the *fanciulli* insured a stable *res publica*. The professional or bureaucratic tone extended from the courtly pedagogues of the north into Florentine circles. Alberti believed "man was born in order to be useful to other men"; his recommendation to his *giovani* nephews remained representative of post-Cosiminian pedagogy: "E datevi a conoscere quelle che sono necessarie a chi desideri essere, quanto merita la virtù vostra, pregiato e amato da' nostri cittadini, e adoperato in le admministrazione della republica" ("De Iciarchia," in *Opere Volgari*, ed. C. Grayson [Bari, 1966], 2:214). ("And give him to understand what things are necessary to him who wants to be, in so far as your virtue merits, praised and loved by our citizens, and employed in the administration of the republic"). For a different view, see Garin, *Pensiero*, xi-xii, xiv; *L'educazione*, 1-4; *Italian Humanism* (New York, 1965), 37-77.

[150] "Aggiungi che i giovani sono anche di animo compassionevole, senza malignità, e di umore benigno, perchè, nati da poco, credono che gli altri siano come loro, che hanno commesso piccoli peccati, e ritengono quindi di vederli soffrire ingiustamente. . . . Bisogna impiegare un conveniente sistema d'educazione, facendo in modo che mano a mano acquistino buoni costumi e che siano attenuati o, meglio ancora, sradicati del tutto i cattivi" (Garin, *L'educazione*, 61) ("Add that youth are also of a compassionate mindset, without malignity, and of a benign humor, because, born recently, they think that others are like them: that they have committed little sins and believe therefore that they suffer unjustly. . . . A suitable system of education is necessary, which will bit by bit have them acquire good habits and lose or, still better, have eradicated all the bad ones").

[151] "Sono, infatti, i giovani naturalmente splendidi e liberali, perché non hanno ancora provato il bisogno, e non si sono guadagnate con le loro fatiche le ricchezze in cui nuotano. Non è solito infatti scialacquare il proprio, chi lo mise insieme col suo sudore" (ibid., 58f). ("Indeed, youth are naturally splendid and liberal, because they have not yet felt need, and have not earned through their own work the riches in which they swim. Indeed, he who sweats to possess will not usually squander").

[152] Platina, cited in Garin, *Pensiero*, 676, 683; see also ibid., 611-13, 677-79.

about subsistence. Any controls over food and board must be imposed for pedagogic, not financial, reasons. Financial integrity once insured, the master had to guard his charges from circumstances which might open the door to sensuality, so destructive of order and learning. The student was to be allowed neither isolation nor solitude nor unoccupied time. For it was in such unattended moments that the boys lost their chastity; and, "before all, the boys must be kept chaste."[153]

The medieval monastery had also faced this eternal problem of the youth group. Set up to remove boys from the sensuality of the streets, its monosexual composition provided an ideal setting for homosexuality. Even if women could be avoided in such a setting, and the pedagogical illusion be created that learning was asexual and unerotic, the problem of association was not automatically solved. Solitude allowed boys to be procured—masturbation was only slightly hinted at.[154] Association with older boys was discouraged by one writer, for they knew about sex while the young did not.[155] Grave, older men, who had left sexual passions behind, were more fitting companions.[156] Leisure time created a vacuum into which only sensuality could rush, so the teacher had to know what a boy was doing every minute, and the boy's time had to be compartmentalized to the fullest extent.[157] This includ-

---

[153] Vergerio, cited in Garin, L'educazione, 62. For examples of the model of the abnegatory master financially aiding his students and even their parents, see Garin, Pensiero, 517, 603, 693, 701, 703.

[154] A boy off by himself is chained by one thought, said Vergerio. "E come non è bene lasciar soli quelli che sono tentati dalla disperazione, così neanche quelli che hanno l'animo assilato dal piacere" (Garin, L'educazione, 62) ("And as it is not good to leave alone those who are tempted by suicide, so neither those whose spirit is spurred by pleasure"). For solitude, "maximum ad vitia lenocinium," see Prendilacqua, cited in Garin, Pensiero, 598; also Vegio, ibid., 180. Cato's warning that boys left alone were in danger of being approached by bad men was seconded by Alberti, in Garin, L'educazione, 129. Idleness, solitude, lasciviousness or sensuality were the vices regularly described as the worst "illness" of adolescents.

[155] Palmieri, cited in Garin, L'educazione, 115f. The delicacy of the educated was supplemented by the directness of the preachers; both were talking about the same thing (on the preachers, see above, 86f. and below, 104).

[156] See Vergerio, in Garin, L'educazione, 65. The patriarchal proclivities of Alberti need no mentioning. The main difficulty with exposing young people to the average master was the latter's reputation for corruption. Bernardino told his listeners about the pedagogues' reputation for homosexual behavior: "A Genova è uno statuto che niuno toscano può essere maestro di scuola solo per tal caso" (cited in Herlihy, "Vieillir à Florence," 1349) ("In Genoa there is a statute that no Tuscan can be a school master, because of this situation"). This helps to explain Vittorino's fame for producing good and pious teachers, as well as the Albertian myth of the concerned, yet patriarchal pedagogue-father.

[157] "Itaque neque noctu, neque interdiu ab his discedere. Si qua necessitas dabatur, spectatae virtutis ac fidei custodes adhibebat; saepe enim dicere solitus est, neminem, nisi sapientem, tuto sibi posse committi" (Prendilacqua on Vittorino, in Garin, Pensiero, 598) ("Thus do not leave them alone day or night. If some necesssity arises, employ custodians of evident virtue and faith; for often it is customary to say that no one except a savant should be assigned as a tutor"). "Fuit in Victorino summa dividendi temporis diligentia, ut singulis exercitationibus singula ferme momenta designarentur, neve inertiae quicquam

ed time away from studies, which was to be carefully organized to teach princely students battle skills and inure all students to physical hardship. At all times, said Vergerio, the students should be submitted to some norm.[158] Sexual activities, the likely alternative to a carefully planned program of recreations, fatigued and wasted the sexless virility thought necessary to learning.[159] Vittorino, ascetic and virginal though he was reputed to be, would reluctantly encourage marriage for those students who were sensually inclined. As for those who became involved in homosexual activities, they were immediately excluded from the school.[160]

The subject matter in these schools was not narrowly technical, as that of the traditional schools was, but liberal. Consequently, acculturative instruction in religion and in the social graces was an important part of the whole. Indocility made intellectual progress impossible. It was essential that God be spo-

---

permitteretur" (ibid., 628) ("Vittorino had a great gift for parcelling time, so that single moments were designated for single exercises, and thus no time for inertia was permitted"). Francesco da Castiglione wrote in the same vein (ibid., 544). See also Vergerio in Garin, *L'educazione*, 62.

[158] "Ma poichè non possiamo sempre attendere a qualche lavoro, e qualche volta bisogna concedersi un certo respiro, anche per questo voglio darti qualche norma" (Garin, *L'educazione*, 100; on the same subject, see ibid., 90–100, 112, 116f.; *Pensiero*, 585, 683).

[159] "Infatti l'amore gustato anzi tempo contamina anima e corpo" (Vergerio in Garin, *L'educazione*, 62); "Adolescentes ab usu venereo, quoad fieri poterat, coercebat, continua opera, sobrietate; quod hinc firmari corpus et ingenium, illinc enervari et mentem tolli diceret" (Platina describing Vittorino in Garin, *Pensiero*, 676) ("As much as possible, he coerced the adolescents away from every sexual practice by continual effort and sobriety; he said that in this way the body and spirit were strengthened, while the other way lay enervation and loss of intellect"). These views are similar to those of Savonarola: "E nella parte sensitiva non è alcuna potenza che più tolga la operazione delle altre potenze dell'anima e massime delle potenze della ratione, che la potenza del tatto nell'atto della lussuria. . . . La libidine è cosa veementissima che è data agli animali per conservare la specie . . ." (cited in Scremin, "Savonarola educatore," 87). ("In the sensual part there is no force that more readily eliminates the operation of the other powers of the soul, and especially the power of reason as does the power of touch in the act of lasciviousness. . . . The libido is a most vehement thing, given to animals to preserve the species").

[160] "In mares quos ferri vidisset, eos omnino ex gymnasio summovit, quod hoc crimine nil tetrius aut flagitiosius putaret" (Garin, *Pensiero*, 676) ("He summarily dismissed from school all males whom he had seen acting together, for he thought there was no crime more repulsive or shameful"). "Nunquam uxorem habuit; nunquam in aliquo concupiscentie genere lascivisse memoratur. Abhorrebat precipue vitium soddomiticum. Si quem adolescentum qui apud se erant illo infectum esse offendisset, nulla poterat vel magna in eum animadversione satiari. Narravit mihi quidam summe sinceritatis vir, qui a Victorini confessore hoc audierat, illum scilicet usque ad mortem perpetuam celibem perdurasse: que profecto quanto rarior est inter mortales, tanto gloriosior est laus" (Francesco da Castiglione describing Vittorino, in Garin, *Pensiero*, 540) ("He never had a wife; he was never known to have fallen into any type of concupiscence. If he found some adolescent to be infected with this, his aversion to him could never be sated. A man of the highest sincerity told me what he had heard from Vittorino's confessor, namely that he remained a virgin up to his death, which certainly, being so rare among mortals, deserves the more glorious praise"). On Vittorino's lifelong attachment to his mother, see Herlihy, "Vieillir à Florence," 1344. For his abhorrence of powders and perfumes, see Garin, *Pensiero*, 677.

ken of with the greatest reverence, and that cult ceremonies not be held up to ridicule. "What in fact would ever remain venerable and venerated among men if the divine majesty were to lose its value?" On the other hand, the silly emotions of women in things of religion had to be avoided.[161] To achieve this balance, the dedicated Vittorino led his boys to church and taught them the proper behavior in the presence of the divine majesty.[162]

In addition to this training in religious behavior, the humanistic schools imparted instruction in the normative social and intellectual graces of contemporary society. The theater for their performances was usually composed of their fellow students and master. Success consisted in acting the perfect adult in front of one's adolescent colleagues.[163]

To accomplish this, the boys learned that spontaneity of expression was undesirable: "Quickly said is poorly said."[164] The same was true for writing. "There is never a need to begin to write without first having warmed and stimulated the mind by reading that which one proposes to imitate." Vittorino insisted upon this with great warmth.[165] This approach to speaking and writing was naturally carried over from content to physical action:

> [Vittorino] was scrupulous in carefully correcting in the youth not only defects of pronunciation, accustoming them to an agreeable, fluid, clear [and] sweet pronunciation if their diction was too closed or open, harsh or shrunken, hard or weak, but he rendered harmonious the step, the act of the body, the movement of the head, of the feet, of the hands, into a graciousness full of decorum.[166]

The results of this incessant training in manners and gesture were gratifying to the teacher and a joy to the parents. What consolation it was that the

---

[161] Vergerio, cited in Garin, *L'educazione*, 64; see also Vegio and Aeneas Piccolomini in Garin, *Pensiero*, 177, 229–31.

[162] Ibid., 545, 609, 611, 679.

[163] Ibid., 189, 527. A passage in Alberti is highly instructive:
O giovani studiosi, Dio buono, beati voi quando qui e quivi e dirimpetto sederanno mille e mille più volte mille omini *in teatro* o in qualche altro *publico spettaculo*, o giovani, beato a qualunque di voi potrà dire seco: "Qui, fra tanto numero di nati simili a me, niuno è omo tale a cui merito io volessi *potius* esser simile che a me, e a quelli che sanno più di me. . . ." O gaudio maraviglioso! O incredibile contentamento! ("De Iciarchia," 214f. [my italics]).

[164] Garin, *Pensiero*, 234, 641, and *L'educazione*, 60.

[165] Garin, *Pensiero*, 691; see also ibid., 187.

[166] Platina, in Garin, *Pensiero*, 691. Cf. Alberti's advice: "Queste sono el cavalcare, el danzare, l'andar per via, e simili. Ma vi bisogna soprattutto moderar e gesti e la fronte, e' moti e la figura di tutta la persona con accuratissimo riguardo e con arte molto castigata al tutto, che nulla ivi paia fatto con escogitato artificio, ma creda chi le vede che questa laude in te sia dono innato dalla natura" ("De Iciarchia," 229f.) ("These are riding, dancing, walking down the street, and such. But you have especially to moderate gestures and the face, and movements and the figure of the whole person, with the most careful attention and the simplest art in everything, so that nothing appears to have been done with aforethought, but rather one who sees him should think that this praiseworthiness in you is a gift inate in your nature"). Alberti's own displeasure at gauche public presentation follows the above passage, adopted from a "prudente antiquo."

petulance of a young noble like Carlo Gonzaga could be tamed. Panegyrists recorded how the boy had repented his misdeeds before Vittorino and his fellows—with the greatest poise, of course.[167] Vittorino's training of Alessandro Gonzaga had been so successful that the boy could not bring himself to join in infantile games in Vittorino's absence, "because I have him always before my eyes, observer and judge of all my thoughts."[168] But the greatest star in Vittorino's firmament was Federigo, future ruler of Urbino. "Judged by many as dowered beyond the human condition," even in his childhood Federigo's "precocious indolence" caused people to flock to the court to see him:

> Tempering with singular courtesy his regally shining spirit, calling each by his name, greeting each with extreme gentility, often going to meet others, he was accustomed to attract the attention and spirit of all to such an extent that nothing was considered more decorous and marked with such affability.[169]

Vittorino cried in the face of such natural spirit and indolence. And in addressing the now mature Federigo, the master's panegyrist saw his rhetorical skills put to the test in assessing Vittorino's contribution to the formation of this student:

> To Vittorino belongs only a part of your glory. But as much of the beautiful as is owed to him—and it is much—just as much he owes to the reflection of your splendor. With his care he has educated you, bettered you, made you more handsome, you who by natural disposition were oriented toward the highest dignity. And you, through the grandness of your innumerable virtues, have rendered him immortal among those who come after.[170]

Such results could not help but be a consolation to civil society at large. The schools enabled men to rely on justice from their educated princes, and selfless service from the princes' courtiers, "creatures" first of the pedagogue, then of the prince.[171]

Humanist education and the new urban confraternities had much the same social causes and methods, a similar tone and acculturative content. There were fundamental and obvious differences: part, as against full-time segregation, an essentially moral as against a primarily scholastic curriculum, and so forth. For all that, both were seen as contributing to a re-masculinization of the family line in the face of styles and customs which obscured the differences between male and female. Both produced young people who could con-

---

[167] Garin, *Pensiero*, 609.

[168] Ibid., 608.

[169] Ibid., 613.

[170] Ibid., 616. The writer was Prendilacqua.

[171] Federigo d'Urbino was considered the prime example of a prince whose education had contributed to an enlightened rule; see ibid., 614.

tribute to the moral regeneration of the family and society at large. Both were based on the assumption that through the repression of sensual and aggressive appetites in biologically mature adolescents, careful training in segregated atmospheres could produce father images in youth of tender years. Their methods were also similar: the avoidance of solitude and of contacts with older boys, the systematic utilization of all leisure time, training in gesture and expression, in acting and oration.

In all this there is a definite echo of monastic institutions. Society still required the corporate separation of some group to the end of preserving the extant order of things. But among the humanistic students and the *confratelli*, the suppression of sex and aggression was to be ingrained in adolescence, whereas in traditional monasticism heroic and individual asceticism had been a day-to-day, lifelong struggle with the enemy of the human race. This task was from now on a generational, rather than a corporative, function. In this relocation of institutional rites of passage from a monastic corporation to an adolescent generation to come, only the teacher remained the traditional monk: virginal, emotional, ascetic for life, a continual flagellant.

During the quattrocento, the "little angels" or *giovangeli* slowly became a societal ritual object, one whose correct manipulation could result in the preservation, even salvation, of the natural and civil order. Parents had always been consoled by the prettification of their children at home, just as they derived a sense of solidarity by dressing up the statues and paintings of their patron saints which they kept in their homes. Now, in the quattrocento, the energies of the adolescents were being institutionally harnessed in much the same way that the society authenticated its more traditional ritual objects: through silken clothes, angels' robes, and other accoutrements designed to preserve the "shining brilliance" of powerful ritual objects, while neutralizing the anarchy in the breast of undisciplined adolescents.[172]

Their position in the ritual panoply of the commune was unique. In one sense they were pure object: manipulated by pedagogues, compared to horses, plants, and clay, the boys of the ideal confraternal group responded to directions in much the same way as the machines used to feign natural mo-

---

[172] For elaboration, see my article, "Ritual Behavior." In the following remarks on acting and ritual, I have benefitted from the classic work by Huizinga, *Homo Ludens* (Boston, 1950), and the fine work by R. Caillois, *Les jeux et les hommes* (Paris, 1958). In certain areas, however, I have supplemented their works with modern sociological and anthropological literature. The latter distinguishes between young and old people at play; attributes important sociocultural functions to the play of the younger generation; recognizes the sacramental function of certain masques, mimes, and plays; and considers the role of the play's lawgiver (without imputing to him a non-metaphysical, purely technocratic attitude toward the players). For bibliography and the new approach to formalized behavior, see Julian Huxley's symposium, "A Discussion on Ritualization of Behaviour in Animals and Man," *Philosophical Transactions of the Royal Society of London*, ser. B, 251 (1966): 247–526. On the persistent association between technique and ritual in pre-industrial society, see the remarks by K. Thomas, "Work and Leisure in Pre-Industrial Society," *Past and Present*, no. 29 (1964): 50–62. For the dual function of youth as repository and purist manifestation of established values, see S. N. Eisenstadt, "Archetypal Patterns of Youth," in E. Erikson, ed., *The Challenge of Youth* (New York, 1963), 32f.

tion in the festivals and representations. And Florentines reacted to these actors' ability to reproduce an adulthood which showed none of the signs of the indoctrination behind such art, with much the same amazement rendered these machines, all of whose parts and motors were hidden from the naked eye.[173] Still they were their parents' children, and in their humanity supplemented and replaced the ritual position of the monks and the government in the placation of the godhead.

Adolescence became a new fetish of a deeply religious society. The teacher was the individualist, the manipulator of this sacred stuff. The essentially new aspect in this realignment of sacrality was that the new cult object was a purer and more direct reflection of societal values and personages, a direct affirmation of the present, while at the same time a generational guarantee of the future. In their dramatic performances the confraternal adolescents presented Everyman: the saint, the obedient son and mother, the patriarchal father, the whore and lost son, the devil, the greedy man, even the Virgin who fears Joseph will find her with the handsome Annunciation angel. These youngsters imitated in the *sacra rappresentazione* all the bad as well as the good.[174] The inevitable victory of obedience and chastity was the victory of the social organization of innocent youth; as in the best drama, the play controlled the actors.

By the 1490s, the Italian peninsula was full of prophets and humanists speaking of a new age and of the destruction of the old.[175] The image of youth and adolescence as being the salvation of the world was *au courant*. The

---

[173] D'Ancona refers to the union in the *sacre rappresentazioni* of "l'industria de'meccanismi e la venustà della dizione" (*Origini*, 1:217). For an epilogue to the contemporary wonder at these machines which made them seem not feigned, but "verissimo," see Vasari's *Vita* of Cecca.

[174] For the anxious Maria, see D'Ancona, *Origini*, 1:249. The author of the "Dì del Guidizio" thought it necessary to present the bad in order to choose the good:

  E farem quelle rappresentazioni
che si dice che fian nel detto giorno,
con certe contenzion tra' rei e' buoni
che faran più divoto e più adorno
quest'atto, e per le predette quistioni
potrá comprender chi sarà da torno
el gaudio che procede da far bene,
e quanto è vizii sien cagion di pene.
    (L. Banfi, *Sacre rappresentazione*, 113).
  And we will perform those representations
that are said to be done on the said day,
with certain competitions between the good and the bad
which will make this act more devout and more ornate.
And by the said questions
one will be able to understand who will profit from
the joy that comes from doing good
and how much vices are the cause of punishment.

[175] For Florence, see C. Vasoli, "L'attesa della nuova èra in ambienti e gruppi fiorentini del quattrocento," in *L'attesa dell'età nuova nella spiritualità della fine del medioevo* (*Convegno del centro di studi sulla spiritualità medievale*, vol. 3) (Todi, 1962), 370–432; D. Weinstein, *Savonarola and Florence* (Princeton, 1970), 57–66.

nineties were to impose upon the Florentines a choice between two kinds of salvation by adolescence. Savonarola was to bring a new type of boys' movement with him, one that built on the past, but looked to an innocent, utopian future. Before considering the innovations of these prophetic years, let us summarize the world image which the boys' clubs had offered their viewers.

That image was apolitical. The "little old men" of the confraternal stage showed a society where political masks were unnecessary because the bonds of authority were clearly recognized and eulogized. How much elders could learn from such innocent obedience![176] The preservation of the social order and of the family name was best achieved through submission to a prince whose fatherly characteristics were carefully worked out by Lorenzo himself in his "S. Giovanni e Paolo."[177] The old society had been marred by the sexual and political eroticism of an undisciplined youth and adolescence. The old David had confused the perverse judges of the older generation. The confraternal David, it was proclaimed, would *save* these elders.[178]

It was a private image, one of idiosyncratic imitations upon a private, not a public, stage. In the old order, sinful men had manipulated God through their ritual processions. God had been pleased by this processional reflection of the political base of Florentine civic organization. The Innocents—and innocence is a private virtue—the "children of [the] new age" were, men had now learned, the only ones who could "sooth an angered God."

> Deh, Jesu, apri el pecto tuo et piovi
> quel tanto tuo pretioso liquore
> di gratia tal che horamai si rinnovi
> la tua Pistoia nel tuo puro amore:
> el nostro dono, a lei come a noi giovi;

---

[176] The feeling was expressed in a letter of Castiglione after seeing a performance at Urbino: "Io non dico ... nè come una delle commedie fosse composta da un fanciullo, recitata da fanciulli, che forse fecero vergona alli provetti, e certissimo recitarono miracolosamente, e fu pur troppo nuova cosa vedere vecchiettini lunghi un palmo servire quella gravità, quelli gesti così severi" (cited in D'Ancona, *Origini*, 1:402) ("I won't go on ... about how one of the plays was written by a boy [and] recited by children—which would perhaps shame the experienced. And most certainly they recited miraculously, and it was really a novelty to see little ancients a palm high employ that gravity, those so severe gestures"). There is a slight difference between this praise of the perfectly acting boy and the more traditional theme of the man who had never been a boy; for examples of the latter, see R. Ridolfi, *The Life of Francesco Guicciardini* (New York, 1968), 7; Vespasiano, *Vite*, 355 (Donato Acciaiuoli); I. Gråberg da Hemsö, ed., "La vita di Giovanni da Empoli ... scritta da Girolamo da Empoli suo zio," *ASI* 3, *Appendice* (1846): 22.

[177] P. Toschi, "La teoria del principe nella rappresentazione sacra di Lorenzo de' Medici," *Rivista Italiana del Dramma* 4 (1940): 3-20.

[178] "Come altra volta fu suscitato el spirito di Daniello giovinetto da Dio in confusione delli antiqui iudici perversi, così pare che suscitassi Dio el spunto di questi pochi giovinetti ... non in confusione ma in salute delli loro seniori et del popolo pistolese" (Vigo, *Confraternità ... pistoiesi*, 4) ("As in olden times the spirit of the young Daniel was resuscitated by God to the consternation of those ancient perverse judges, so it seems that God resuscitates the fire of these few young boys ... not to the consternation but for the salvation of their seniors and of the Pistoian populace").

> qual ti sia accepto, che ti diamo, el quore,
> et voi ci date venia de defecti.
> qual mertiamo essendo giovanetti.[179]

Oh Jesus, open your heart and pour out
   enough of your precious liquid
   of grace so that from henceforth your
   Pistoia will be resurrected in your pure love;
   our gift is useful both to you and to us;
   Let what we give you be acceptable, the heart,
   and you grant us forgiveness of sins,
   which, being young people, is our due.

> Se si mostra adirato
>   ad ragione el Signore
>   deh fa che sia placato
>   dal pueril decore,
>   di purità amatore ...[180]

If our lord shows himself angry,
   with reason,
   see that he is placated
   by this childish decorum,
   which loves purity.

The new ideology of youth and adolescence was vigorously proselytized, not only by Lorenzo, Poliziano, and other new Jesuses teaching in the temple, but by the confraternities. The Pistoian brotherhood of the Purità carried banners reading: *Ex ore infantium, Ecce ancilla Domini, Exultavit infans in utero meo,* and of course, *Sinite parvulos venire ad me, talium est enim regnum celorum*[181] (From the mouths of babes, Behold the Lamb of God, The Infant in my womb is joyous, Suffer the little children to come unto me, for theirs is the kingdom of heaven). They preached to the city fathers the idea of salvation by the young:

> Godi dunque città di Cathilina
>   di questo puro et pueril consortio
>   a le cui prece la bontà divina
>   fa che tu fai da quel demon divortio.[182]

> Onde la adulta età dal età verde
>   resta, come vedete, subiugata;

---

[179] Ibid., 13.
[180] Ibid., 15.
[181] Ibid., 10f.
[182] Ibid., 21.

> beato è dunque quello el qual mai perde
> questa excellente dote a Dio sì grata ...[183]

> Enjoy, therefore, city of Catiline
> this pure and childlike group
> to which the divine goodness preaches:
> take steps to divorce yourself from that deamon.

> Thus the adult age remains subject
> to the green age, as you see;
> and so, blessed is he who never loses
> this excellent endowment, so pleasing to God....

How strikingly different was the view expressed in this verse from the traditional belief that the salvation of the family and of the commonweal depended on the good example set by parents for their children. A role reversal of sorts had taken place, and the organized and educated young people now saved what of the old society could still be salvaged. Never before had the "reverence for age" been so scrupulously and publicly manifested as in the dramatic action of quattrocento Florence.[184] Yet increasingly, Florentines looked to the condition of the young to determine the future of the planet. There were signs:

> And on the said sixteenth day [of July 1497], there were about thirty cases of plague, and quite a few died of fever as well. Note that all those who died were heads of households from about twenty to fifty years [of age], and not *fanciulli*. This appeared to verify the dictum of the Frate about the renovation of the church and of the world.[185]

Videt ne contemnatis unum ex his pusillis[186] ("See that you do not condemn one of these children").

In his description of a public function of the Pistoian Purità, a contemporary remarked:

> It was considered a spiritual success. They gave the *popolo* quite an example and edification by marching in procession so composed and devoutly. Certainly example is more moving than speaking.[187]

Savonarola presented Florentines with just this alternative: ordered processional motion rather than fixed representational acting. As the city fathers had once processionally placated the ire of God, so now would the Florentine young people. The difference was innocence and purity.

---

[183] Ibid., 20.
[184] See Giovanni di Carlo's pleasure at this fact in Hatfield, "Magi," 150.
[185] Landucci, *Diario*, 155, 158.
[186] Vigo, *Confraternità ... pistoiesi*, 11.
[187] Ibid.

I tell you, the Lord wants these boys. From among the elders he will take one here and there, [but] the others will be discarded, for they have become old in evil.

I tell you boys that you have to be the good citizens who will enjoy the good which God has promised this city. A time will come when you will see many officials come to ask your advice on governing [the city]. And they will choose to govern as you govern yourselves.[188]

With Piero de' Medici's departure in November 1494, the Dominican Girolamo Savonarola, spiritual leader of Florence, assumed a political and social importance in the life of the city which no religious personage before him had ever attained. From the first, the friar insisted on a general moral reformation in Florentine society. Without it, no reorganization of the *res pubblica*, important as that was, could have any hope of success.

A central theme of this moral reform was the redirection of children and adolescents toward Christian virtue. Two successive phases can be distinguished during which the prophet approached the realization of this goal from different angles. The first period lasted until early 1496. During this time, Savonarola emphasized the parents' role in reforming the young. In the subsequent period, he relied more and more on the virtue of children who had come of age in the new dispensation and been subjected to the stern but sweet piety of a reformed city. The politization of the young fell within this latter period, and was partly the result of Savonarola's realization that a majority of the men who had grown up in the old corruption were incapable of reform.[189] It is this later period of the prophet's activity which will be the focus of our attention. Who were the Savonarolan boys? What were their activities? Who opposed them? What function did the prophet's boys fill in this supercharged period of political activity? How did these boys fulfill a century of hope invested in the young, and in what way did events transform the character of that hope?

The average age of Savonarola's *fanciulli* was lower than that of the earlier boys' confraternities. Three independent contemporary sources estimated the ages of the boys in the procession of carnival, 1496 (16 February). The Milanese ambassador said the oldest was not more than fourteen, while a Florentine observer believed that they ranged in age from six to sixteen or seventeen. Another stated that all the *fanciulli* were aged from five or six up to sixteen.[190] From Savonarola's sermon of four days later, we know that in

---

[188] Savonarola, cited respectively in Scremin, "Savanarola educatore," 98, and P. Luotto, *Il vero Savonarola* (Florence, 1900), 222.

[189] This was shown most clearly in the preacher's continual diminution of those included within the Ark and the New Jerusalem.

[190] Respectively: P. Villari, *La Storia di Girolamo Savonarola e de' suoi tempi*, 2 vols. (Florence, 1926), 1:cxiii–cxiv (Paolo Somenzi); U. Scoti-Bertinelli, "Il carnevale del 1495 a Firenze," in A. V. Cian. *I suoi scolari dell'università di Pisa* (Pisa, 1909), 89f. (Bruno di Nicholaio di Matteo Lagi); the author erred in dating the document 1495 (it refers to 1496); Landucci, *Diario*, 135.

church, boys over twenty were excluded from the stands.[191] The final indication of the upper age limit comes from Jacopo Nardi, who probably had himself been a Savonarolan *fanciullo*. This historian estimated that in one day some 1300 boys eighteen and under had received communion from Savonarola in the cathedral.[192]

The extensive participation of the very young was considered the greatest miracle of all. The Milanese ambassador, for example, after giving his exaggerated estimate of 10,000 boys, noted that 4000 were between the ages of six and nine.[193] And the Florentine diarist Landucci's statement that "all were between the ages of four or six and sixteen" suggests this same wonder.[194]

The chronicler Piero Parenti intimated that the age group from eighteen to thirty warily eyed, but did not participate significantly in the movement. After describing the burning of the vanities by the *fanciulli* in 1497, the historian noted that opinions on this and other Savonarolan policies had split families down the middle. "And not only [were] the *cittadini del regimento* [divided], but the *garzoni* from eighteen to thirty [years old] had divergent opinions."[195] Their support or disdain for the friar's activities was expressed in the time honored Florentine fashion: two groups of *garzoni* elected *messeri* and prepared to "combat each other in soccer and defeat each other."

The assumption that Savonarola's boys were eighteen and below is confirmed by three independent sources who depict the *fanciulli* as Savonarolan and the *giovani* as those generally opposed to the asceticism of the friar. All

---

[191] "Però farete che quelli che sono da dieci anni in giù, voi gli teniate a casa, e quelli che sono da dieci in su lassateli venire alla predica; ma non si vuole che là nel tribunale de' fanciulli vi vadino quelli che sieno maggiori di venti anni, e gli guardiani delle compagnie stieno là e proibischino che non si facessi scandolo" (*Prediche sopra Amos e Zaccaria*, ed. Paolo Ghiglieri, [Rome, 1971], 1:115 [*Predica* 4, 20 February]) ("But arrange it so those who are less tham ten years old be kept at home, and let those who are above ten years old come to the sermon; but one does not wish those more than twenty years old be in the tribunal of the boys. The guardians of the confraternities will stand there and prevent any scandal"). When the reform of the boys was drawn up, the *ordinatori* had the authority "di scacciare e' maggiori che non erano del loro collegio" (Ginori Conti, *Vita . . . Savonarola*, 122).

[192] J. Nardi, *Istorie della città di Firenze* (Florence, 1888), 1:91 (II, 21).

[193] "Et li maggiori non passavano li 14 anni de etade; de anni 6 fin in 9 gene era circa 4 ^{m}" (Villari, *Storia,* 1:cxiii–cxiv).

[194] "E note che furono stimati seimila fanciugli o più, tutti da 5 o 6 anni insino in 16" (Landucci, *Diario*, 125). The estimates of the number of boys in this procession varied from the 10,000 of Somenzi to the 1700 of Lagi. On the following Palm Sunday, the estimates were much closer. The contemporary Fra Placido Cinozzi explained why: "El numero de'quali ascese a più che a cinquemila, e quali di industria furon numerati, perchè in fatto questa fu giudicata cosa molto mirabile e stupenda" (cited in P. Villari and E. Casanova, *Scelta di prediche e scritti di Fra Girolamo Savonarola* [Florence, 1898], 10). ("Their number ascended to more than 5,000. These were precisely counted, because indeed this was judged a most admirable and stupendous thing"). Still, a subsequent biographer makes the same crowd-counters total up 8000 boys (Ginori Conti, *Vita . . . Savonarola*, 128). For the best description of the Palm Sunday procession, with emphasis on the "si tenera età" of the boys, see Hieronymo Benivieni, *Commento di . . . sopra a piu sue canzone e sonetti dello amore et della belleza divina* (Florence, 1500), cc. cxi^{v}–cxii^{r}.

[195] Cited in Schnitzer, *Quellen*, 4:160.

these sources, consequently, permit a cautious statement about Savonarola's policy: Firstly, he aimed at exposing children to his political pedagogy from the time they reached the age of reason and started school. Secondly, he seems to have recruited a substantial if not the preponderant part of his *fanciulli* from those not yet past puberty. The prophet's emphasis was on unsullied purity. Even in choosing the leaders of the boys, Savonarola's trusted colleague Fra Domenico considered "not so much age as purity of life and natural judgement."[196] The institutionalization of boys aged six to eighteen as against those thirteen to twenty-four may have been dictated by the disinterest of the older boys or perhaps preferred by the friar because this age limit more clearly marked off the innocents from those who had sexual experience.

The boys' strong sense of group cohesion arose from their common participation in processions. In certain other activities, however, participation was limited by age. Savonarola did not want any of them taking communion before they were eleven, and this excluded many from one of the *fanciulli* rituals most consoling to the parents.[197] In addition, he excluded boys below ten from his sermons.[198] The famed responsory *laudi* and the equally famous disciplined attendance at sermons was, consequently, a theater limited mostly to young adolescents. Luotto has further suggested that the inquisitorial activities of the *fanciulli*, who searched out vanities and broke up games, was the province of the older boys. Certainly they played the leading role among their *confratelli*.[199] It may well be that they were responsible for more directly political activities.

Contemporaries were just as unable to agree on the social composition of Savonarola's *fanciulli* as on the makeup of the prophet's following as a whole. The characterizations range from *plebe* to *tutti nobili giovani*.[200] A reasonable assumption would be that their makeup was similar to the confraternities of

---

[196] Benivieni, *Commento*, c. cxv^r. The three sources mentioned were the *Piagnoni* Landucci, Cambi, and Nardi, who says flatly that the *giovani* were opposed to Savonarola; *Istorie*, 1:99 (II, 25). Parenti adheres to this division between *fanciulli* and *giovani* except at one point; see Schnitzer, *Quellen*, 4:227.

[197] Luotto, *Il vero Savonarola*, 191. Luotto made this point of selective participation in *fanciulli* activities to counter Pastor's and Perrens's criticism of Savonarola for allegedly indiscriminately exposing the very young to the seamy side of life.

[198] See above, n. 191.

[199] Benivieni tells how Fra Domenico da Pescia, charged by Savonarola with the organization of the boys, "raccolti subito epiu experti e epiu ad questo effecto non tanto per anni quanto per purita di vita e naturale iudicio accommodati giovanetti, incomincio come dilligentissimo pastore ad investigare el desiderio, la inclinatione e el consiglio di ciaschuno circha ad questa loro nuova reforma: Et considerato per la uniformita di tutti e per el maturo loro consiglio ..." (Benivieni, *Commento*, c. cxv^r) ("He immediately brought together the most expert young men, suitable not so much because of their years as because of their pure lives and natural judiciousness. Like a diligent pastor, he began to investigate the desire, inclination and counsel of each regarding their new reform. And having considered their uniform and mature counsel ...").

[200] On the natural *Piagnone* claim that the boys were noble, see Schnitzer, *Quellen*, 3:38. Parenti describes 4000 boys processing on carnival, 1496, "tra nobili et ignobili, di cui la maggiore parte erano" (ibid., 4:94).

the earlier quattrocento, a mélange of aristocrats, burgher patricians, and smaller artisans, with the leaders being the older boys of superior social standing.[201] The report that no one dared trouble the boys seeking out vanities because they were the sons of nobles might lead one to suspect that just such high-standing youngsters were placed in these delicate, more political tasks.[202]

In considering the organization of these boys, our first question would naturally be, what was their organizational relationship to the older groups? A biography of Giovanni d'Empoli written in 1530 by his uncle provides our only source. This contemporary observer wrote:

> On feast days, he always went to the Company of the Vangelista. And note that at that time all the *fanciulli*, and especially those of the Companies, met together through the exhortation of Father Frate Ieronimo da Ferrara, who at that time preached against the low vices and sins committed in the said city, especially games [of chance] and blasphemy. They had constituted from among themselves officials, that is *messeri*, counsellors, and other officials who went around extinguishing games [of chance] and other vices. A son of Messer Luigi della Stufa, called Prinzivalle, was made *messere* for their company, and Giovanni was made one of the counsellors. He was the right hand man of the said *messere* and his performance was praised.[203]

This passage makes sense if one bears in mind the fact that the inquisitorial activities of the Savonarolan *fanciulli* were underway before the prophet's first attempt to gain governmental recognition for his new organization of the boys. Originally, it would seem, the boys' activities centered in the traditional confraternal groups. In addition to the Vangelista, we know that the Purification (in San Marco) was functioning in 1495.[204] Then, in Mardi Gras, 1496, the boys ordered themselves according to quarter for their procession.[205] Shortly thereafter Savonarola made the decision to incorporate them according to the political subdivisions of the city. We do not know whether the

[201] See above, 215.

[202] "Eron questi figliuoli di persone da bene et nobili et per questo davon grandissimo spavento" (Ginori Conti, *Vita ... Savonarola*, 124) ("These were the sons of rich and noble persons, and as a result were much feared").

[203] Gråberg da Hemsö, "Vita," 22. The author goes on to say: "E spesso i fanciulli si ragunavano in San Marco a consigliarsi" (ibid.). At the end of Lent, 1496, Savonarola told the *fanciulli*: "Voglio che abbiate un luogo fuora di San Marco dove vi raduniate e che stiate da voi" (Luotto, *Il vero Savonarola*, 226) ("I want you to have a place outside of San Marco where you can get together and which you control"). Whether the subsequent organizations ever had their own quarters is unknown.

[204] Without evidence, D'Ancona says that the Vangelista was reformed by Savonarola (*Origini*, 1:411). For the aggregation of the Purification to the spiritual benefits of the Observant Dominicans in 1495, see Richa, *Notizie*, 5:330f. According to Passerini, the confraternity del Ceppo was "one of the fraternities" which took part in the burning of the vanities (Passerini, *Storia ... beneficienza*, 192).

[205] Landucci, *Diario*, 124f.

traditional groups were submerged by the new organization, but the new political organization dominated men's minds.

"Woe to the city administered by *fanciulli*," cried the Augustinian preacher Gregorio da Perugia from the pulpit of Santo Spirito, when the city council considered the request of the *fanciulli* that their new organization be approved by the commune.[206] The petition had been brought to the Palace by a solemn embassy of *fanciulli*, who ascended the steps of the city hall, saying they were sent by Christ and Mary, and demanded that their petition be heard.[207] In itself this curious act must have concerned many older Florentines, for the individual *fanciulli* had no legal status. More unsettling still was the purpose and content of the proposed reform. Savonarola explained that the proposed political structure would "begin to order the *giovani* [sic] in a good life style, and from the tender years on [such a model] would show them how they will have to govern in the future. For it is of the utmost importance which habits they form."[208]

Across the river Fra Gregorio thundered that such a constitution meant establishing "a small government of the Republic," that is, a puppet government.

> I am amazed that the Florentines, who are considered so expert, [and] men of the most acute spirit, have come into such decline and lowness, that the very *fanciulli* emerge with the upper hand and want to govern.[209]

To this author's knowledge Florence had never had a company or confraternal structure based on the political geography of the city. It is almost certain that no such division or groups had ever been approved by the government. Consequently, this *novità* appeared to the Florentines as something much more than the traditional communal approval accorded new religious sodalities. It must have seemed an attempt to enforce the *fanciulli* morality upon the citizenry with governmental authority, using the internal political structure of the city as a base for this reform. Each quarter's company was to be fitted out with a custodian, counsellors, confessors, etc. as well as with two purely social magistrates, the correctors, whose task was to hunt out vanities and luxuries, and the *elemosinieri* or alms collectors, whose aggressive tactics did not endear them to some Florentines.[210] One other official, the *paciere* of each quarter, was to keep peace among the boys of the quarter. Though this office's authority may have been meant to extend only to members of the quarter's *compagnia*, the catholic claims of the Savonarolan boys to represent

---

[206] Cited by Parenti in Schnitzer, *Quellen*, 4:112. This took place in March 1496. See J. Schnitzer, *Savonarola* 1:314, 320, n. 51.

[207] Ginori Conti, *Vita . . . Savonarola*, 125f. Parenti in Schnitzer, *Quellen*, 4:105.

[208] Parenti in Schnitzer, *Quellen*, 4:106.

[209] Ibid., 105.

[210] The most extensive description of the new quarter organizations is in Ginori Conti, *Vita . . . Savonarola*, 122f.

the fanciulli of Florence meant that it would function as a control element for all the neighborhood's *fanciulli*.[211]

The very dedication of the boys, depressing to some in its earnestness, frightened many Florentines. All the youngsters had cut their hair above the ears. All had taken to simple, clearly masculine clothing; there was to be no question as to their gender, their innocence, their group appurtenance.[212] All had vowed to give up the excursions to Fiesole and Monte San Gaggio to see and participate in the *rappresentazioni*[213]: in normal times these plays were considered devout, said Savonarola, but to his sons they appeared completely carnal.[214] No schools of dancing and fencing for them.[215] And they were such implacable foes of homosexual behavior that during the boys' heyday people feared even to mention the unmentionable sin.[216] Overnight, it seemed, the boys changed from undisciplined individuals to pious and grave examples to all the *saeculum*.

To give a political base to an organization with these liabilities was asking too much of enough members of the Grand Council to ensure the petition's defeat.[217] As Savonarola and his boys learned, fathers reared in Medici tyranny did not easily surrender their private pleasures. The prophet also understood very well the determination of the older generation to exclude the young from high political office and from important magistracies—and if the young, how much more so the children! The city patriarchs were anguished by reports that foreign people were amusing themselves over the boy government of Florence.[218]

Savonarola had no intention of instituting a government of young people. Yet as the year 1496 wore on, he increasingly identified the New Jerusalem with the *fanciulli*, and used them as political activists. They lobbied at home and in the Palace for the implementation of their program.[219] During this year, they became the active element in Florentine public life in a socio-ritual sense. In place of the privacy of the old theatrical confraternities, Savonarola stressed the public activity of his boys. In procession they assumed the emphasis on order which had once been the dominant property of public ritual. They represented again the public order of the commune rather than the sce-

---

[211] "Haveano a tenere et comporre pace infra loro et fuora di loro, fra gli altri fanciulli del lor quartiere . . ." (ibid., 122).

[212] Ibid., 119f.

[213] Ibid., 122.

[214] Ibid., 46.

[215] Ibid., 122.

[216] Landucci, *Diario*, 124.

[217] See Cerretani, cited in Schnitzer, *Quellen*, 3:38.

[218] Parenti, cited in Schnitzer, *Quellen*, 4:105ff.; see also Luotto, *Il vero Savonarola*, 186f. For the discomfort over the stories that the city was governed by friars, see ibid., 137.

[219] Savonarola often cautioned the boys to exercise restraint and intended that their liberty of action be strictly supervised by their magistrate. To those who objected to the *fanciulli's* sociopolitical activity, Savonarola responded: "Tell me, are the boys magistrates? Are they of the Eight?" See Luotto, *Il vero Savonarola*, 186, 194–206.

nographic elements of the private world of the confraternities. Christ, king of
Florence, and Mary, its queen, looked down upon the republic and saw, as in
an earlier time, the political order of the city offered to them—by innocent activists. And they were pleased. The crucifix of redemption was "in the hands
of holy purity."[220] Placation and salvation had again become a public thing.

At this juncture, the one male age group with no political weight in the
commune were the *giovani*. Their younger brothers and their fathers were involved in civic affairs. But of the *giovani*, only those aged twenty–nine and
above had access to the Grand Council. Since only members of that Council
had the right to fill the important officialities of the commune, *giovani* below
twenty–nine were effectively excluded from honorable positions in the communal bureaucracy. With little concrete evidence to support me, I suspect
that the Savonarolan period saw a reaction away from the preciosity of golden
youth which had marked the Lorenzan period.

Savonarola could sympathize with the political plight of the *giovani* while
remaining dubious about their moral redemption. Perhaps at his urging, an
exception had been included in the law instituting the Grand Council which
permitted the annual selection of twenty-four *giovani* aged twenty-four and
above as candidates for election to the Grand Council.[221] The stated purpose for this yearly rejuvenation of the Council was "to encourage the *giovani*
and incite the *uomini* to virtue."[222]

Giovani were in these as in other times and places the bellweathers of the
political winds. Virile, passionate, and often otherwise unoccupied, they could
influence how long, and how strongly, the wind would continue to blow from
San Marco. This explains Parenti's interest in their own type of festive politics, and the *Piagnone* Pagolantonio Soderini's decision to place one of his
sons among the Compagnacci, a group of *giovani* dedicated to the humiliation of the Dominican friar.[223] Savonarola and his followers realized the importance of this group, and many of them supported moves designed to ease

---

[220] Landucci, *Diario*, 124. The procession of the Savonarolan quarters was not a
perfect reproduction of the traditional procession of the administrative sections of the
city. The latter was based on the *gonfaloni*, four to a quarter, whereas the former was
probably organized only according to quarters. The only tradition of quarter organization
for processional purposes was a quattrocento festival division which is only imperfectly
documented (see Hatfield, "Magi," 115–20). See also Vasari, cited in D'Ancona, *Origini*,
1:234. On the political evangelism of the *fanciulli*, see G. Gnerghi, "Gerolamo Savonarola
e i fanciulli," *Rassegna Nazionale* 117 (1901): 345–70, esp. 362.

[221] On 13 December 1496, Savonarola told his listeners that when the Council was
instituted, he had favored "everyone" entering, "because liberty was then in its beginnings, and it was necessary to experiment" (Villari, *Storia*, 1:502). The following information on the Grand Council is based on N. Rubinstein, "I primi anni del Consiglio
Maggiore di Firenze," *ASI* 112 (1954): 154–229, 321–47; for the exception to the basic
law, see ibid., 166f.

[222] Villari, *Storia*, 287f.

[223] For Parenti, see Schnitzer, *Quellen*, 4:160; for Soderini, see Guicciardini, *History*,
137.

their admission to the Grand Council and therewith the right to hold office.[224]

A first modest step in that direction was taken in November 1495, with the reordering of the bags from which members of the Grand Council were drawn to fill most important offices in the communal bureaucracy. Whereas before no age distinction had been made among those in the council, now the council was divided into three age groups. Each member over 45 had three chits deposited in the bags for the offices. Those between 35 and 45 had two such chits, and, most important, those from 25 to 35 had one.[225] From a practical point of view, this was the first time that *giovani* of this age had any access to these offices. In the very same days, however, the same council rejected the recommendation of one of its committees to open doors to *giovani* twenty-four years old and above. Despite the pressing need for this action, the council maintained the standard minimum of twenty-nine years.[226]

What made such a step seem important to the commission was the fact that the Grand Council, the supreme instrument of the new republic, was plagued by non-attendance, but more seriously, by the all too limited number of those eligible to take part in council deliberations and voting. Together, these problems meant that quorums were difficult to meet. Two legal conditions for participation could be modified to increase the number of those who were eligible. One was to soften the requirement that members be paid up in taxes. The other was to drop the legal age minimum. Not surprisingly the council, after a great deal of deliberation, opted for their sons over the lesser propertied.[227]

The election of the arch-*Piagnone* Francesco Valori as *gonfaloniere della giustizia* was the signal for Savonarola's followers to carry through this and other pending reforms. Three crucial acts of his two-month office should be mentioned. The first was the purging from the Grand Council of certain "bad," pro-Medicean members who had obtained seats illegally.[228] The second was the passage of the constitutions of the boys, left in abeyance for almost a year because of the strong majority opposition to their implementation.[229] The third was lowering the legal age minimum for the Grand Council from twenty-nine to twenty-four for any successive three-month period in which a

---

[224] It is unclear whether Savonarola himself was in favor of this move (see below, n. 231).

[225] Rubinstein, "I primi anni," 331.

[226] Ibid., 186. This had been maintained despite the cooption each year of some *giovani* aged twenty–four and above. The minimum age for entitled appurtenance had remained twenty–nine.

[227] The law was passed 18 January 1497; ibid., 197.

[228] Dated 1 February; ibid., 190. Savonarola had called for these ousters in a sermon on 13 December 1496 (see the passages in Villari, *Storia*, 1:502f.).

[229] This was forced through in January after repeated readings (Parenti, cited in Schnitzer, *Quellen*, 4:155; see ibid., 3:38).

statutorily fixed minimum of eligibles could not be reached.[230]

Certainly the long-awaited communal approval of the boys' constitutions was gratifying to Savonarola. But lowering the age for participation was probably not as warmly endorsed by the prophet as it was by many of his followers on the council. According to the *Piagnone* historian Jacopo Nardi, a *fanciullo* himself in these years, Valori "and other men of good mind" believed that the younger *giovani* were less open to the threats of vengeance used by dissatisfied factions in the council. Adding them to it would preserve the commune.[231] In other words, the *Piagnoni* felt that the young *giovani* would side with them, partly in thanks for now having greater access to the council and to the magistracies.

> But a result followed which was quite different from that which the said Francesco [Valori] and the other men of good mind had believed. For the degenerate *giovani*, [once] multiplied in the Council, allied themselves in the elections of magistrates on the side of the *Arrabbiati* [opponents of the *Piagnoni*], and consequently they ruined or at least had little love for the Council.[232]

This pattern of *giovani* opposition to the prophetic impulse of Savonarola clearly affirmed itself in the remaining year and a half of Savonarola's life. It was a company of *giovani*, the so-called *Compagnacci*, which became the principle extragovernmental opponent of the *frate*.[233] They smeared the pulpits where the Dominicans preached, created rackets during sermons, circulated defamatory writings, defied his moral asceticism by staging lavish and ostentatiously obscene banquets, and attacked the boys in processions. In the sources for the period, as has been mentioned, impieties were almost uniformly ascribed to the *giovani*, which were put into clear relief to contrast them with the saintliness of the *fanciulli*. Certainly there was much stereotyping in such opinions, but as much truth. It is a striking fact that in no account of any Savonarolan procession is there any indication that *giovani* participated.

True to his prophetic calling, Savonarola from the first had sought out the holy purity of the very young. He had turned the *fanciulli* to evangelistic social activism before puberty, educating them in Christian militancy at a time when children were traditionally still under the influence of their mothers. His influence over the young adolescents had not been meager: we have seen

---

[230] Rubinstein, "I primi anni," 187 (18 January 1497). The *giovani* had to be paid up in taxes, and this reduced the otherwise admissible *giovani* from about 500 to about 200.

[231] "Credendo pure d'acconciarlo meglio col farlo di maggior numero, e perciò manco esposto alle offese di chi per via di sètte lo volesse alterare" (Nardi, *Istorie*, 1:38 [II, 25]). It has been assumed that Savonarola was opposed to admitting the *giovani* (see for example R. Ridolfi, *Vita di Girolamo Savonarola* [Rome, 1952], 1:276; Villari, *Storia*, 1:505). Yet the language of Savonarola in his political sermon of 13 December 1496, upon which this assertion is based, is ambiguous. In his work on the Grand Council cited above, Rubinstein does not express an opinion.

[232] Nardi, *Istorie*, 1:38 (II, 25).

[233] Villari says that it was the Compagnacci who benefited from the age lowering (Villari, *Storia*, 1:505).

that he was able to marshal 1300 young people between the ages of eleven and eighteen to a solemn communion one Christmas morning. His failure to attract a militant segment of the *giovani* to his banner was the failure of a peaceful man who indoctrinated his followers with an abhorrence of aggression. The confraternities of the quattrocento had not produced a docile *gioventù*. Neither did the Dominican, nor did he really try. His hopes rested with the children and young adolescents, and those hopes failed. It was just a little time, said the diarist Landucci, but "God be praised that I lived in this little bit of holy time."[234]

Ritual is creative for a community to the extent that it reflects both structure and the formless energy upon which vital order rests. The moment that ritual is emptied of those elements in which spectators see some formless element of themselves reflected, it becomes "mere ritual," "very beautiful, but devoid of spirit," as the *Piagnoni* were wont to say.[235] Creative ritual's motion is never arrested. On the other hand, the ritual in which direction is not arrested, but diverted, threatens always to lose its formal nature, and become "destructive." The ritual contract broken, the results of such destruction can in themselves be creative—a new social order may result.[236] Within the social order, however, creative ritual must contain elements of both play and action, a dialectic of form and anti-form, if it is to survive, and if it is to engage both participants and observers.[237]

For a short period in 1496 and 1497, the processions in Florence accomplished this end. Contemporaries were incredulous upon seeing how successfully the processions achieved their task of "eliminating all confusion," as the historian-politician Parenti put it.[238] The conditions for this success were optimal: the city was threatened from abroad, the city's spiritual guide seemed above reproach in these years, and the Florentines generally agreed on the necessity of recreating the republic. Consequently, the processions of these years could reflect the citizens' unity of purpose while eliminating the confusion over means.

The Florentines did not simply parade their *fanciulli*, their hopes for the

---

[234] Landucci, *Diario*, 124.

[235] Luotto, *Il vero Savonarola*, 145; Cambi, *Istorie*, in *Delizie*, 22:45. Erikson calls "true ritualization" "an unexpected renewal of a recognizable order in potential chaos. Ritualization thus depends on that blending of surprise and recognition which is the soul of creativity, reborn out of the abyss of instinctual disorder, confusion of identity and social anomie" (E. H. Erikson, "Ontogeny of Ritualization in Man," in Huxley, "A Discussion of Ritualization," 349).

[236] See the interesting articles by F. E. Williams, "The Vailala Madness and the Destruction of Native Ceremonies in the Gulf Division," *Territory of Papua. Anthropology*, report no. 4 (1923), and "The Vailala Madness in Retrospect," in *Essays Presented to C. G. Seligman*, ed. E. Evans-Pritchard et al. (London, 1934), 369–79.

[237] A typical game example of this interplay is the breakthrough in American football, where the skilled runner evades the structures set up to restrain him. This brings the crowd to its feet. In the world of religious cult, this principle is seen in the continued renewal of cult by the addition of new miracle-producing relics or images.

[238] Schnitzer, *Quellen*, 4:62f.

future, in these processions. When we recall the socio-political activities of these same *fanciulli*, we see that the boys portrayed not only the future, but also the present. They were engaged in real political action, and not merely the immortalization of the idiosyncracies of politically powerless fathers.

The organization of these devotional activities betrayed a prophetic and thoroughly public processional community. Private confraternities of men found no entrance to them.[239] Women were not permitted to lean out the windows to watch processions, and were sometimes excluded from sermons altogether.[240] At other times, Savonarola insisted on a rigid separation of the sexes.[241]

It is sometimes assumed that the processions of the Savonarolan period were for the boys alone. This is not at all the case. In fact, only the Carnival processions of 1496 and 1497 seem to have been limited to *fanciulli*.[242] These processions were intended as invectives toward the devil, who usually reigned on this date, and were considered the boys' own ersatz *feste*.[243] But all the other public processions of the period, including the Carnival procession of 1498, comprised men and women, girls and boys.[244] The boys came first, organized according to quarter, each company carrying the quarter's banner. From the Palm Sunday procession of 1496 on, they were dressed as angels, a costume assumed as well by the little girls on that memorable day.[245] In subsequent processions, the order was fixed: first the companies of boys in twos; then the men, then the young girls, and finally the women. Each of these groups was ordered according to height.[246]

Contemporary chroniclers placed so much emphasis upon the boys in these processions because of their incredible discipline and docility. Some called the processions "processions of *fanciulli*," when they were in fact much more than that; one observer called one of them "the most solemn proces-

---

[239] The traditional adult companies are mentioned only once during the Savonarolan period: according to Nardi, they took part in a procession of 27 October 1496, when the miraculous image of Impruneta was brought into the city (*Istorie*, 1:87 [II, 19]).

[240] Landucci, *Diario*, 90-94.

[241] Ibid., 107 (Nardi, *Istorie*, 1:47 [I, 19]). The separation of the sexes at church was traditional, but seems to have eased during the quattrocento; for an earlier example of the separation of the sexes in procession, see above, n. 81. For the Savonarolan period, see below, 110).

[242] No mention of other than boys was made by either Landucci (*Diario*, 124f.), or Lagi (Scoti-Bertinelli, "Il Carnevale" [full citation above, n. 190]). The same is true for 1497 (Nardi, *Istorie*, 1:92f. [II, 21]); Ginori Conti, *Vita . . . Savonarola*, 129-35; Parenti, cited in Schnitzer, *Quellen*, 4:159-61.

[243] Benivieni, *Commento*, c. cxvi^v; Ginori Conti, *Vita . . . Savonarola*, 130, 134.

[244] For the 1498 Mardi Gras, see Villari, *Storia*, 2:lii; Parenti, cited in Schnitzer, *Quellen*, 4:232; and Ginori Conti, *Vita . . . Savonarola*, 132f.

[245] Landucci, *Diario*, 128. In the earliest processional appearance of the *fanciulli*, they had processed "sanza veste"; see Scoti-Bertinelli, "Il carnevale," 89f.

[246] The most extensive descriptions: Parenti, cited in Schnitzer, *Quellen*, 4:159-61; Ginori Conti, *Vita . . . Savonarola*, 127ff., 129-35; Benivieni, *Commento*, c. cxi^v; Somenzi, cited in Villari, *Storia*, 2:lii.

sion of the quarters," when it seems that only the boys were arranged in quarters, while the rest of the men, women, and girls were arranged according to sex and size.[247] Clearly, the boy activists had become the desired representation of the city's segments before God. Their processional behavior was the parents' assurance that they were in or were nearing the New Jerusalem.

The Savonarolan processions were both propitiatory and celebratory. Propitiatory certainly in their order: the boys led the procession as the priests usually did, and "the people" came behind. Yet organizing these activist innocents into quarters made the processions celebrations of the new polis. The parents who followed bore witness that only public commitment could open the gates of the New, innocent, Jerusalem.

During the quattrocento Florentines learned that the segregated indoctrination of adolescents outside the family and away from the streets could reproduce ideal adult types. This discovery did not, however, modify society's opinion of the natural proclivities of the adolescent. When Alberti described hunting as a "childish toy," he was disparaging that pastime in a thoroughly traditional fashion.[248] The Renaissance in Italy discovered no new values in uninhibited childishness and adolescence. No Florentine father revelled in the juvenile behavior of his children as does the modern father. If mothers did, they always had, and such maternal coddling was understood as another example of the basic sensuality and light-headedness of the weaker sex. The artistic putto, and not the vivacious infant Christ, imaged the ideal young person: *vecchiettini* with the wings of angels.[249]

How could society make its adolescents into utopian fetishes, while conceding no inherent value to their spontaneous behavior? From one point of view, the answer is evident: Parents' joy in their children's individual growth is a private joy; the young person's self-expression can be socially valued only in a culture where the rights of the private realm are taken to be natural. Yet throughout Europe the emergence of this private realm and this new joy in children, so well described by Ariès, was accompanied by growing political absolutism.

In Florence, the quattrocento saw the debilitation of the decision-making powers of the old political class, and its slow conversion to bureaucracy and professional service to the Medici. Such an evolution could not be accom-

---

[247] A good example of the equation of the processions with the boys is Landucci, who calls the Palm Sunday, 1496 procession "for boys," and then describes its incorporation of all elements (*Diario*, 128). Simone Filipepi refers to the "procession of the Quarters" (Villari and Casanova, *Scelta*, 486).

[248] "Nè ti chiamerò bene operoso se tu consumerai tutto il dì allo sparviere a'cani, alle reti e simili. Simile occupazioni sono trastulli fanciulleschi, concessi ora agli omini gravi per recreare d'animo . . ." (Alberti, "De Iciarchia," 239) ("Nor will I say you have done well if you spend the whole day hunting with dogs, fishing, etc. Such occupations are childish pasttimes that are allowed to grave men to relax the spirit . . .").

[249] For a different view, see Garin, *Pensiero*, xiv; Goldthwaite, *Private Wealth*, 264. Ariès examines the different types of representations (*Centuries*, 34–37, 43–48).

plished without the greatest strains being placed upon traditional life patterns. In earlier times, family prestige had been solidly based on political influence, and the ritual procession of family and civic glory before God and men had reflected the communal organization of real power. With the increasing subversion of political forms by the Medici, this old union of ritualistic and political action came to an end. Lorenzo's opponent Alamanno Rinuccini complained about the honored families being driven into their homes by the new "Caesar": "Both by example and words he did away with all the things which in the old days had graced and given reputation to the citizens, like marriage feasts, dances, *feste*, and ornate dress."[250]

At a stage when public manifestation still seemed a natural part of political activity, the confraternities of adolescents stepped into this breach between the traditional publicity of the republic and the familial privacy of the new world of political authoritarianism. These grave boys represented on the one side a world of private virtues, but on the other a hope of public salvation for families whose survival had been customarily tied to processional prestige. To do this successfully, youthful asceticism, not boyish miscreance, was the order of the early Florentine Renaissance. The socialized and indoctrinated adolescent on the stage and in procession was ritually efficacious before he became privately consoling. He was a social ideal before becoming a private, familial diversion.

Addendum

After finishing the final draft of this paper, I found a reference to a company of *fanciulli* called the Purità, founded about 1474 in the Dominican church of Santa Maria Novella and composed, according to the source, of sons of *gentili uomini e di stato*. The following is a letter of 12 May 1476 to a Rinuccini, ambassador in Rome for the Florentine government: "A Santa Maria Novella è nuovamente una congregazione di fanciulli, chiamasi Purità, per quello nuovo miracolo di che se' informato. Sono tutti figliuoli di gentili uomini e di stato, hanno qualche dubitazione che per utilità di quello altare nuovamente fatto nel luogo del miracolo, i frati del convento non faccino regnare costì qualche supplicazione contro all loro libertà. Quando t'accaderà dira'ne qualche parola alla Santità del papa, in modo che quando ne fussi supplicato, la Santità Sua sia informata, ed a questa compania sia conservata la loro libertà" (*Ricordi storici di Filippo di Cino Rinuccini dal 1282 al 1460 colla continuazione di Alamanno e Neri suoi figli fino al 1506*, ed. G. Aiazzi, [Florence, 1840], 246). On the Florentine group *della Pura*, see S. Orlandi, *"Necrologio" di S. Maria Novella* (Florence, 1955), 2:332, 338 ("Recently a group of children has been installed in Santa Maria Novella. It is called Purity because of that new miracle you've been informed of. They are all children of gentlemen of status. They are concerned lest, because of the altar recently installed where the miracle took place, the friars of the friary would launch some petition

---

[250] *Ricordi . . . Rinuccini*, cxlviii.

down there directed against [the group's] independence. When you get a chance say a word about it to His Holiness the pope, so that when he is supplicated on that score, His Holiness will be informed and the independence of this confraternity will be preserved").

"The Youth are Coming!" Nonsense in Florence during the Republic and Grand Duchy*

G IOVANI ARE TAKING OVER! IN SUCH EXAGGERATED TERMS THE MORALISTS and politicians of trecento and early quattrocento Florence warned their contemporaries against the influence of youth. The city's *novelliste* chimed in, displaying their fear and resentment of the young by making individual boys the butts or perpetrators of countless practical jokes.[1] Of course there were class and age tensions in Florence. Still, neither youth nor the variously aged *garzoni* or shopboys with whom they are so often associated talked back as a group. They did not take to the street to threaten their elders or masters with ridicule if the latter did not wine and dine them. There were no charivaris.

The Rough Music of Florence's *contado* and *distretto* was but an echo in the city.[2] Charivaris are completely absent from the city's rich historical litera-

---

* This essay appeared previously in *Le Charivari. Actes de la table ronde organisée à Paris (25–27 avril 1977) par l'Ecole des Hautes Etudes en Sciences Sociales et le Centre National de la Recherche Scientifique*, ed. J. Le Goff and J. -C. Schmitt (Paris, 1981), 165–76. This is its first appearance in English.

[1] For anti-youth feelings see Franco Sacchetti, *Il trecentonovelle*, ed. V. Pernicone (Florence, 1946), 51, 290, 572; Filippo Villani in *Croniche di Giovanni, Matteo, e Filippo Villani*, 2 vols. (Trieste, 1857), bk. XI, chap. 65 (1363); *Cronica di Buonaccorso Pitti*, ed. A. Bacchi della Lega (Bologna, 1905), 135 (1402); G. Cavalcanti, *Istorie fiorentine*, ed. G. di Pino (Milan, 1944), 40 (II, 22); 108 (IV, 108). I thank my erstwhile research assistant Anthony Di Iorio and my former colleague Frederic Jaher for their valuable help.

[2] The wedding *serraglio* was practiced in Florence in the 1490s; cf. *La vita del B. Geronimo Savonarola* (Ps. Burlamacchi), edition attributed to P. Ginori Conti (Florence, 1937), 123; and in nearby Prato about 1535 if no charity was forthcoming (Agnolo Firenzuola, *Le novelle*, ed. E. Ragni [Rome, 1971], 318–27). For evidence of early modern *scampanate* or charivaris in Tuscany and Italy see C. Corrain and P. Zampini, *Documenti etnografici e folkloristici nei sinodi diocesani italiani* (Bologna, 1970), 100f., 396f.; B. Del Vecchio, *Le seconde nozze del coniuge superstite* (Florence, 1885); G. C. Pola Falletti Villafalletto, *La juventus attraverso i secoli* (Monza, 1953), 133–70; and the same author's *Associazioni giovanili e feste antiche*, 4 vols. (Milan, 1939), esp. 1:561, where he indicates the

ture, from its laws and festivals, from its *novelle* and carnival songs. Misrule
rarely soothed the young, nor was that mischievous lady's play kingdom a
staging area for Ciompi solidarity. A search of the city's judicial archives will
certainly turn up examples of group ridicule in the neighborhoods, but the silence of Florence is convincing: that particular configuration of noise, youth,
and ridicule called charivari had no importance to the city at large.

The Florentines must have wanted it that way; political considerations must
partly explain such urban silence in the midst of country clamor. This paper
searches out these political motivations by sketching the public activity of
youth and *garzoni* in successive periods of Florentine history. Three elements
emerge as paramount. First, the locus of political power in the city: Florence's
republican governments characteristically suppressed neighborhood solidarities in the interest of public authority. Second, the extent of political roles:
No substantial youth or *garzoni* roles in Florentine public life were possible so
long as individual city fathers bowed to peer pressure and common interest
by not courting those virile powers. Third, the relation between ridicule and
power: The commune of Florence monopolized ridicule to enforce law and
demonstrate power. Masterful students of their city, the Medici finally sub-
verted the republic in part by courting youth and workers in their neighborhoods. Borne by glittering youth and *garzoni*, Lady Misrule rode through now
proud neighborhoods to meet her authoritarian spouse. By the Cinquecento,
Florence had finally found her lord.

Activities Documented before Lorenzo

The most common games of boys (*pueri, fanciulli*) in the trecento were
rock, fist, and truncheon fights staged downtown or on the Arno bridges. The
carnival period featured stone fights, the bishop in 1365 cancelling curial activities on Mardi Gras because on that day "men do not like to go out because of the games of rocks or throwing of rocks."[3] Large fist fights seem to
have been concentrated in April, neighborhood gangs called the Berta and

---

difficulty of finding the so-called *badie* (youth groups) outside Piedmont. In Florence the
closest I came to the charivaris was a statutal prohibition against persons throwing rocks
at houses during wedding feasts (*Statuti della repubblica fiorentina*, ed. R. Caggese, vol. 2,
Statuto del Podestà dell'anno 1325 [Florence, 1921], 200). This was substantially unchanged
in 1415; see *Statuta populi et communis Florentiae* (Fribourg, 1778), 1:371. There are also
rubrics limiting *citarizentes et mattinatas*, respectively, 276, 403. See now C. Klapisch-Zuber,
"The 'Mattinata' in Medieval Italy," in her *Women, Family, and Ritual in Renaissance
Florence*, 261–82.
    [3] D. Manni, *Osservazioni istoriche sopra i sigilli antichi* (Florence, 1770), 21:32. "Fare a'
sassi" in the Mercato Nuovo in 1438, accompanied by the destruction of several roofs; cf.
L. Artusi and S. Gabbrielli, *Feste e giochi a Firenze* (Florence, 1976), 97. Rock fights were
probably already associated with Carnival bonfires; the latter were "common" in the
fifteenth century. See e.g., the rock fight of 1457 "occasione certe treggie que comuniter
in die Carnisprivi de sero in civitate Florentie comburi solet" (*Archivio di Stato, Firenze*
[*ASF*], *Atti del Capitano del Popolo*, 3826, fol. 22r). My thanks to Samuel Cohn for this
reference.

Magroni fighting it out every evening for a fortnight in the 1380s and 1390s.[4] Poorly documented during the quattrocento, brawls of this type were thought ineradicable at the end of that century, and chroniclers regularly described them in the cinquecento and seicento.

Young men and *garzoni*, as distinct from *fanciulli*, favored a different activity: festive role-reversal. At certain times of the year youth of good family or artisan groups dressed up and played their elders or betters. Antonio Pucci gives an interesting account of one such event in the 1380s: *buon briganti* congregated in the Mercato Vecchio in December, appointed a *signore* or *messere* over their *reame*, and then rode around on horses celebrating themselves.[5] On New Year's Day they dressed in shirts showing their emblem, then "baptised" themselves by jumping into the Arno. Now pretend knights, they ate watermelons before, trumpets blaring (one searches in vain before the cinquecento for *strumenti scordati* or Rough Music in the Florentine records), they went to a great bonfire where all the brigades ate a rich meal.[6]

Fanciulli, *giovani*, and *garzoni* had two ways to finance these games and the fires and meals which went with them. Participants could erect barriers (*stili*) and tax passersby and those whose shops lay around the field of activity.[7] If one neither paid nor heeded the trumpet announcing the coming fracas, one had only oneself to blame for eventual damages. Alternatively, a group could secure the financial backing of a patron. How important the patron was, even for fights, can be seen in the fact that the commune, in order to stop them, forced leading citizens who sponsored such events to post bond which would be forfeited if the fights occurred.[8]

In these activities boys proved to their audience that "boys will be boys,"

---

[4] *Biblioteca Nazionale, Firenze (BNF), fondo Panciatichi*, 158, fol. 172r. This anonymous diary has now been edited by A. Molho and F. Sznura: *Alle bocche della piazza: Diario di anonimo fiorentino (1382–1401)* (Florence, 1986). See also *ASF, Consulte e Pratiche (CP)*, 26, fols. 3r, 23r, 26v, 27r; 28, fol. 38v; 30, fol. 22r, with details on the fist and rock fights of this time. Gene Brucker generously sent me these texts, referred to in his "The Florentine *Popolo Minuto* and Its Political Role," in L. Martines, ed., *Violence and Civil Disorder in Italian Cities, 1200–1500* (Berkeley, 1972), 172.

[5] Antonio Pucci, "Le Proprietà di Mercato Vecchio," in *Delizie degli eruditi toscani* (1775), 6:272ff.

[6] The first reference I find to *strumenti scordati* is in 1551; see M. Plaisance, "La politique culturelle de Côme I et les fêtes annuelles à Florence de 1541 à 1550," in *Les fêtes de la Renaissance*, ed. J. Jacquot and E. Konigson (Paris, 1975), 3:150.

[7] The earliest Florentine reference to *stili* is in the later 1490s; see J. Schnitzer, *Quellen und Forschungen zu Geschichte Savonarolas* (Leipzig, 1910), 4:94 (Parenti); the Ps. Burlamacchi mentions them as marriage *serragli* and as a Carnival practice (123, 130). By this time another activity of boys had started to emerge in the sources, *calcio alla palla*. The earliest references I find are in a poem of Giovanni Frescobaldi (fl. 1460s–1480s), "La Palla al Calcio," in *Lirici Toscani del Quattrocento*, ed. A. Lanza (Rome, 1973), 601–7 (*la festa della palla grossa* [*pallone*?]), and in a 1472 list of *feste* by Benedetto Dei (*ASF, Manoscritti*, 119, fol. 3v). Players from the quarter of Santo Spirito clash with those from the Prato or Meadow in the quarter Santa Maria Novella. From B. Varchi, *Storia fiorentina*, 2 vols. (Florence, 1963), XIII, 14 one gets an idea of how rough the *calcio* of the mid-cinquecento could be.

[8] *ASF, CP*, 26, fols. 24v, 27r (19 April 1387).

while artisans proved their levity. Fist fights and mock cavalcades convinced the mature political males that they ruled by necessity and reason. There is no evidence in this period that participants in these games directly ridiculed, castigated, or outwardly opposed particular individuals or groups outside the game. The joke was, as Pucci knew, on the participants. The pretend knights, he said, returned to a simpler reality. After New Year's Day they ate radishes instead of venison, and their *signore*, his play kingdom dissolved, gave up his baton and his pretensions. Pucci's account thus reflects one important view of such activities: Rather than being directed against an audience, they were staged for its amusement. The mock knights, in Pucci's words, ate "out of others' pockets."[9]

The action was therefore confined to the game; groups of rockthrowers or riders competed with or opposed each other and not someone else. Still, two competing neighborhood groups of *garzoni* could represent the political divisions of their betters or elders. Boys' fist fights could be a metaphor for, or could simply be, adult politics. A cavalcade of artisans in the neighborhood of the Alberti matched by another from that of the Castellani was understood as a contest between competing political factions at the same time that it confirmed the prejudices against artisans and youth.[10] Political force or potential, not the moral suasion of the charivaris, could be the message. Using "bestial" boys or artisans, great citizens could demonstrate their force with that very group of urban inhabitants whose ferocity at certain times of the year was thought unavoidable and thus excusable. The image of social difference between actors and audience, inhabitants and citizens, masked a potential political reversal effected by vertically integrated clientage which cut across those social differences. The government of Florence had every reason to oppose such demonstrations, and did.

It makes sense that a regime in power would resist such threats to its dignity and authority. Nonetheless the Florentine governments which opposed such manifestations remained fundamentally ambivalent toward them. Governments consisted of nothing more than the heads of the great families or their clients, and each Signoria ruled for only two months. Claims of honor and order conflicted. On the one hand family honor, and indirectly, communal honor, depended upon the families' ability to demonstrate a numerous clientele, and that clientele naturally came from the artisans and youth of the neighborhoods. On the other hand family fathers or patrons in government recognized the need for merchant solidarity against the 80% of the city excluded from the political process, against their sons, workers, and women. This ambivalence between family-based and communally-based solidarities, between neighborhood and city-wide associations, between organic and class solidarity, was a constant in Florentine history.

The ultimate danger was evident. Florentines believed that activated youth

---

[9] "All'altrui spese," in *Delizie*, 6:272ff.

[10] The chapter, "The Ritual of Celebration," in Trexler, *Public Life in Renaissance Florence* (New York, 1980), contains extensive data on this subject.

gangs or artisanal groupings would protect the highest bidder in exchange for charity or tips. They constantly feared, therefore, that one patron, strong in his own neighborhood, could flatter other neighborhood associations and become in the end the single patron of all neighborhoods. Organic and structural bonds could be combined. Under a tyrant the social force of festive boys and *garzoni* in their neighborhoods could be the main political force of a single city ruler.

The duke of Athens posed just such a threat in 1343. To augment his power Walter of Brienne created a bodyguard of 300 "needy *giovani* of good family" and organized six festive brigades of neighborhood *sottoposti* or non-citizens.[11] These groups' "forced vanity" in that year's Mayday and San Giovanni festivities, their geographical base, and their stone fights were not soon forgotten; the lower classes and youth of good family, both constitutionally excluded from the political process, readily served powerful men. The nightmare of a city full of bonfires with groups of toughs doing battle, all for the amusement and profit of a single patron, haunted citizens' minds.[12] Governments of fearful *vecchi* had long tried to keep their boys and *garzoni* outside politics. The experience of Walter of Brienne reinforced that bias: neighborhood identities were dangerous, so were the *garzoni* and youth who represented them, so was any family patron who sought to court these ferocious groups. Political tyranny and neighborhood identities seemed to go together. To combat the former, the city had to be ritually unified around its community of merchant rulers.

The struggle to ritually unify the city was largely successful. There were no neighborhood saints or processions, little in the way of neighborhood confraternities, and remarkably little neighborhood symbolism. Members of the adult citizen class belonged to city-wide rather than parish voluntary associations and went to the Mendicant churches rather than parish ones.[13] Societies of youth, common in the early duecento, vanished from the scene.[14] Organizations of *sottoposti* were prohibited. Any type of brigade organized for certain feasts, said the Statute of 1322, could have no more than twelve mem-

---

[11] G. Villani, XII, 8; *Ricordi storici di Filippo di Cino Rinuccini dal 1282 al 1460, colla continuazione di Alamanno e Neri suoi figli fino al 1506*, ed. G. Aiazzi (Florence, 1840), xxiv.

[12] The proportions such city-wide battles could take can be glimpsed in the stone fight described by G. Cambi, *Istorie fiorentine*, in *Delizie*, 21:136.

[13] Citizens belonged to parish *opere* by definition. But with rare exceptions these organizations met only to patch roofs and elect rectors. They had little status, minimum religious character.

[14] Boncompagno da Signa writing about 1215 said: "Ista consuetudo ... [iuvenum societates] ... fortius in Tuscia viget"; "Cedrus," in L. Rockinger, ed., *Briefsteller und Formelbücher des elften bis vierzehnten Jahrhunderts (Quellen zur Bayerischen und Deutschen Geschichte* 9, part 1) (Munich, 1863), 122 ("This custom of societies of youth ... is strongest in Tuscany"). See also R. Davidsohn, *Firenze ai tempi di Dante* (Florence, 1929), 517. But *societates iuvenum* are not found again until early quattrocento; see Trexler, "Ritual in Florence: Adolescence and Salvation in the Renaissance," in *The Pursuit of Holiness in Late Medieval and Renaissance Religion*, ed. C. Trinkaus with H. Oberman (Leiden, 1974), included in the present volume.

bers.[15] By the end of the century laws against *facciendo messere* are encountered.[16] Fiscal and judicial subdivisions within the city obviously had to be maintained, but they too had weak symbolic identities.

Neighborhood solidarities being undermined, and youth and *garzoni* being largely excluded from the representational sphere in the trecento, Florence was a poor candidate for charivaris. Unlike Genoa, it had only one baptistry and one *pieve*. Late medieval Florence fostered brotherhood, as Dino Compagni wanted to believe, only around one font.[17]

The charivari was absent in trecento Florence because the organic neighborhood solidarities that it required were suppressed. Other factors mitigated against such groups as well, but politics were determinant. The ritual unity of the city meant that if the boys or *garzoni* were to seek an object of ridicule outside their group, they would have to find it at the communal level, outside the neighborhoods. And in fact, the closest we come in pre-Medicean records to charivari Misrule is in a third area of boyish or *garzoni* activity, which took place on a communal judicial, rather than on a neighborhood stage. Here, in fact, citizens were ridiculed by outsiders. Florentine *fanciulli* occasionally shredded the bodies of criminals sentenced and usually already executed by the government. At the end of the duecento families guarded the bodies of relatives to prevent such indecencies.[18] In 1383 some 200 boys decimated the body of a follower of Giorgio Scala, and a diarist tells us that the *furia del popolo* would have done the same to the populist Scala himself if the government had not protected his body.[19] The practice continued in the quattrocento. *Fanciulli* twice disinterred Pazzi conspirators in 1478, ridiculing their bodies while adults watched, and in 1493 an image defiler's body was insulted by both boys and grown men.[20]

Here as in the charivari individual transgressors were ridiculed by boys acting for their elders. But notice the difference from the popular justice of the charivari: the boys' violence against these bodies simply reaffirmed a judgment already made by their elders and betters in government. True, boys who humiliated a corpse were, in doing so, admonishing the family of the dead man. The warning consisted in a preview of the punishment, first communal and only then popular, which awaited future transgressors. In the ritually unified city, the one regularly verifiable ridiculing activity of the young and *garzoni* simply confirmed and made more terrible the judgments of elders and betters.

[15] Those feasts were Mayday, S. Giovanni, Christmas, and Easter (*Statuti*, vol. 1: *Statuto del Capitano del popolo degli anni 1322–25* [Florence, 1910], 309).

[16] *ASF, Provvisioni* 81, fols. 211r–v (22 August 1393).

[17] D. Compagni, *Cronica delle cose occorrenti ne' tempi suoi* (Milan, 1965), 73 (II, 8). For the current Siennese practice of welcoming the newborn into the parish, see A. Dundes and A. Falassi, *La Terra in Piazza* (Berkeley, 1975), 37ff.

[18] I. Del Lungo, "Una vendetta in Firenze il giorno di San Giovanni del 1295," *Archivio Storico Italiano (ASI)*, ser. 4, 18 (1886), 387ff.

[19] Naddo da Montecatini, *Memorie Storiche*, in *Delizie*, 18:38.

[20] Luca Landucci, *Diario fiorentino*, ed. I Del Badia (Florence, 1969), 21f., 66.

We should not however imagine that a visual or moral contrast existed between the grave judgment of governmental elders and an "irresponsible" or ferocious ridicule on the part of the boys. The boys' ridicule simply extended the ritual ridicule used by the government to demonstrate its power. The proof of government's authority, after all, was its ability to shamelessly, incalculably, arbitrarily, spontaneously, and vindictively make fun of its enemies.

We see this insult ritual used in diplomatic and military affairs—the defamatory paintings, the horse- and whore-races run around the walls of enemy cities, the wagons of buffoons sent on military expeditions, the coins struck in enemy lands.[21] We find it part of the normal festive life in the city: How else are we to interpret the commune's celebration of the feasts of St. Anthony and St. Sebastian as other than ridicule of the lower classes whose revolts had been suppressed on those saints' days?[22] Most important, however, we find governmental ridicule in the judicial sphere. Indeed the government tried to monopolize the right to ridicule, perhaps in part to make boyish activity superfluous. From the moment a traitor, bankrupt, homosexual, prostitute, iconoclast, or heretic was condemned until the moment of execution or release, the Signoria of Florence insulted them. The most typical public humiliation was being made to wear the miter, a paper cap painted with dancing devils, and an equally ridiculous coat. Those pardoned by the commune wore them on their way to the church where they would be excused. Those tainted with heresy stood outside church with the miter, exposed to the humiliation of the crowd. Those going to execution wore them, as did those going to prison. One Pacchierotto was found guilty in 1492 of homosexuality and badmouthing:

> Quite a large miter was put on his head. Then he was whipped around the Piazza. Taken to the scene of his many crimes, miter on head, the victim was whipped publicly at each spot. Then he was taken to the Stinche [jail], confined perpetually, and he was put in the prison of the sodomites, thieves, and blasphemers. They waited for him with joy. When he arrived there, they made him their new captain, all happily singing for a bit of recreation. Having been so lovingly fondled, he was then forcibly put at the head of the table wearing another new miter, bigger than the first. The poor Pacchierotto cried for shame as well as from the pain of the whipping.[23]

To summarize. In this ritually unified city, elders fearful of youth and *garzoni* even if attracted to them generally sought to maintain the primacy of communal law and justice by suppressing neighborhood solidarities. Yet on the communal stage these grave men indulged in the very Misrule or ridicule they condemned in outsiders, for it was through vindictive frivolity that grave ger-

---

[21] See "The Ritual of Diplomacy" in my *Public Life.*

[22] See for example *ASF, Prov.* 74, fols. 240r–241r (25 January 1385/86).

[23] P. Villari and E. Casanova, ed., *Scelta di prediche e scritti di fra Girolamo Savonarola* (Florence, 1898), 501f.

ontocracies showed virility. By decimating bodies already ridiculed to death by their elders and betters, youth and *garzoni* imitated, rather than corrected, their elders and betters.

Lorenzan and Savonarolan Florence

From 1497 until 1502 the city of Florence was wracked by an explosion of youthful ridicule of established persons and institutions unique in republican history.[24] Savonarola's brigades of innocent *fanciulli* started it, censoring and burning books and paintings, castigating "shameless" girls, perhaps even attacking their fathers' card games. The *fanciulli*'s older brothers, wined and dined by well-off patricians (the *Compagnacci* or *Vecchi*), responded by attacking the Savonarolan children during procession, smashing sacred things both outside and inside sacred places at sacred times. Sermons were conducted amidst the smell of sulphur and manure, the racket of *giovani* troublemakers (apparently without Rough Music), and the presence of horses and goats introduced by the friar's opponents. While Savonarola and his two companions burned in the main square in 1498, *fanciulli*, by now converted to the opposition, tried to bring down the bodies with stones so that they could decimate the remains. The years after the execution were, in one chronicler's words, "as if hell had been opened."[25] Transvestites created scandals among pious widows. City toughs forced sympathizers of the dead prophet to kneel before live owls meant to ironically represent the "true light" of which Savonarola had so often spoken. Obscene literature about the friar's alleged sexual exploits with novices was hawked in the streets. Not until the papal emissary Giles of Viterbo came to the city in late 1502 was some order restored.[26] In these *anni mirabiles* one finds *fanciulli* and *giovani*, together or in opposition, acting for adult society, upholding one morality or another not only in the wake of communal justice, but as true executors. How does one explain this unprecedented explosion in the light of the quiescence of youth and *garzoni* in previous Florentine history?

Part of the answer lies in the fact that during the quattrocento adolescents, youth, and *garzoni* were assigned public roles in Florentine communal life that they had never before enjoyed. Something similar was happening everywhere in Europe, but neither the links to European developments nor the causes of this development in Florence can be examined here. We must be satisfied with a mere description. First, *giovani* of good family became identified as those who celebrated communal victories as well as welcomed and entertained visiting foreigners. Ephemeral Florentine groups of *giovani*, known by names like "the Helmet," "Globe," and "Flower," seem to be of the same

---

[24] Compare what follows with Natalie Zemon Davis's view that the events of the 1490s represented the "persistent" spirit of *scampanata* ("Some Tasks and Themes in the Study of Popular Religion," in *The Pursuit of Holiness in Late Medieval and Renaissance Religion*, 324).

[25] Landucci, *Diario*, 71.

[26] In Parenti's view; see Schnitzer, *Quellen*, 4:300.

genre as the contemporary Venetian *Compagnie delle Calze* which also played a significant role in their city's relations with the outside world.[27] In both cases, "polished youth" increasingly served as intermediaries or "disarmers" who facilitated the cities' relations with foreign powers.

Secondly, adolescents were identified in the quattrocento as important to their parents' individual and group salvation. Organized into age-specific confraternities, these teenagers through their sacred plays and processions contributed to the perpetuation of their families and their fathers' commune.[28] The adolescent confraternities endured as corporations while their older brothers' societies died soon after their festive cause had passed, always suspect because of the *giovani*'s potential for violence. But both the organized pious adolescents and the festive *giovani*—neither indulging in ridicule—expressed a central truth about Florentine society at the end of the quattrocento: foreign visitors, cities, governments, and families could not be honorable or endure without youthful approbation. In the midst of dire signs from heaven in 1492, the *popolo* could think of no other way of placating God than a procession of *fanciulli* dressed in white. Clearly aware that Florence's children had, disgracefully, become the city's salvation, a Guicciardini commented on this procession of angelic children: "You see what we have come to."[29] In the same years another grave male, Piero Parenti, recorded the fact that boys now sat together in church—that they had in effect surfaced as a distinct part of a broadened community—and branded this queer sight "both ridiculous and devout."[30] Ridicule, in the garb of innocence, had come to the old republic.

Underway from the early quattrocento, this incorporation of the young into the concept of the community was immeasurably furthered in 1469 by the unprecedented accession to power of a boy, Lorenzo de' Medici ("still an adolescent," says one near contemporary, "since he was only twenty") and his still younger brother Giuliano.[31] Their very position in Florentine society revolutionized the status of all youth, and the two Magnificents nurtured their age-cohorts. It was they who attended the adolescents' plays, they who as *messeri* of *giovani* brigades outfitted their youthful friends with devices, coats-of-arms, food, and other amusements, they who appointed their sons *messeri* of confraternities. Savonarola was the heir of Lorenzo. When he told his listeners that the hope of Florence was in its young, he only repeated what Medici sychophants had been saying for years. The end of the quattrocento therefore represented a culminating turn away from the cultural hegemony of the

---

[27] The Florentine companies are named in G. O. Corazzini, ed., "Diario fiorentino di Bartolomeo di Michele Del Corazza," *ASI*, ser. 5, 14 (1894): 254f. On the Venetian Calze, see L. Venturi, "Le compagnie della Calza (secc. XV–XVI)," *Nuovo Archivio Veneto* (*Archivio Veneto*, ser. 3, 16–17 [1908–9]: 161–221, 140–233).

[28] On the confraternities, see my "Adolescence and Salvation."

[29] R. Ridolfi, *Studi savonaroliani* (Florence, 1935), 263.

[30] Schnitzer, *Quellen*, 4:96 (Parenti).

[31] N. Valori, *Laurentii Medicii Vita*, in F. Villani, *Liber de civitatis florentiae famosis civibus* (Florence, 1847), 166.

elders or *vecchi*. In the Savonarolan years, *fanciulli* were the moral beacons of the commune, their older brothers the spokesmen for traditional mores. In the Last Republic (1527–1530), the *giovani* emerged as the moral saviors of Florence.

The Cinquecento and Grand Duchy

When Giles of Viterbo came to Florence in 1502 with the task of ending the "hell" of youthful activity, there could be no question of returning to that ritually unified, *vecchi*-dominated city of yore. Not only had youth and adolescents become important forces in the city, the *garzoni* or shop boys as well had begun to assume comparable importance. Further, all these groups were taking on neighborhood colorings which they had not had since the time of Walter of Brienne. Savonarola's boys, for example, were organized according to the city's quarters, their officers including a peacemaker to settle arguments among the *fanciulli* of each quarter.[32] Hints of developing neighborhood associations of shop artisans abound, though they have not been studied. A society of wool carders existed in the later 1480s and early 1490s, for example, one of several groups with neighborhood and occupational focuses which were tolerated by the Medici regime.[33] A century before, organized *Ciompi* were feared. Now they organized with the blessing of the regime. By the cinquecento, the descendants of Lorenzo would maintain their power through neighborhood groups of *garzoni*, as well as through youth groups.

The cinquecento was the golden age of the so-called *potenze*, the first neighborhood festive associations in Florence since the time of the duke of Athens. Plebeian by definition—though sometimes with a youth of good family associated for status—these artisan groups seem to have grown up under the wing of Lorenzo, perhaps as Singleton has suggested playing a large part in the increasingly elaborate Carnival celebrations of the last dozen years of the quattrocento.[34] With the expulsion of the Medici in 1494, these groups seem to have become the darlings of powerful families competing for authority in the refurbished republic. When in 1501 we first encounter them by name, their activity reflects at once a carnival, familial, and official orientation: the Melarancia group performed on Mayday—a carnival-type day—but Mayday was also the date a new Florentine government entered office, and this group celebrated that entrance. Finally, it was obviously financially supported by the Frescobaldi family, since one of that family's children had an honored place in its presentation.[35] With the return of the Medici in 1512, however, the *potenze* soon became neighborhood instruments of Medici power. Under that family's aegis, they developed into social welfare organizations for the *sottoposti*, some-

[32] Trexler, "Adolescence and Salvation," 255.
[33] A. D'Addario, *Aspetti della controriforma a Firenze* (Rome, 1972), 66.
[34] C. Singleton, ed., *Nuovi canti carnascialeschi del Rinascimento* (Modena, 1940), 11.
[35] Cambi, *Istoria*, 21:159.

thing quite new in Florentine history. They disappeared from the city's records in the 1620s.

The interaction of the *potenze* and the Medici is already clear in a carnival song written before the family's expulsion in 1494. In it, a feigned Spanish embassy comes to Florence to celebrate the conquest of Granada (1492) and presents gifts to a play emperor—doubtless the Emperor of the Meadow (*Prato*), sovereign of all the *potenze* throughout the succeeding century.[36] Through the *Imperatore del Prato*, members of the ruling family are praised, as in another pre-1494 song where "the son of Clarice," probably Piero di Lorenzo, is vaunted.[37] Foot-*potenze* armed with fake helmets, swords, and lances came out of their neighborhood kingdoms, duchies, and counties to receive their flags from Pope Leo X (Medici) in 1515, and mounted *potenze* celebrated Clement VII's (Medici) election in 1523.[38] Probably suppressed during the Last Republic (1527-1530) as "creations of tyrants," they were revived by Alessandro de' Medici in 1532, who gave them rich gifts in exchange for their celebration of his marriage to the German emperor's daughter.[39] From that point on, the link between the *potenze* and the ruling family could not have been more explicit. By funding one or two *potenze*, the grand dukes stimulated other rich men to compete in dressing up others. All then came before their emperor and promised this play sovereign "to shed their blood and give their lives in the service of" the real sovereign, the prince of Florence and Tuscany.[40]

There were inconveniences. One power might seek to strike alliances with neighboring powers. It might set up barriers to tax those passing its borders. Several *potenze* might engage in pitched battles to determine in whose "kingdom" a Medici palace lay.[41] But the Medici had learned that the neighborhood youth and *garzoni* helped legitimate their power. By controlling the appointment of the *Imperatore del Prato*, the family could regulate these neighborhood disputes through that Grand Sovereign's *libro di confini*. If all else failed, the grand duke could call out his mercenaries.[42] The Medici had developed two elements of the charivaris, neighborhood solidarities and moral roles for outsiders. As the richest family in the city, they above all others ran no risk of ridicule, for, meeting the stock threat of such groups, they could always turn latent ridicule to approbation through liberality. The city stage, finally, could support the ridicule of the neighborhoods.

---

[36] C. Singleton, ed., *Canti carnascialeschi del Rinascimento* (Bari, 1936), 75.

[37] Ibid., 85.

[38] Cambi, *Istoria*, 22:249f.

[39] Ibid., 23:117. Donato Giannotti recommended abolition of the *potenze* in 1527 or 1528 because of their tyrannical origins and because they "tolgono riputazione al publico, ed acresconla a' privati" (G. R. Sanesi, ed. "Un discorso sconosciuto di D. G. intorno alla milizia," *ASI*, ser. 5, 8 [1891]: 25) ("take reputation away from the public and increase it among private [persons]").

[40] Plaisance, "Politique culturelle," 143f.

[41] Giuliano de' Ricci, *Cronaca (1532-1606)*, ed. G. Sapori (Milan, 1972), 222f.

[42] Ibid., 223.

Misrule found her throne in absolutist Florence. We will not know her neighborhood shapes until the *potenze*'s neighborhood activities are studied, but her presence on the civic stage is quite clear. Already in 1493 a wagon full of Fools had graced the celebration not of Carnival but of St. John's Day, most sacred of all Florentine feasts.[43] On the feast of that patron in 1514 the Fools can be viewed in action. Flanked on all sides by a hoard of devils, Cambi tells us, the Ship of Fools was pulled through the streets on 23 June.[44] In preparation for the fun, the sponsor of this apparatus had arranged the night before for one particular person to be arrested by the police so that he could be ridiculed the following day. And as the festive bark went through the city that day, a second person was seized from the crowd, hooked onto the Ship by the devils, put to oar, and whipped with an air-filled leather truncheon.

Cambi tells us why these two men were ridiculed. Maestro Antonio di Pierozzo da Vespignano was

> ... a hood maker who was a bit of a half-wit, but wordy and amusing.... They put him on the said ship in a coat and black hood, his normal attire, for he was quite raggedly dressed, for he was poor. And those devils tore [the clothes] from his back. I think they gave him new clothes [later].

Giovanni Tancredi on the other hand was a wool porter from Santa Croce:

> He was much more stupid than the said maestro Antonio, for he could not do anything but carry wool. He had never thought about becoming a master, for in fifty years he never changed his trade.

This single example of particular ridicule in the festive history of republican Florence was directed, we see, not against "crimes" typically associated with charivari ridicule, nor against the regime, but against individuals who, economically immobile, were stupidly poor. Republican Florence had had little use for adolescents, youth, or *garzoni*, because it feared them. Grand ducal Florence would watch the *potenze* vaunt economic virtues, ridicule themselves, and take alms from a political power they took for granted. When the kingdoms of Misrule did finally issue from their neighborhoods, they wore the stockings of the Medici and fooled no one.

---

[43] The *carro sive trionfo de' buffoni* was built by Francesco di Piero Baldovini (*ASF, Monte Comune*, 2088, 14 June 1493).

[44] *Istorie*, 22:45, for this and the following citations.

Bibliography

Alberti, Leonbattista degli. "De Iciarchia." In *Opere Volgari*, edited by C. Grayson, vol. 2. Bari: G. Laterza, 1966.
——. *I Libri della Famiglia*. Turin: Einaudi, 1969.
Alighieri, Dante. *La divina commedia*. Florence, 1896.
Archivio storico italiano (ASI).
Ariès, P. *Centuries of Childhood*. New York: Random House, 1965.
Bakan, D. *Slaughter of the Innocents*. San Francisco: Jossey-Bass, 1971.
Bandini, A. *Specimen Literaturae Florentinae Saeculi XV*. Florence, 1751.
Banfi, L. ed. *Sacre Rappresentazioni del Quattrocento*. Turin: Union Tipografico-Editrice Torinese, 1963.
Bec, C. *Les marchands écrivains. Affaires et humanisme à Florence 1375-1434*. Paris: Mouton, 1967.
Benivieni, Hieronymo. *Commento di . . . sopra a piu sue canzone e sonetti dello amore et della belleza divina*. Florence, 1500.
Bergues, H. et al. *La prevention des naissances dans la famille*. Paris: Presses Universitaire de France, 1960.
Bernardino da Siena. *Le prediche volgari inedite*. Edited by D. Pacetti. Siena, 1935.
Boccaccio, Giovanni. *Corbaccio*. In *Opere*, edited by C. Segre. Milan: U. Mursia & C., 1966.
Bode, H. "Die Kindestötung und ihre Bestrafung im Nürnberg des Mittelalters." *Archiv für Strafrecht und Strafprozess* 61 (1914): 430–81.
Boncompagno da Signa. "Cedrus." In *Briefsteller und Formelbücher des elften bis vierzehnten Jahrhunderts (Quellen zur Bayerischen und Deutschen Geschichte 9, part 1)*, edited by L. Rockinger. Munich, 1863.
Bossi, Egidio, *Aegidii Bossii patritii mediolanensis . . . tractatus varii, qui omnem fere criminalem materiam. . . .* Venice, 1574.
Boswell, John. *The Kindness of Strangers: The Abandonment of Children in Western Europe from Late Antiquity to the Renaissance*. New York: Pantheon, 1988.

Brissaud, Y. -B. "L'infanticide à la fin du moyen âge, ses motivations psychologiques et sa répression." *Revue historique de droit français et étranger* 50 (1972): 229–56.

Brouardel, P. *L'infanticide.* Paris, 1897.

Brucker, G. "The Florentine *Popolo Minuto* and Its Political Role." In *Violence and Civil Disorder*, edited by L. Martines.

——, ed. *The Society of Renaissance Florence.* New York: Harper & Row, 1971.

Bruscoli, G. *L'archivio del R. Spedale di Santa Maria degl'Innocenti di Firenze.* Florence, 1911.

——. *Lo spedale di Santa Maria degl'Innocenti di Firenze.* Florence, 1900.

Caillois, R. *Les jeux et les hommes.* Paris: Gallimard, 1958.

Calzolai, C. C. *Frate Antonio Pierozzi.* Rome: Ars grafica editorialis presbyterum, 1960.

Cambi, Giovanni. *Istorie fiorentine.* In *Delizie*, vols. 20–23.

Cavalcanti, Giovanni. *Istorie Fiorentine.* Edited by G. Di Pino. Milan, 1944.

Chiassino, G., and M. Natale. *Ricerche sulla mortalità infantile.* Rome, s.d.

Chojnacki, S. "Political Adulthood in Fifteenth-Century Venice." *American Historical Review* 91 (1986): 791–810.

Cianfogni, P. *Memorie istoriche dell' ambrosiana imperial basilica di S. Lorenzo di Firenze....* 3 vols. Florence, 1804–1817. Assembled and continued by D. Moreni.

Clavasio, Angelo de. *Summa Angelica de casibus conscientiae.* Venice, 1487.

Coleman, E. "L'infanticide dans le Haut Moyen Age." *Annales E.S.C.* 29 (1974): 315–35.

——. "Medieval Marriage Characteristics." *The Journal of Interdisciplinary History* 2 (1971): 205–19.

——. "A Note on Medieval Peasant Demography." *Historical Methods Newsletter* 5 (1972): 53–58.

Compagni, Dino. *Cronica delle cose occorrenti ne' tempi suoi.* Milan: Rizzoli, 1965.

Corrain, C. and P. Zampini. *Documenti etnografici e folkloristici nei sinodi diocesani italiani.* Bologna: Forni, 1970.

D'Accone, F. "A Documentary History of Music at the Florentine Cathedral and Baptistry during the Fifteenth Century." Ph.D. diss., Harvard University, 1960.

D'Addario, A. *Aspetti della controriforma a Firenze.* Rome: Ministero dell'Interno, 1972.

D'Ancona, A. *Origini del teatro italiano.* 2 vols. Turin, 1891.

——, ed. *Sacre Rappresentazioni dei secoli XIV, XV e XVI.* 3 vols. Florence, 1872.

Davidsohn, R. *Firenze ai tempi di Dante.* Florence, 1929.

——. *Forschungen zur Geschichte von Florenz.* 4 vols. Berlin, 1896–1908.

——. *Storia di Firenze.* 8 vols. Florence: Sansoni, 1956–68.

Davis, N. Zemon. "The Reasons of Misrule: Youth Groups and Charivaris in Sixteenth-Century France." *Past and Present* 50 (1971): 41–75.

——. "Some Tasks and Themes in the Study of Popular Religion." In *The Pursuit of Holiness in Late Medieval and Renaissance Religion*, edited by C. Trinkaus with H. Oberman, Leiden: E. J. Brill, 1974.

Debenedetti, S. "Sui più antichi doctores puerorum a Firenze." *Studi Medievali* 2 (1906-7): 338-42.

Del Corazza, Bartolommeo. "Diario Fiorentino di Bartolommeo Del Corazza, anni 1405-1438." Edited by G. O. Corazzini. *ASI*, ser. 5, 14 (1894): 233-98.

Del Lungo, I. *Dino Compagni e la sua cronica*. Florence, 1879.

——. *Florentia. Uomini e cose del quattrocento*. Florence, 1897.

——. "Una vendetta in Firenze il giorno di San Giovanni del 1295." *ASI*, ser 4, 18 (1886): 355-409.

Del Migliore, Ferdinando. *Firenze città nobilissima illustrata*. Florence, 1684.

Del Vecchio, B. *Le seconde nozze del coniuge superstite*. Florence, 1885.

Delaruelle, E. "La vie religieuse dans les pays de langue française à la fin du XVᵉ siècle." In *Colloque d'histoire religieuse (Lyon, octobre 1963)*. Grenoble: Imprimerie Allier, 1963.

Delaruelle, E., et al., *L'Église au temps du Grand Schisme et de la crise conciliaire (1378-1449)*. Fliche et Martin, 14, part 2. Paris: Bloud & Gay, 1964.

Delizie degli eruditi toscani. Edited by I. da San Luigi. 24 vols. Florence, 1770-1789.

Demographic Yearbook 19 (1967).

Dominici, Giovanni. *On the Education of Children*. Edited by A. Coté. Washington, 1927.

Dundes, A., and A. Falassi. *La Terra in Piazza*. Berkeley: Univ. of California Press, 1975.

Durkheim, E. *L'évolution pédagogique en France*. Paris, 1938.

Eisenbichler, K. "Plays at the Archangel Raphael's." *Fifteenth-Century Studies* 13 (1988): 519-34.

Eisenstadt, S. N. "Archetypal Patterns of Youth." In *The Challenge of Youth*, edited by E. Erikson. New York: Doubleday, 1963.

Erikson, E. H. "Ontogeny of Ritualization in Man." In *A Discussion of Ritualization. See* Huxley.

Fedele, F. *De relationibus medicorum*. Palermo, 1602.

Felber, A. "Unzucht und Kindsmord in der Rechtsprechung der freien Reichsstadt Nördlingen vom 15. bis 19. Jahrhundert." Ph.D. diss., Univ. of Bonn, 1961.

Ficino, Marsilio. *Opera Omnia*. Turin: Bottega d'Erasmo, 1962.

Firenzuola, Agnolo. *Le novelle*. Edited by E. Ragni. Rome: G. Salerno, 1971.

Gardner, L. I. "Deprivation Dwarfism." *Scientific American* (July, 1972): 76-82.

Gargin, L., ed. *Lo studio teologico e la biblioteca dei Domenicani a Padova nel tre e quattrocento*. Padua: Editrice Antenore, 1971.

Garin, E. "Desideri di riforma nell'oratoria del quattrocento." In his *La cultura filosofica del Rinascimento Italiano*. Florence: Sansoni, 1961.

——, ed. *L'educazione umanistica in Italia*. Bari: G. Laterza, 1949.

——. *Italian Humanism*. New York: Harper & Row, 1965.

——, ed. *Il pensiero pedagogico dello umanesimo*. Florence: Sansoni, 1958.

Garzoni, T. *La piazza universale di tutte le professioni del mondo*. Venice, 1665.

Gavitt, P. *Charity and Children in Renaissance Florence: the Ospedale degli Innocenti, 1410-1536*. Ann Arbor: Univ. of Michigan Press, 1990.

Giannotti, Donato, "Un discorso sconosciuto di D. G. intorno alla milizia." Edited by G. R. Sanesi. *ASI*, ser. 5, 8 (1891): 3-27.

Ginzburg, C. *I benandanti*. Turin: Einaudi, 1966.

Gnerghi, G. "Gerolamo Savonarola e i fanciulli." *Rassegna Nazionale* 117 (1901): 345–70.

Godefroy, D. *Codicis Iustiniani ... libri 12*. Lyon, 1662.

Goldthwaite, R. *Private Wealth in Renaissance Florence: A Study of Four Families*. Princeton: Princeton Univ. Press, 1968.

Gori, P. *Le feste fiorentine attraverso i secoli. Le feste per San Giovanni*. Florence, 1926.

Gråberg da Hemsö, I., ed. "La vita di Giovanni da Empoli ... scritta da Girolamo da Empoli suo zio." *ASI* 3, *Appendice* (1846).

Guasti, C. *Le feste di San Giovanni Battista in Firenze*. Florence, 1884.

Guasti, C., and A. Gherardi, eds. *I capitoli del comune di Firenze*, vol. 2. Florence, 1893.

Guicciardini, Francesco. *The History of Florence*. New York: Harper & Row, 1970.

Hanway, J. *Letters on the Importance of the Rising Generation of the Laboring Part of our Fellow-Subjects*, vol. 1. London, 1767.

Hatfield, R. "The Compagnia De' Magi." *Journal of the Warburg and Courtauld Institutes* 33 (1970): 107–61.

Hausfater, G., and S. Blaffer Hrdy, eds. *Infanticide: Comparative and Evolutionary Perspectives*. New York: Aldine, 1984.

Hawes, J., and N. Hiner. *Children in Historical and Comparative Perspective: An International Handbook and Research Guide*. New York: Greenwood, 1991.

Henry of Susa (Hostiensis). *Summa Aurea*. Turin: Bottega d'Erasmo, 1963.

Herlihy, D. *Medieval and Renaissance Pistoia*. New Haven: Yale Univ. Press, 1967.

——. "Vieillir à Florence au Quattrocento." *Annales E.S.C.* 24 (1969): 1338–52.

Herlihy, D., and C. Klapisch-Zuber. *Les toscans et leurs familles*. Paris: E.H.E.S.S., 1978.

Hoffer, P. *Murdering Mothers: Infanticide in England and New England, 1558–1803*. New York: New York Univ. Press, 1981.

Hügel, F. S. *Die Findelhäuser und das Findelwesen Europas*. Vienna, 1863.

Huizinga, J. *Homo Ludens*. Boston: Beacon Press, 1950.

Hunt, D. *Parents and Children in History: The Psychology of Family Life in Early Modern France*. New York: Basic Books, 1970.

Huxley, J., ed. *A Discussion on Ritualization of Behaviour in Animals and Man. Philosophical Transactions of the Royal Society of London*, ser. B, 251 (1966): 247–526.

Institoris, Heinrich, *Malleus Maleficarum*. 1486.

Jacquot, J., and E. Konigson. *Les fêtes de la Renaissance*. 3 vols. Paris: C.N.R.S., 1956–75.

Kertzer, D. "Gender Ideology and Infant Abandonment in Nineteenth-Century Italy." *Journal of Interdisciplinary History* 22 (1991): 1–25.

Kirshner, J. "Papa Eugenio IV e il Monte Comune." *ASI* 127 (1969): 339–82.

Klapisch-Zuber, C. *Women, Family, and Ritual in Renaissance Italy*. Chicago: Univ. of Chicago Press, 1985.

Kohler, J. *Studien aus dem Strafrecht. Das Strafrecht der Italienischen Statuten vom 12. bis zum 16. Jahrhundert*. Mannheim, 1896.

Kohler, J., and W. Scheel, eds. *Die Bambergische Halsgerichtsordnung* (1507). Halle, 1902.

Kristeller, P. O. "Lay Religious Traditions and Florentine Platonism." In his *Studies in Renaissance Thought and Letters.* Rome: Edizioni di Storia e Letteratura, 1956.

Kumer, Z. *Balada o nevesti detomorilki.* Ljubljana: Slovenska akademija znanostiin umetnosti, 1963.

Lallemand, L. *Histoire des enfants abandonnés et délaissés.* Paris, 1885.

Lami, J. *Sanctae Ecclesiae Florentinae Monumenta.* Florence, 1758.

Landucci, Luca. *Diario Fiorentino dal 1450 al 1516 di Luca Landucci.* Edited by I. Del Badia. Florence: Studio Biblos, 1969.

Langer, W. "Checks on Population Growth: 1750-1850." *Scientific American* (February, 1972): 92-99.

———. *Political and Social Upheaval, 1832-1852.* New York: Harper & Row, 1969.

Lanza, A., ed. *Lirici Toscani del Quattrocento.* Rome: Bulzoni, 1973.

Lastri, M. *Ricerche sull'antica e moderna popolazione della città di Firenze per mezzo dei registri del battistero di S. Giovanni dal 1451 al 1774.* Florence, 1775.

Lea, H. C. *Materials Toward a History of Witchcraft.* 3 vols. Philadelphia, 1939.

Léauté, J., ed. *Recherches sur l'infanticide (1955-1965).* Paris: Dalloz, 1968.

Leges Henrici Primi. Edited by L. J. Downer. Oxford: Oxford Univ. Press, 1972.

Litovskii statut 1588 goda. Edited by I. Lappo. Vol. 22. Kaunas, 1938.

Litovskii statut v Moskovskom perevode-redaktsii, Edited by I. Lappo. Iur'ev, 1916.

Luotto, P. *Il vero Savonarola.* Florence, 1900.

Machiavelli, Niccolò, *History of Florence.* New York: Harper and Brothers, 1960.

Manni, D. *Osservazioni istoriche sopra i sigilli antichi.* Vol. 21. Florence, 1770.

Marinelli, O., ed. "La Compagnia di Disciplinati di S. Domenico in Firenze." *Bolletino della deputazione di storia patria per l'Umbria,* ser. 1, 66 (1969): 211-40.

Martines, L. *The Social World of the Florentine Humanists.* Princeton: Princeton Univ. Press, 1963.

———, ed. *Violence and Civil Disorder in Italian Cities, 1200-1500.* Berkeley: Univ. of California Press, 1972.

Mathes, H. "On the Date of Lorenzo's *Sacra Rappresentazione di San Giovanni e Paolo.* February 17, 1491." *Aevum* 25 (1851): 324-29.

Meersseman, G. "Disciplinati e penitenti nel duecento." In *Il Movimento dei Disciplinati.*

Molho, A. *Florentine Public Finances in the Early Renaissance.* Cambridge, Mass: Harvard Univ. Press, 1971.

Molho, A., and F. Sznura, eds. *Alle bocche della piazza: Diario di anonimo fiorentino (1382-1401).* Florence: Leo. S. Olschki, 1992.

Molinari, C. *Spettacoli fiorentini del quattrocento.* Venice: N. Pozza, 1961.

Monti, G. M. *Le Confraternite Medievali dell'Alta e Media Italia.* Florence, 1927.

Moorman, J. R. H. *The Grey Friars in Cambridge, 1225-1538.* Cambridge: Cambridge Univ. Press, 1952.

Morçay, R. *Saint Antonin. Archevêque de Florence (1389–1459)*. Paris, 1914.

Moreni, D. *see* Cianfogni, P.

Il Movimento dei Disciplinati nel settimo centenario dal suo inizio. Perugia: Deputazione di storia patria per l'Umbria, 1962.

Murray, M. "Child-Sacrifice among European Witches." *Man* 18 (1918): 60–62.

Nardi, Jacopo. *Istorie della città di Firenze*. Florence, 1888.

Nevizzani, Giovanni, *Silva nuptialis bonis referta non modicis*. Lyon, 1545.

Newbigin, N., ed. *Nuovo Corpus di Sacre Rappresentationi fiorentine del Quattrocento*. Bologna: Commissione per i testi di lingua, 1983.

Niccoli, Ottavia, "Le Compagnie di Bambini nell'Italia del Rinascimento." *Rivista Storica Italiana* 101 (1989): 346–74.

Njal's Saga. Edited by M. Magnusson and H. Pálsson. Baltimore: Penguin, 1966.

Noonan, J. *Contraception*. Cambridge, Mass: Harvard Univ. Press, 1966.

Origo, I. "The Domestic Enemy: Eastern Slaves in Tuscany in the Fourteenth and Fifteenth Centuries." *Speculum* 30 (1955): 321–66.

———. *The Merchant of Prato*. New York: Knopf, 1957.

Orlandi, S. *S. Antonio*. Florence: Il Rosario, 1960.

Paatz, E., and W. Paatz, *Die Kirchen von Florenz*. 6 vols. Frankfurt, 1940–54.

Passerini, L. *Notizie storiche dello spedale degl'Innocenti di Firenze*. Florence, 1853.

———. *Storia degli stabilimenti di beneficienza e d'istruzione elementare della città di Firenze*. Florence, 1853.

Penlikäinen, J. *The Nordic Dead-Child Tradition*. Helsinki: Suomalainen tiedeakatemia, 1968.

Pertile, A. *Storia del diritto italiano*. Vol. 5. Bologna: A. Forni, 1966.

Picotti, G. B. *La jeunesse de Léon X*. Paris, 1931.

Pinaeus, S. *De virginitatis notis, gravitate, et partu*. Lyon, 1650.

Pinto, G. "Il personale, le balie, i salariati dell'Ospedale di San Gallo di Firenze, negli anni 1395–1426. Note per la storia del salariato nelle città medievali." *Ricerche storiche* 4 (1974): 113–68.

Pitti, Buonaccorso. *Cronica di Buonaccorso Pitti*. Edited by A. Bacchi della Lega. Bologna, 1905.

Plaisance, M. "La politique culturelle de Côme I et les fêtes annuelles à Florence de 1541 à 1550." *See* Jacquot and Konigson, *Les fetes*, vol. 3.

Platz, W. *Geschichte des Verbrechens der Aussetzung*. Stuttgart, 1876.

Pola Falletti Villafalletto, G. C. *Associazioni giovanili e feste antiche*. Vol. 1. Milan, 1939.

———. *La juventus attraverso i secoli*. Monza: Fratelli Bocca, 1953.

Pucci, Antonio. "Le Proprietà di Mercato Vecchio." In *Delizie*, 6:272–74.

Ransel, D. *Mothers of Misery: Child Abandonment in Russia*. Princeton: Princeton Univ. Press, 1988.

Relazione storica-descritiva del regio spedale degli Innocenti (Brefotrofio) di Firenze. Florence, 1912.

Reumont, A. von. Note in *ASI*, ser. 3, 20 (1874): 190–91.

Ricci, Giuliano de'. *Cronaca (1532–1606)*. Edited by G. Sapori. Milan: Riccardo Ricciani, 1972.

Richa, G. *Notizie istoriche delle chiese fiorentine*, 10 vols. Florence, 1754–62.

Ridolfi, R. *The Life of Francesco Guicciardini*. New York: Alfred A. Knopf, 1968.

———. *Studi savonaroliani*. Florence, 1935.

———. *Vita di Girolamo Savonarola*. Rome: Bellardetti, 1952.

Rinuccini, Filippo di Cino. *Ricordi storici di Filippo di Cino Rinuccini dal 1282 al 1460, colla continuazione di Alamanno e Neri suoi figli fino al 1506*. Edited by G. Aiazzi. Florence, 1840.

Rodericus de Castro, *Medicus-Politicus*. Hamburg, 1614.

Rossi, V. *Il Quattrocento*. Milan: F. Vallardi, 1964.

Rubinstein, N. "I primi anni del Consiglio Maggiore di Firenze." *ASI* 112 (1954): 154–229, 321–47.

Sacchetti, Franco, *Il trecentonovelle*. Edited by V. Pernicone. Florence: Sansoni, 1946.

Salimbene De Adam, *Cronica*, ed. G. Scalia. Bari: G. Laterza, 1966.

Santoni, L. *Raccolta di notizie storiche riguardanti le chiese dell'arci-diogesi di Firenze*. Florence, 1847.

Savonarola, Girolamo, *Edizione nazionale delle Opere*. General editor, R. Ridolfi. Rome: A. Belardetti, 1955–.

Schnitzer, J., ed. *Quellen und Forschungen zur Geschichte Savonarolas*. 4 vols. Munich and Leipzig, 1902–10.

———. *Savonarola*. Milan, 1931.

Scot, Reginald. *The Discoverie of Witchcraft*. Edited by M. Summers. Great Britain, 1930.

Scoti-Bertinelli, U. "Il carnevale del 1495 a Firenze." In *A. V. Cian, I suoi scolari dell'università di Pisa*. Pisa, 1909.

Scremin, L. "Savonarola educatore e la psicologia sessuale." *Genesis. Rassegna di studi sessuali ed eugenica* 12 (1932): 86–100.

Seay, A. "The 15th-Century Cappella at Santa Maria del Fiore in Florence." *Journal of the American Musicological Society* 11 (1958): 45–55.

Semichon, E. *Histoire des enfants abandonnés depuis l'antiquité jusqu'à nos jours*. Paris, 1880.

Sherwood, J. *Poverty in Eighteenth-Century Spain: The Women and Children of the Inclusa*. Toronto: Univ. of Toronto Press, 1988.

Shorter, E. "Illegitimacy, Sexual Revolution, and Social Change in Modern Europe." *The Journal of Interdisciplinary History* 2 (1971): 237–72.

Singleton, C., ed. *Canti carnascialeschi del Rinascimento*. Bari, 1936.

———. *Nuovi canti carnascialeschi del Rinascimento*. Modena, 1940.

Somogyi, S. "Sulla mascolinità delle nascite a Firenze dal 1451 al 1774." *Rivista italiana di demografia e statistica* 4 (1950): 465seq.

Starn, R. "Francesco Guicciardini and his Brothers." In *Renaissance Studies in Honor of Hans Baron*, edited by A. Molho and J. A. Tedeschi. Dekalb: Northern Illinois Univ. Press, 1971.

Statuta populi et communis florentinae (1415). 3 vols. Fribourg, 1778.

Statuti della repubblica fiorentina. Edited by R. Caggese. Vol. 1: *Statuto del Capitano del popolo degli anni 1322–25*. Florence, 1910. Vol. 2: *Statuto del Podestà dell'anno 1325*. Florence, 1921.

Statutum bladii Reipublicae Florentinae (1348). Edited by G. Masi. Milan, 1934.

Strozzi, Alessandra Macinghi negli, *Lettere di una gentildonnna fiorentina del secolo XV ai figliuoli esuli.* Edited by C. Guasti. Florence, 1877.

Tacchi Venturi, P. *Storia della compagnia di Gesú in Italia.* Rome: Civiltà Cattolica, 1950.

Tansillo, Luigi. *La Balia.* Vercelli, 1767.

Thirsh, J. "The Family." *Past and Present* 27 (1964): 116–22.

Thomas, K. "Work and Leisure in Pre-Industrial Society." *Past and Present,* 29 (1964): 50–62.

Thomson, A. *Barnkvävningen.* Lund: C. W. K. Gleerup, 1960.

Thorgillson, Ari. *The Books of the Icelanders.* Edited by H. Hermannson. Ithaca, 1930.

Tomagni, G. D. *Dell'eccellentia de l'huomo sopra quella de la donna.* Venice, 1565.

Torrente, C. *Las Procesiones Sagradas.* Washington D.C., 1932.

Toschi, P. "La teoria del principe nella rappresentazione sacra di Lorenzo de' Medici." *Rivista Italiana del Dramma* 4 (1940): 3–20.

Traversari, Ambrogio. *Latinae epistolae....* Vol. 2. Edited by L. Mehus. Florence, 1759.

Trexler, R. "Le célibat à la fin du Moyen Age: Les religieuses de Florence." *Annales E.S.C.* 27 (1972): 1329–50.

——. "Charity and the Defense of Urban Elites in the Italian Communes." In *The Rich, the Well-Born and the Powerful: Elites and Upper Classes in History,* edited by F. Jaher. Urbana, 1973.

——. *Public Life in Renaissance Florence.* New York: Academic Press, 1980.

——. "Ritual Behavior in Renaissance Florence: The Setting." *Medievalia et Humanistica* 3 (1972): 125–44.

——. *Synodal Law, in Florence and Fiesole, 1306–1518.* Vatican City, 1971.

Trinkaus, C., with H. Oberman, eds. *The Pursuit of Holiness in Late Medieval and Renaissance Religion.* Leiden: E. J. Brill, 1974.

Tudeschi, Niccolò dei. *Lectura super quinque libros Decretalium.* Basel, 1487.

Valori, Niccolò. *Laurentii Medicii Vita.* In F. Villani, *Liber de civitatis florentiae famosis civibus.* Florence, 1847.

Van Der Meer, F. *Augustine the Bishop.* New York: Harper & Row, 1961.

Van Dülmen, R. *Frauen vor Gericht: Kindsmord in der frühen Neuzeit.* Frankfurt am Main: Fischer Verlag, 1991.

Varchi, Benedetto. *Storia Fiorentina.* Florence: Salani, 1963.

Vasari, Giorgio. *Le opere.* Edited by G. Milanesi. 9 vols. Florence: Sansoni, 1973.

Vasoli, C. "L'attesa della nuova èra in ambienti e gruppi fiorentini del quattrocento." In *L'attesa dell'età nuova nella spiritualità della fine del medioevo* (*Convegno del centro di studi sulla spiritualità medievale* 3), 370–432. Todi: L'Accademia Tudertina, 1962.

Venturi, L. "Le compagnie della Calza (secc. XV–XVI)." *Nuovo Archivio Veneto* (*Archivio Veneto,* ser. 3, 16–17) (1908–9): 161–221, 140–233.

Vespasiano da Bistici. *Vite di uomini illustri del secolo XV.* Florence, 1938.

Vigo, P., ed., *Una confraternità di giovanetti pistoiesi a principio del secolo XVI.* Bologna, 1887.

Villani, Filippo. *Liber de civitatis florentiae famosis civibus*. Florence, 1847.

Villani, Giovanni, Matteo, and Filippo. *Croniche di Giovanni, Matteo e Filippo Villani*. 2 vols. Trieste, 1857.

Villari, P. *La Storia di Girolamo Savonarola e de' suoi tempi*, 2 vols. Florence, 1926.

Villari, P., and E. Casanova, eds. *Scelta di prediche e scritti di Fra Girolamo Savonarola*. Florence, 1898.

La vita del beato Ieronimo Savonarola. P. Ginori Conti, ed. attrib. Florence, 1937.

Vitalani, Bonifazio de'. *De maleficiis*. In *Tractatus diversi super maleficiis*. Venice, 1560.

Viviani, G. F. *L'assistenza agli 'esposti' nella provincia di Verona* (1426–1969). Verona: Huber, 1969.

Weinstein, D. *Savonarola and Florence*. Princeton: Princeton Univ. Press, 1970.

Werner, O. *The Unmarried Mother in German Literature*. New York: Columbia Univ. Press, 1917.

Williams, F. E. "The Vailala Madness and the Destruction of Native Ceremonies in the Gulf Division." *Territory of Papua. Anthropology*, report no. 4 (1923).

——. "The Vailala Madness in Retrospect." In *Essays Presented to C. G. Seligman*, edited by E. Evans-Pritchard et al. London, 1934.

Woodward, W. H. *Vittorino da Feltre and Other Humanist Educators*. Cambridge, 1897.

Zacciae, P. *Questiones medico-legales*. Rome, 1621.

Zanelli, A. *Le schiave orientali a Firenze nei secoli XIV e XV*. Florence, 1885.